THE FIFTH
PILLAR

By the same author

Finland at Peace & War
With the Prince of Wales's Own
Dwin Bramall: The Authorised Biography of Field Marshal
The Lord Bramall

THE FIFTH PILLAR

THE LIFE AND PHILOSOPHY OF
THE LORD BRAMALL, KG

MICHAEL TILLOTSON

FOREWORD BY SIR ALISTAIR HORNE

SUTTON PUBLISHING

This book was first published in 2005 under the title
Dwin Bramall by
Sutton Publishing Limited · Phoenix Mill
Thrupp · Stroud · Gloucestershire · GL5 2BU

This revised paperback edition first published in 2006

British Library Cataloguing in Publication Data
A catalogue record for this book is available from the British Library

ISBN 0 7509 4239 8

Typeset in 10.5/12.5pt Goudy.
Typesetting and origination by
Sutton Publishing Limited.
Printed and bound in Great Britain by
J.H. Haynes & Co. Ltd, Sparkford.

Contents

List of Plates and Maps

Foreword

by

SIR ALISTAIR HORNE CBE

Somebody once remarked 'Dwin has had a charmed life'. It is an observation that holds up on several levels. Anyone who has ever met him will recognise at once that special brand of personal charm, utterly uncontrived, as effective on women as on men. Michael Tillotson describes well that 'slightly crooked, self-deprecating smile' that greets acquaintances old and new. Perhaps strangely for so powerful a figure, Dwin genuinely sought to be liked – and so he was across a wide span of the Army, as well as in his social life, and in the Lords.

His professional career was, indeed, a charmed one – in at least two senses. At almost every point in it the Gods seemed to be smiling on Dwin, and pointing the way ahead to the very summit. From earliest days that seemed predestined. But reading Michael Tillotson's vivid account of Dwin's early life, as a young platoon commander in Normandy in 1944, one realises the full force of the 'charmed life'. The last Chief of the Defence Staff to have seen action in the Second World War, Dwin landed with his motor platoon of the 60th in Normandy on D+1. He had several extremely narrow escapes in the fighting that ensued, and was wounded in the fight for Caen. By the time the battle had reached Belgium, Dwin was back in action. He had a miraculous escape stepping on a Schu-mine, which failed to explode, and ended the war with another wound and a well-earned Military Cross.

For Dwin, however, his experiences fighting the elite of the *Wehrmacht* in Normandy became more than the anecdotage of an old soldier. All through his career he reflected upon, and put to excellent use, what he had learned first hand about the particular skills of the Germans fighting a defensive battle, heavily outnumbered in men, material and air power. The lessons were particularly relevant to the kind of battle that the British Army might have had to fight (but, thank God, did not) against the Soviets in central Germany. When commanding his division in Germany in the 1970s it was partly his battle experiences that made him seek out the closest possible association with his opposite numbers in the *Bundeswehr*. He formed a very special relationship greatly beneficial to NATO.

He was, in every sense, a fighting and a thinking general – with the keenest of brains behind that bluff exterior. The papers he wrote in the 1970s left a permanent mark on British military doctrine and the art of leadership, impressing such hard-eyed critics as Professor Sir Michael Howard.

If there was any serious 'blip' in Dwin's charmed professional life, it came – most regrettably – in the Heseltine era. Here his biographer pulls no punches. Rashly (one might almost say, foolishly) the hugely talented politician went ahead with his planned major reforms without consulting his Chief of the Defence Staff – or even keeping him informed. Tillotson speaks of 'a conscious decision not to take the CDS into his confidence, but to present him with a *fait accompli*', as does Heseltine in his autobiography *Life in the Jungle*. It seems the most extraordinary lapse: badly misjudging the timbre of the soldier with whom the politician was dealing.

During the Falklands War of 1982, Dwin was just completing his three-year tour as Chief of the General Staff. General Tillotson has some provocative, historical thoughts to offer here. Dwin had reservations about the risks associated with the landings and potential casualties of this hazardous undertaking. When the crucial, political decision to despatch the task force was taken, he was away in Northern Ireland. The Chief of the Defence Staff, Admiral of the Fleet Sir Terence Lewin, was visiting New Zealand, and also out of town was the Chief of the Air Staff, Air Chief Marshal Sir Michael Beetham – whose reservations about lack of air power complemented Dwin's. So it was that Prime Minister Thatcher's resolve was pre-eminently based on the forcefully positive (and, in the event, most courageous) advice of the more hawkish First Sea Lord, Admiral Sir Henry Leach.

If Dwin had been present, his advice would almost certainly have comprised elements of caution. Now suppose he had been Chief of the Defence Staff at the time; might his advice have swung Thatcher against even sending the task force? It is an interesting speculation; certainly history would have taken a different course. But, as Dwin quickly appreciated, even if a political solution was favoured, a task force would be needed to project the requisite power in the South Atlantic, and once it had arrived off the Falklands and with no political solution by then in sight, then the military risks associated with repossession of the Islands would have had to be faced.

The Army was far from being the only strand in Dwin's amazingly full life, and in it he was fortunate to be supported – very quietly, but nonetheless forcefully – by a wonderful wife, Avril. He was a painter, and a passionate (performing) cricketer. His energy in fund-raising, and getting things done, as Chairman of the Imperial War Museum was legendary.

Whenever he got up to speak, whether in the Lords or at public meetings, his was (and, happily, still is) always the voice of authority and good sense. I for one always sat up and listened. What a pity it was that the present government was not of the same mind when Dwin spoke out so vigorously against the war in Iraq. Here he echoed in a letter to *The Times* Field Marshal Templer's question before the Suez operation, 'Of course we can get to Cairo, but what I want to know is what the bloody hell do we do when we get there!' Long may his voice be heard in the land.

It is indeed an honour to be invited to contribute a foreword to a fine biography of such a great soldier and human being.

Alistair Horne

Author's Note

When T E Lawrence's 'Seven Pillars of Wisdom' was printed privately in 1926 it excited great interest and led readers to ask, 'So what were the Seven Pillars?' Thanks to his brother Arnold's preface to later editions, we now know the title taken from Proverbs 'Wisdom hath builded a house: she hath hewn out her seven pillars' had been intended for an earlier manuscript about seven cities, but never published. Use of the intriguing title for his account of the Arab Revolt in the Hejaz and defeat of the Turks in Palestine in 1917 probably owes much to T E's obsession with obscurity. The rationale for Britain's failure to honour her undertakings to Emir Feisal is more simply understood: what had seemed an urgent necessity in the stress of war proved inconvenient in the comfort of peace.

Lord Bramall first put forward his concept of the 'Fifth Pillar' in the 1980s, when the Soviet Union was perceived to present the paramount threat to peace. British defence policy then rested on four pillars: maintenance of the nuclear deterrent, defence of the United Kingdom, ground and air contributions to the defence of NATO's European Central Region and naval and air contributions to the defence of the eastern Atlantic. These commitments virtually drained the defence budget, but Bramall foresaw new threats to Western interests and security emerging from South-West Asia and the Middle East. Consequently, as Chief of the Defence Staff, he saw it his responsibility to argue for preparations to meet them.

His proposed 'Fifth Pillar', comprising a dynamic British foreign policy supported by military expertise and facilities, was intended to provide a structure capable of development into a policy of containment of the new threats he foresaw. It had the additional merit of being realistic financially in the context of overall defence expenditure at the time. The end of the Cold War has since brought the requirement for a nuclear deterrent again into question and rendered defence of the NATO Central Region and the eastern Atlantic redundant. In contrast, the security of the United Kingdom – with its increasingly diverse population – has become the principal area of concern.

The dangers Bramall foresaw in the 1980s have appeared in the Middle East and, more widely, from the Muslim perception of a malevolent influence of Western sub-culture and political philosophy on their world, into which armed force has been ruthlessly intruded.

My biography *Dwin Bramall*, published in 2005, explained his concept of the Fifth Pillar in the final chapter but without the focus that subsequent developments now demand. I therefore welcome the opportunity of this revised edition to provide a more comprehensive exposition of his ideas and proposals. I do not contend this will complete the story but I hope this new version of the book will be a useful contribution to the debate on how to deal with today's problems of national security, other than by the crudest application of force.

To those I thanked for their help with the earlier book, I should now add Sir Michael Quinlan, formerly Permanent Under-Secretary of State at the Ministry of Defence, for his authoritative explanation of why and how Britain moved from the Polaris to the Trident II D5 nuclear weapons delivery system, and former ambassador Peter Unwin for thoughts provoked by his book *1956: Power Defied*, published earlier this year.

I should also acknowledge the comments of those who spotted errors in the earlier book such as my mistaking 'Florians' in Venice for 'Harry's Bar' and the solecism of incorrectly defining Marylebone Cricket Club. Field Marshal Sir John Stanier's amused acceptance of my apology for carelessly describing him as a mere General is also appreciated.

Michael Tillotson
Wylye, Wiltshire

Prologue

One of the generals in the bar was getting some good-natured ribbing. It was the biennial conference for infantry commanders at the School of Infantry at Warminster, with a fair number of senior officers present. The butt of the banter did not match the popular image of a general. Of medium height and stooping a little, he had a pale, humorous face with a rebellious lock of hair falling over his forehead, which he only occasionally troubled to push back.

It had just leaked out that Major-General Edwin Bramall, known as 'Dwin' since boyhood, was to be promoted at the end of his command of the 1st Armoured Division in Germany to become Commander of British Forces in Hong Kong. This meant he would skip a second appointment as a major-general and be a full step ahead of his contemporaries, so some of the badinage may not have been quite as jocular as it sounded.

The principal reason behind his advancement lay nine years ahead. At this time – the early 1970s – the three armed services provided the Chief of the Defence Staff (CDS) in rotation, the individual stepping up from having been the professional head of the Navy, Army or Air Force. It was therefore important for each service to monitor the situation to ensure a man of the right calibre was available when the time came. The then head of the Army (Chief of the General Staff) General Sir Michael Carver, a man of powerful intellect and relentless efficiency, would shortly become CDS himself. He had in mind two young generals to succeed to the top post nine years ahead but recognised that he would have to force the promotion pace for one of them. After visiting both at their respective divisional headquarters in Germany, he decided on Bramall. But by announcing only his selection for Hong Kong and consequent early promotion, Carver was keeping options open for anything unexpected; the message was nevertheless clear to read.

Even as a young officer, Bramall was widely known in the Army. This was due in part to his ability but more to his spontaneous friendliness. His slightly crooked, self-deprecating smile would greet acquaintances old and new, conveying an impression of joint complicity in some enterprise in which they could safely share confidence.

He had no time for affectation, so his superiors grew to recognise his friendliness as a bonus to his searching mind. Not only did he think clearly and constructively, but the warmth of his approach could persuade others to discard prejudices for ideas they would otherwise reject without a second thought. He was more sombrely dressed than most others at the Infantry Conference dinner in 1973. He wore the 'mess kit' of the King's Royal Rifle Corps – the 60th Rifles – more usually known simply as the '60th'. It was of the darkest possible green, appearing almost black, with black buttons, a soft rather than starched shirt and no badges of rank. This last idiosyncrasy indicated there was no rank within the 60th mess, where all officers were equal – a band of brothers.

At the time of his battalion command on active service, Bramall wrote a pamphlet entitled 'Leadership the Green Jacket Way' and later, having commanded a brigade, a wide-ranging politico-military thesis: 'The Application of Force'. Both indicate deep but liberal-minded thought about his profession and, the thesis in particular, on the humane and moral issues with which those who make war are faced and would increasingly face in the future. There are two opinions on these writings and the many lectures and informal talks he gave. The first claims him unequivocally as an original military thinker with a mind free of bias or prejudice. The second accords him the facility of a good listener, a detector of points for development and expansion on the ideas of others. The truth lies not between these two extremes but in the evidence that he fulfilled them both.

In seeking the central issues of his philosophy, one would not go wrong in settling on 'humanity' and 'candour'. When invited as

PROLOGUE

Chief of the General Staff to speak at the Royal United Services' Institution on 'The Future of Land Forces' in early 1982, he began, 'I don't have to remind this audience that war settles nothing. It may have its moments, it may bring out the best in some people but, apart from the suffering it causes in human and economic terms, it usually creates more problems than it solves.'

Most significantly, perhaps, in the same address he questioned whether in the closing years of the twentieth century full-scale war could still be regarded as a rational extension of a country's foreign policy. He concluded that it *might be* if full-scale military force could achieve the political objectives in a matter of days as, for example, in the Israeli pre-emptive war of 1967, but he questioned whether opposed, closely contested and *therefore prolonged* military conflict could any longer be regarded as a legitimate means of pursuit of a country's foreign policy goals.

1

The Fifth Pillar

'It could be that the material, economic and moral costs of using violence will have become so great that no nation state will be able to use it, however much it might be tempted to do so, and if force is to be applied at all it will have to be *in a rather different form.*'

These words were central to Edwin Bramall's thesis 'The Application of Force', written in 1970. Later, as Chief of the Defence Staff in the 1980s, he sought to turn the minds of Cabinet Ministers and his fellow Chiefs of Staff away from their fixation with the threat then posed by the Soviet Bloc and persuade them to look towards future challenges to our security and vital interests arising in the Middle East and South West Asia.

Two decades later, six months before the American-led invasion of Iraq, he published a letter in *The Times* on the balance of likely advantage of such an initiative in prosecuting the international 'war against terrorism'. While accepting that a swift removal of Saddam Hussein might result in a more pacifically-minded Middle East, he conjectured the conflict would be more likely to produce 'the very display of massive, dynamic United States activity which provides one of the mainsprings of motivation for terrorist action in the region, and indeed over a wider area. Far from calming things down, enhancing any peace process and advancing the 'war on terrorism', which could and should be conducted internationally *by other means*, it would make things infinitely worse.' This is precisely what has occurred.

In his 1970 thesis, he had argued that in the past, once all attempts to reach an acceptable solution through diplomatic manoeuvre had been exhausted, violence had been the commonly accepted means of resolving international disputes. In the ultimate situation where the very life and breath of a nation are plainly and indisputably under threat this may still hold true, but Bramall is on record as saying 'war usually creates more problems than it solves'. The damage to a nation's economic well-being, danger to its citizens at home and abroad, whether or not they are personally engaged in the conflict, and the nation's international reputation and relationship with others incurred by the use of violence, are now at such critical risk that common sense dictates that an alternative to outright violence must by sought. We must find the *other way*.

The essential component of Bramall's 'other way' is a dynamic, pro-active, foreign policy based on objectively assessed information on the activities of our potential opponents, and on their capabilities and likely intentions. ('Objectively assessed information' is, of course, 'intelligence', but the word has acquired a disreputable character in the context of the Anglo-American approach to Saddam Hussein and it should not be inferred that Lord Bramall would suggest its use in a similar 'political' manner again). He argues that such information would enable the national leadership to keep several steps ahead of the potential perpetrators of antagonism or unrest, thereby allowing time for political initiatives to be launched and discreet military adjustments to be made.

When he first advanced this theory of the Fifth Pillar in the early 1980s, the international situation was to a broad extent stabilised by the Cold War. Each significant diplomatic initiative or move had to be cautiously weighed in advance to ensure this delicate balance of power was not disturbed. The collapse of the communist structure in Moscow in 1991, and subsequently that of the military threat from the Warsaw Pact, brought an end to this over-arching, uneasy equilibrium. There was a downside, political forces repressed or restrained by the Soviet regime began to break free and create tensions or havoc locally.

In this new and far more volatile situation, diplomacy – in

particular pre-emptive diplomacy – has greater freedom of manoeuvre when attempting to deal with an international crisis. Bramall understood this but also knew changes in the direction of foreign policy, or defence policy in support of it, could not be accomplished quickly. Even so, the ground had to be prepared beforehand. In the days of the Four Pillars (nuclear deterrent, defence of the UK, European Central Region and the eastern Atlantic), only the crumbs of our defence resources remained after their allocations. There was scope for exercises and attachments to strengthen service ties with selected countries and for training teams to be sent to help to modernise their armed forces. This would put a significant extra load on service attachés who, with FCO co-operation, might receive some enhancement to their staffs and status. While relatively minor, such an innovative policy could, so he judged, open up a new way of thinking on how to deal with a regime, country or region potentially hostile or in turmoil ahead of the next crisis. He characterised this as 'helping our friends to help themselves'.

Although he had not worked in the field of politico-military intelligence – and it is unwise to try to deal with these separately as they are the two sides of the coin of aspiration and capability – Bramall appreciated and valued its importance. Above all, he recognised that pre-emptive diplomacy must start from an unprejudiced understanding of the possible or actual opponent's intellectual rationale and consequent point of view. To regard, for example, leaders in the Muslim world exclusively as religious zealots would be to deny oneself any hope of grasping their outlook on life or, equally important, perspective of time. Patience is their strength and impatience the West's self-imposed handicap.

To evaluate Bramall's proposition for what, in his first Ministerial approach, he termed a 'Fifth Role', it is necessary to measure the impact his proposal for a dynamic foreign policy with military support might have had in averting or moderating the emergencies and crises that have arisen since 1985. This demands a critical assessment of its potency in a world no longer stabilised by super power balance, but up for ransom by any fanatic with hold over a core of zealots, as careless for their own lives as for those of others.

There is also a widening rift between the industrialised nations and the less well developed but no longer poor Muslim world, estimated to be one fifth of the world's population. Much has changed since the Fifth Pillar concept was first advanced, but the new dangers show Bramall's prophetic assessments to have been disturbingly correct and the Fifth Pillar strategy appropriate to addressing them.

Long before the Israeli systematic encroachment onto Palestinian lands had provoked the *intafada*, accelerating the sidelining of moderate Muslim opinion world wide, Bramall focused consideration on the limitations of military action for solving international disputes. In March 1983, shortly after his appointment as CDS, he drew the attention of the three single Service Chiefs of Staff to the Government's White Paper of June 1981 – which he had helped draft while professional Head of the Army – that had forecast the way ahead for NATO. After a ritual nod in that direction, the White Paper offered a wider discussion: *'Military effort cannot be the sole instrument, but it has an inevitable part to play.'*

Writing to the Chiefs of Staff on the extent to which events, in particular continued obsession with the threat from the Soviet bloc, had severely restricted any significant action towards developing *some other way* of dealing with threats to British interests and security, he brought to their notice the largely un-coordinated nature of what little had been done. The overriding difficulty was that the disparate elements of the proposed 'Fifth Role' lacked a coherent framework with which government ministers could readily identify and so see their way towards implementation. It still drew the 'Yes, but. . . .' line of response.

In an effort to avoid his ideas and proposals being watered down by the customary system of circulating early drafts of policy papers for comment by single-Service departments and other experts, he directed that they be prepared by a small element of the Central Staffs until in near final form. Then, and only then, would he put them to his fellow Chiefs of Staff for opinion. One example of this technique was a schedule of countries for possible Fifth Pillar measures, each categorised according to likely return on investment, rather than on any threat to their security or stability. The grouping of countries so categorised – no doubt deliberately - blurred the boundaries between NATO and out-of-NATO-area defence commitments. Even before the list got anywhere near politicians, the single Service Chiefs of Staff found this factor too radical for them to stomach immediately. Each had grown accustomed to fighting his own Service's financial corner under the Four Pillar rules, so that any step away from them held little appeal, except for the Chief of Naval Staff who saw merit in the categorisation of countries as it boosted the credibility of the Royal Navy's world-wide role. Undeterred by this lukewarm response, Bramall began to look round for a new way to launch his iconoclastic campaign against the near-total preoccupation with the NATO geopolitical arena that had stultified defence debate for four decades, rather as the Western Front in France had numbed minds during the First World War.

A new and potentially powerful persona then appeared on the world stage in the form of Mikhail Gorbachev. His policies of *glasnost* (openness) and *perestroika* (restructuring) shone a light beneath the Iron Curtain that forecast at least a relaxation, if not yet an end, to East-West tension. When Gorbachev became General-Secretary of the Communist Party of the Soviet Union in March 1985 Bramall had just six months to run as Chief of the Defence Staff, but he could see how an end to the East-West stand-off would render two if not three of the Four Pillars redundant. Only 'defence of the United Kingdom home base' would remain wholly credible – and with no positively identified threat at that time beyond the Provisional IRA. His concept of the 'Fifth Pillar' could no longer be parodied as the fifth wheel of the coach, it had the potential to lead the way towards the closely co-ordinated foreign and defence policies he foresaw for the future.

Earlier he had explained the Fifth Pillar to the Chiefs of Staff as the:

'Sweeping up in one all-embracing phrase the whole spectrum of our out-of-(NATO) area activities, not covered by the other four pillars, to provide a focal point for a co-ordinated approach to strategy.'

Now his difficulty was how to re-launch his ideas in the time left to him as CDS while the Gorbachev Spring had yet to blossom. As the financial considerations under the existing policies had inhibited his fellow Chiefs of Staff in giving their wholehearted approach to his Fifth Pillar concept, he decided to concentrate on drawing the attention of Ministers to the dangers he foresaw and to his proposals of how they might be addressed and even moderated before they became critically serious.

Looking at the page and a half Minute he had put to the Defence Minister – Michael Heseltine – in March 1983, one is struck both by its economy of words and latent potential. He knew his man, recognising that it would be a waste of time to introduce his idea as a major stride in defence strategy, a subject in which Heseltine had virtually no interest. But if he was able to plant the seeds of an idea both credible and relative to problems of the day, there was a chance that they would take root. This is what he wrote:

Secretary of State
UK DEFENCE POLICY BEYOND THE NATO AREA – THE FIFTH ROLE

1. *The Current White Paper explained that the UK has four main defensive roles and that additionally we exploit, as far as our resources permit, the flexibility of our forces to meet both specific British responsibilities and the growing importance to the West of supporting our friends and contributing to world stability beyond the NATO area. For various reasons, not least our pre-occupation with the defence budget and lack of resources, implementation has fallen far behind intention. Where action has been taken it has been largely uncoordinated. The various constituent parts of our capability beyond the NATO area have never been placed into one coherent framework, which MoD and FCO Ministers could then direct. Moreover the maintenance of strict priorities, with Priority 1 allocated to the UK's NATO commitments and Priority 2 to those beyond the NATO area has led, particularly at any time of financial stringency, to an unfortunate reduction in emphasis and resources to activities beyond the NATO area. The Falklands Islands reminded us of the cost of unexpected aggression and has caused us to re-appreciate our approach to out of area activities.*

10

2. *The Chiefs of Staff discussed these issues on 2 March (1983) and concluded that our Defence Policy had not been implemented fully to meet the wide range of our commitments and interests beyond the NATO area where we are vulnerable to Soviet opportunism and local threats. While we appreciate that the allocation of resources must recognise clearly the primacy of the Soviet threat to NATO, and the importance of the four main defence roles, we agreed that a more flexible and co-ordinated approach is needed to the implementation of present defence policy.*

3. *At present we engage in a great deal of military activity outside the NATO area. This ranges from our commitments in the Falkland Islands, Belize and Hong Kong, through loan service and seconded personnel, training teams, assistance to sales and the provision of high calibre defence attachés, all of which are designed to maintain stability in these areas and to increase British influence. In the context of no more than a slight shift in strategic emphasis, and without downgrading our NATO capability, the Chiefs of Staff are agreed unanimously that these limited forms of involvement can represent some of the most economical and cost effective ways of meeting our commitments and protecting and advancing UK interests beyond the NATO area. But to get maximum advantage for our foreign policy and strategic interests, and also to make best use of the limited resources, these activities need to be properly co-ordinated.*

4. *We have therefore given instructions for work to be undertaken by the end of May (1983) to identify more clearly all aspects of existing activities beyond the NATO area and to propose how best they can be managed and coordinated. In the longer term, after further study in conjunction with the FCO, we aim to establish priorities for our involvement with countries or areas outside the NATO area, against which changing demands for limited resources may be assessed.*

5. *I conclude that the activities and limited resources which can be brought to bear to protect our essential interests worldwide should be acknowledged as constituting an important **Fifth Role** of our defence*

policy, all elements of which must be considered, of course, as a whole. I would ask you to endorse this conclusion in principle because I believe it should be reflected in your forthcoming statement on Defence Estimates.

6. *I have discussed all this with the Permanent Under-Secretary who is in broad agreement with this approach, and we suggest you may wish to have an early meeting with us on this subject.*
   25 March 1983   *(Signed) ENWB CDS.*

Unfortunately, throughout the spring, summer and autumn of 1983 and the following winter, the Secretary of State for Defence and Chief of Defence Staff were pursuing separate agendas. The former was throwing his principal effort into the essentially political campaign against activities of the Campaign for Nuclear Disarmament (CND), while the latter continued to plough a lonely furrow for planting the seeds of his Fifth Pillar philosophy. Michael Heseltine's battle with CND was not won until the first successful road test exercise of cruise missiles from Greenham Common in March 1984. This had demanded much personal commitment and, as explained in Chapter 16, he was concurrently working behind closed doors with his Private Secretary, Richard (later Sir Richard) Mottram on organisational changes to the Ministry of Defence he had already cleared in general terms with the Prime Minister, Margaret Thatcher.

Bramall did not let his case rest after an inconclusive discussion with the Secretary of State. He knew that to gain political endorsement for his ideas he must win over the Foreign and Commonwealth Office as a partner. In any liberal democracy the routes of diplomacy and military planning and preparation tend to diverge and all too often one can impede the other. In Britain, this dichotomy has fostered mutual reserve between the Foreign and Commonwealth Office and the Ministry of Defence for generations.

An example of this, conducted at the highest level, occurred at the time of the United States' intervention in the Commonwealth island of Grenada. On the morning before the US operation to remove the newly-installed Revolutionary Military Council in October 1983, Bramall mentioned to the Prime Minister, Margaret Thatcher, that he 'had a feeling in his bones' that Washington was about to make a move using armed force. 'Why on earth would they want to do a thing like that?' she asked and inquired of the Foreign Secretary, Geoffrey Howe, whether he could give any credence to Bramall's concern. Howe replied with a firm negative, leading the Prime Minister to shrug off Bramall's suggestion with, 'There you are, you see.'

The British Government had received no prior notice of the US plan to intervene in Grenada, indeed assurances had been given until the last moment that there was no such intention. In the middle of that night, however, with signals coming in confirming the invasion was imminent, Bramall was summoned to Downing Street. At 1.45 am he ordered a signal to be sent to warn HMS *Antrim*, which otherwise would have been in the middle of the American operation, and asked the Prime Minister – furious about the United States' action – whether she wished to be associated with it in any way. She replied, 'Certainly not.' This is perhaps a more anecdotal than evidential example of a lack of empathy between two great departments of state but it is scarcely encouraging. It is also noteworthy that the Grenada incident, reflecting an acute difference of view between London and Washington, did no apparent harm to Anglo-American relations on this occasion.

Not even the civil service Whitehall brotherhood has been able to do much to bridge the FCO/MoD departmental divide. The two have developed diverse types of individual: the first preoccupied with words and how their different interpretation might allow the smoothing over of a difference of opinion with another government, so maintaining apparent agreement and good working relations. The other is obliged to face a wide range of demands for which sufficient resources are never available. Good manners and mutual respect for the other's difficulties have led to a degree of tolerant co-operation but the fundamental differences of outlook run deep.

It was thinking about the best way of initiating an approach to the FCO that turned Bramall back to the importance of overseas intelligence, the gathering and assessment of which is the function of the Secret Intelligence Service (MI 6), ostensibly an adjunct of the Foreign and Commonwealth Office.

Bramall had contacts with the SIS going back to his service in Egypt in the 1950s and later in Hong Kong. Contact between the CDS of the day and 'C', as the Head of the SIS was historically known, while scarcely routine, were an accepted necessity by both parties and Bramall had the additional advantage of being known by the SIS as an innovative thinker. All this brought some extra piquancy to the meeting he and his fellow Chiefs of Staff had with senior officials of the SIS in 1983.

He opened the round table discussion by explaining that he had received ministerial endorsement for his Fifth Pillar policy. This was factually correct but 'ministerial endorsement' meant little more than tacit acceptance for the pursuit of an idea until the moment arrived for Cabinet approval and grant of financial resources. Undeterred by this, he laid his philosophy on the line. 'Events likely to cause problems for HMG and involve the use of military resources are most likely to occur outside the NATO alliance area,' he asserted, 'It is therefore in our interests – and here 'our' was intended to embrace the SIS – in support of our foreign policy to preserve stability and pre-empt trouble in key areas and so help make our foreign policy as dynamic and effective as possible.' Lest his audience felt that this had little to do with them, he perked them up with, 'This technique is well understood by the Russians and the French.'

Next he turned to the part he felt the Intelligence services could play. He began with an assurance that he believed the type of problems he had in mind could best be overcome not by any large-scale military intervention, but more by means of intelligence – keeping the armed forces ahead of the game – with political and diplomatic activities to create or preserve a reasonable state of affairs, and by personal contact to nudge things in the right direction. This was the nucleus of his policy of *helping our friends abroad to help themselves*.

Bramall's long-term proposals for the Fifth Pillar required, as they do today, close integration of two disparate elements into one harmonious structure. This must then be manipulated jointly by the FCO and MoD working towards mutually agreed goals. It is of particular interest that Michael Heseltine's autobiography, *Life in the Jungle*, published in 2000, contains the following reflection on his three years as Secretary of State for Defence, ' You may not always share the judgements of the Foreign Office but the closer the working relationship that exists between the two departments, the more effective policy-making is likely to be in key areas of interest to the United Kingdom across the globe.' So it is clear he appreciated the essence of Bramall's proposals for a Fifth Pillar at a time when the other pillars still stood at the corners of British defence policy.

Beyond the initial harnessing of armed forces activities as outlined in his Minute to Michael Heseltine in 1983, Bramall had in mind a truly radical change in the manner in which the FCO and MoD conducted their business to ensure national security and protection of our vital interests. He saw the need to bring the two departments of state into closer cohesion, not just when some crisis provoked the convening of the Cabinet Defence and Overseas Policy Committee, but on a day-to-day basis. The need for co-ordinated action could then be detected before a crisis was upon us and some diplomatic finessing, complemented where clearly necessary by military preparations, put in hand. In essence, the two ministries would be proactive together, rather than reactive separately.

Aware that politicians and senior civil servants alike look at military proposals with guarded scepticism, simply on the grounds of suspicion the motive may be to preserve a capability or institution from retrenchment, Bramall proceeded with caution. There was a particular reason for not putting forward his Fifth Pillar concept too emphatically, arising from the then international situation. Today, Moscow's view on an international issue can, on occasion, be harnessed to Western interests; for example in trying to persuade Iran to limit her nuclear programme, even though the views of Russia and the West are not identical on this issue. In 1984 the

Soviet Union was still the heartland of the 'Evil Empire' and through subversion or menace was considered by the West as the principal threat to world peace. To have suggested otherwise could have seriously damaged Bramall's credibility with Ministers and his Service colleagues.

He was to be proved notably perceptive in his assessments of future sources of crisis in his discussion with the Secret Intelligence Service. Some of the prophetic paragraphs in his speaking notes are lined through suggesting that, while representing his thoughts, they were not actually spoken at the time. When dealing with his Fifth Pillar proposal, his notes reflect his particular future concerns, 'Moving now to the area which the Chiefs of Staff paper recognises as the highest priority,' he began, 'let us turn to the Middle East and South West Asia. The armed forces have contributed quite considerably to Britain's foreign policy aims of trying to defuse, or at least stop spreading, the potentially dangerous situation in the Arabian Gulf, while helping our friends build up their self-confidence and stability. It is interesting to note how Oman and the other Gulf States view Saudi Arabia's 'bossiness' every bit as much a threat (to stability) as anything that is likely to come across the Gulf from Iran.'

He then turned his listeners' attention to Afghanistan and Pakistan, the former at that time enduring oppressive occupation by the Soviet Union. 'Pakistan cannot be seen *not* to be giving succour and moral support to the Afghan refugees pouring under duress into their country. Many nations also feel it commendable for Pakistan to be giving the 'freedom fighters' succour and support, but those who wish them to go further, for example the American Congress, might do well to think the problems through very carefully, lest excessive enthusiasm makes the problem worse not better.'

After a *tour d'horizon* of the situation in South East Asia, where he foresaw a diminishing number of problems, he concluded his remarks with the telling phrase which lay at the heart of his philosophy of the Fifth Pillar, *'Let us now move on through the spectrum to what I call pre-emptive diplomacy.'* This was the identical phrase he used in the opening of the section on 'Strategy of Force' in his 1970 thesis. (See Chapter 10).

Over the two decades since he handed over the post of CDS in 1985, Bramall has missed no opportunity to press the arguments for his Fifth Pillar philosophy, that of a dynamic foreign policy with a closely supporting defence policy. During the same period, British diplomatic efforts in the field of safeguarding our vital interests have been largely reactive rather than proactive, an enterprise shortfall no doubt due in part to the claw back in British representation abroad in the interest of economy.

Meanwhile in the international arena, United States dependence on support from the European nations has undergone a fundamental change. In the years of the Cold War and threat from the Soviet bloc, the defence of the American homeland had rested in part on European-based strategic warning and retaliation systems, as well as the stationing of conventional forces on the Continent in a deterrent role. The end of the Cold War brought an end to these aspects of reliance and, consequently, a reduction in American eyes of the usefulness of European nations' opinion on matters of international policy. Now, Washington becomes concerned only when European states might be able to bring influence to bear on American interests elsewhere, votes in the UN Security Council are at a premium or there is a risk Europe might seek to 'go it alone'.

Over the same period, rogue nations – those set against the general trend of world order for ideological or partisan economic motives – have continued to threaten the peace. They are now joined in this by intimidation from political or religious factions dissenting from plights in which they perceive themselves to be locked. Represented by terrorist 'organisations' diffuse in composition, geographically un-attributable and seldom having specifically defined motives, such adversaries are seldom susceptible to negotiation in the generally accepted sense. Governments sympathetic to one side of the dispute or the other may silently applaud terrorist outrages, covertly provide material support or sanctuary for the perpetrators, while striving to stand aloof from implication. Yet it is they who, if approached with diplomatic subtlety, could become the channels if not the actual levers of influence required to bring about a settlement of the dispute.

This is one form of proactive diplomacy at the heart of the Fifth Pillar philosophy.

The first diplomatic approach may have to be backed by the tacit suggestion that force may have to be used, albeit reluctantly, if diplomacy fails. The choice hinges on a careful and essentially objective assessment of whether an implied threat of force is likely to be counter-productive. Then, if diplomacy is seen to be unproductive, force may have to be applied in a carefully measured fashion and, if circumstances allow, with such precision as to keep casualties and damage to a minimum and not alienate friendly states or those neutral in the dispute.

This was the technique adopted at the outset of the American attempt to persuade the Government in Afghanistan to surrender Osama bin Laden following the attacks on the New York World Centre in September 2001. Speaking in the House of Lords on 5 November that year, Bramall said, 'In the context of this infinitely complicated and politically weighted operation in Afghanistan, I am much happier about the comparatively slow tempo of operations than I would be rushing in where angels and wise men fear to tread.' On 17 December, during a further Lords debate on Afghanistan, he gave the more sombre warning, 'I hope that we do not spoil it by forcing formed bodies of British troops on to reluctant Afghans, to do heaven knows what for heaven knows how long. As the realities of non-Muslim forces getting involved in internal domestic power struggles and squabbles sink in, their safety (the troops) could become increasingly precarious. I would therefore plead for the most thorough consultation with the people on the ground and not just in a European forum.'

Here he was indicating the crux of any diplomatic approach: it must be relevant to the self-interest of the state or organisation to which it is being directed. This may apply to issues of security, the regional balance of power, access to vital resources or even economic aid. The sensitivity of the approach will be the key to success. If the approach implies a threat or what amounts to an inducement, either must be so cloaked as to make it acceptable to the government and people, locally and internationally. In essence, if you want to deal with terrorism you are obliged to address its fundamental causes and the people who have the grievance. The failure of the diplomatic approach in Afghanistan does not invalidate this concept. There it was applied to a totally obdurate regime jealous of its authority, while other levers of influence were insufficiently exploited.

The massive military intervention in Iraq was an altogether different matter and, as Bramall gave public warning well in advance, it seriously impeded the so-called 'war on terrorism' and opened up the ground for terrorism and fomented it where it had not previously existed. He went on to criticise this as an example of the 'Dien Bien Phu' strategy – the major deployment of force by the French Union forces in Indo-China in 1953 to tempt the insurgent enemy to concentrate so he could be destroyed by superior firepower. (It failed because the Viet Minh were able to muster the greater weight of artillery and deny the French air-supply).

Such high-risk ventures can produce adverse reactions in neighbouring countries, upset the regional balance of power and, as in the case of Iraq, force the population into revolutionary changes for which they were not prepared. Worse, as with the US and Soviet interventions in Vietnam and Afghanistan respectively, they can end in humiliation.

When a diplomatic initiative is clearly unsuccessful, then a slower-moving containment policy must follow. Countries threatened must look to their security, improve their intelligence networks in scope and reliability, while continuing to try to persuade governments in the region under threat to re-think their political attitudes and allegiances. Much will depend on finding out, through sensitive intelligence, what will make the target governments change their views, either directly or in their attitude towards terrorist organisations depending on their support. Governments disinclined to help the West often need support for their local situation politically and if provided, this may lead to the isolation of terrorist elements.

Within a policy of containment, use of carefully selected military force need not be ruled out, but it must be undertaken only with the sanction of countries where troops, aircraft or naval vessels are to be deployed or based. A containment option will be seen to be in tune with present-day ethics and the stage civilisation has reached in the twenty-first century and deny popular 'legitimacy' to terrorist groups, many of which are criminally or individually motivated, rather than representative of any true ideal.

The 'Fifth Pillar' concept is completely compatible with a containment strategy. Just as the Cold War was won by a skilful combination of patience and containment, so the war against terrorism will only be won by using the same stratagems: to address the causes of terrorism to bring about the internal collapse of the terrorist or insurrectionist organisations whose principal threat is against the very population within which they hide.

2

An Eclectic Boyhood

There is a Chinese saying that the greatest gift a child may have is to be born in interesting times. When Edwin Noel Westby Bramall was born on 18 December 1923, Adolf Hitler was making his first impact as a political force on the streets of Munich and Joseph Stalin had survived Lenin's dying attempt to remove him from the post of General Secretary of the Communist Party of the Soviet Union, leaving him at the centre of power in Moscow. In succession, these two men and Stalin's legacy were to be the dominating influences in world affairs during much of Bramall's professional life. They were indeed interesting times.

Edwin Bramall was born just before Christmas in the small town of Rusthall in Kent, where his mother was visiting her own ailing mother who lived nearby. Although an older brother had been born eight years earlier, Bridget Bramall, always known as 'Bryda' or, after her marriage, as 'Billie', was by that time in her late thirties and so, by the norms of the day, his arrival created something of a stir in the family. As it happened, their GP had advised an abortion, but her natural way of overruling even the best-intentioned advice, declaring 'I want my baby', led to his safe delivery. He subsequently enjoyed a life of good health, unlike his brother, who was slightly delicate during his schooldays. The name 'My Baby' stuck and a little over half a century later the staff in the front office of the Chief of the General Staff were surprised by a call from an elderly lady demanding, 'I wish to speak to My Baby.' 'Mother,' said the Chief when he picked up the phone, 'you really cannot say that sort of thing. Everyone will think we are stark raving mad.' But she declined any rebuke, stating firmly, 'Why not? You *are* My Baby.'

Despite being married conventionally enough in Salisbury Cathedral after a whirlwind courtship during the First World War, the Bramall parents were a distinctly disparate couple. Although Bridget was from an impoverished aristocratic family and lacked any formal education, she was well informed, highly intelligent and fiercely radical. Energetic and extremely strong-willed, she wished to live nowhere other than Kensington or Chelsea. In contrast, Edmund Bramall was of solid trade stock from the Potteries. He was what we would now describe as 'laid back' – an easy-going countryman with a great love of sport of all kind, both country pursuits and team games. He was good at them too, once playing roller-skating hockey for England while up at Pembroke College, Cambridge, an achievement to which Mrs Bramall managed not to give too much publicity. He was a good horseman and a keen shot, but utterly devoid of ambition, tending to drift into things rather than making any definite plan for his life.

There was never any doubt as to the dominant partner, which suited both personalities admirably. The sons, although separated by eight years, were quick to realise that their mother required, indeed demanded, instant agreement with the judgements she invariably took on every conceivable issue of the day. Until the Second World War intervened, the family was based in London, making only brief sorties to the paternal grandparents' large and comfortable house in Sussex.

On leaving Cambridge, Edmund Bramall had gone off to war in 1914 in company with virtually all his generation. He was commissioned into the Royal Artillery and served first as a forward observation officer, then as a battery captain and finally as a battery commander on the Western Front in France. He was at the battle of Ypres, on the Somme, was twice wounded, and contracted rheumatic fever. Subsequently, finding gainful employment in the 1920s proved none too easy, not least because of his wife's insistence that certain types of job were not among those a 'gentleman' should undertake, which inconveniently were those he would have found easiest to master. In consequence, between the two world wars, Edmund had no earned income, but relied entirely on that from shares in the family business to meet the needs of a wife who was an accomplished spender.

The family business was cotton growing in the Fayoum in Upper Egypt. Edmund Bramall's grandfather had married into the family of Sir Robert Peel, the MP for Lichfield, later Prime Minister and responsible, when Home Secretary, for the introduction of the modern police force. The Peels were already one of the great English cotton growers in Egypt, and Edmund's father had gone out to Egypt as a young man, first to be involved in construction of the first Aswan Dam and then to enter the Peel cotton-growing company. This prospered, making a considerable amount of money for the family until the business was sequestrated by President Abdul Nasser in 1956.

Through these earlier events the Bramall family became closely connected with Egypt. Edmund's parents had brought up five children in the rigorous climate of Beni Suef (Bani Suwayf) in central Egypt, where Edmund was born. As the eldest son, he was the obvious choice to take over running the business from his father. Bryda, however, refused to go to Egypt, other than for the briefest possible visits, so responsibility passed to Edmund's youngest brother, a charming and fun-loving man who had nearly as many wives as he owned horses. This situation led Edmund to opt out of the family business to an increasing degree and that family to question whether he had made the right choice of wife, who had such a different inclination.

For her part, Bryda applied her restless energy and innovative brain to hatching money-making schemes that, with a little luck and a partner of greater business acumen, might have significantly altered the family fortunes. She started a car-hire company, specialising in yellow Rolls Royce cars, and a 'boys' kit bureau' for cast-off boys' school clothing that, when renovated, could be sold second-hand to save parents significant sums. She backed 'fix-o-quick' patent furniture for alfresco meals and holiday homes capable, like the furniture in Nelson's men-of-war, of being taken to pieces and quickly reassembled, and a home-made jam and marmalade business marketing under the name 'Simple Simon'. Although the ideas were good, none of the ventures came to anything and the family coffers got lighter by the month.

From the late 1920s to the start of the Second World War, the Edmund Bramalls were obliged to move steadily down market as their money ran out. In 1939, they sold their house in the King's Road, Chelsea, for £3,000 and managed to hang on in London only by relying heavily on Edmund's ever-tolerant parents, who consistently bailed them out, in particular over the children's education.

Dwin went as a day boy to Gibbs School in London, presided over by the patriarchal Charles Gibbs. The teaching was excellent and the games, played on the Harrods ground at Barnes, well coached and enjoyable. His brother Ashley had been there before him and, although not good at games, was academically very bright and benefited greatly from the school before going on to Westminster. Dwin excelled in mathematics under the encouragement of Mr Cummings the maths master, who had played rugby football for Llanelli. Although he was of medium stature, the young Bramall revelled in all games. When he left Gibbs at Christmas 1934, Cummings gave him a copy of *Soccer* by David Jack inscribed, after complimenting the young sportsman on his 'wielding the willow at Barnes or feeding his forwards and in the boxing ring', with the hope: 'May it be said that your life's battles were won on the playing-fields of your first school.'

Dwin was enjoying Gibbs but, probably sensibly as he would have to progress to boarding school, his parents took him away to go to Elstree School, Hertfordshire, as a boarder. He was ten, not seven or eight, which was often the normal age for British children to go away to school, so was able to brush off home-sickness and adjust to boarding-school life quite easily. Academically, he was no better than average, giving his greatest enthusiasm to sports and games. He captained the school cricket side and made two centuries not out in his second season.

Here again, he came into contact with some fine schoolmasters of considerable academic and sporting distinction. These not only kept him up to the mark in both aspects of school life, but provided inspiration. Coming off the rugby field on one occasion, he was mortified to hear a much-respected master who was an Oxford double-blue and a classical scholar say, 'Bramall, you funked that tackle.' Ten years later, when he was about to land on the beach at Normandy, he could, as he put it, hear that voice again and thought to himself, 'My God, I'd better not do that again.'

He had hoped that his parents would choose Harrow as his public school, as Elstree was the preparatory school for Harrow and many of his friends were due to go there. His father had been at Sherborne, but stories of what new boys had to endure there had put his mother off and since, despite her radicalism, she was also a bit of a snob, she chose Eton. Once he was there, his mother became quite obsessive about the school, using – in her ever-simplistic way – various yardsticks to assign public figures to either the Hall of Fame or the Chamber of Horrors. For example: 'If you were black you got good marks, if you were a black Socialist (not unusual), you got better marks still, but if you were a black Socialist Old Etonian (perhaps a little more rare) you got the best marks of all!'

In fact Bryda Bramall did her younger son a great service by sending him to Eton. He revelled in the privacy of a single room, and the unique opportunity that Eton provides for developing personality and real responsibility given progressively in running the school's activities. He was in a house under a caring housemaster with whom he got on extremely well, and he entered into many of the wide range of activities available. He got his House Colours for the field game, was elected to the Library (House Prefect) and became Captain of his House and a member of 'Pop' (School Prefect); he fenced, played fives and cricket for Eton and eventually captained the school XI. He was an under-officer in the Officer Training Corps and became a sergeant in the Home Guard.

The drawing schools allowed him to develop his painting skill, and he had two pictures hung at the Royal Academy while at Eton. Afterwards, he was told by the drawing master that this gave the place some much-needed respectability in the eyes of the headmaster, who had suspicions as to what vice and perversions went on in the music and drawing schools but was reassured by the presence of the Captain of the XI. He read a paper on Wagner and Verdi to the curiously named Junior Archaeological Society and thoroughly enjoyed a life he found full of variety and interest.

If Eton had any penalty for him, it was living together with boys from rich and aristocratic families, some of whom – until the war brought petrol restrictions – were able to visit their sons in excessively smart cars. The Bramall parents, in somewhat distressed circumstances, would turn up in a rather battered second-hand car. This was conspicuous enough, but worse might come in the form of a seven-months'-pregnant sister-in-law, together with the cleaning lady and window cleaner whom his mother, in her personal obsession over Eton, thought would benefit from seeing the school for themselves. He made no protest, welcoming all without embarrassment and perhaps unconsciously preparing himself for the future.

After the largely ignored wake-up call of Munich a year after Bramall had arrived at Eton, war was declared, adding a wholly new element of excitement to all the other activities. With air-raid warnings sounding almost every night, the boys often slept in shelters constructed in the gardens and manned fire-fighting equipment to douse fires started by incendiary bombs that penetrated the roofs of some of the buildings. One evening, a German bomber jettisoned two high-explosive bombs in the very heart of the school, destroying the houses of the senior music master and the organist, as well as flattening a large part of the school hall.

The period 1940–1 was one of great national stress, with invasion by sea and parachute landings regarded as inevitable until Germany turned the other way and invaded the Soviet Union in June 1941. Everyone felt in the front line, not least the older boys serving in the local Home Guard with Windsor Castle so close and an obvious target in any parachute attack. The provost and headmaster dismissed any notion of evacuating the school to some more remote part of the country, as many in London and close to the south coast had been obliged to do.

Bramall's five years at Eton ended on a series of high notes. The cricket team he captained never lost a match, beating both Harrow and Winchester. He was selected to captain the Lords Schools against the other public schools at Lords in 1942, the opposing side being captained by the formidable Trevor Bailey, later to play for England. He was subsequently Bailey's vice-captain in the overall Schools side to play the MCC. On the academic side, he achieved his Matriculation.

There had been disappointments and setbacks, of course. He had had to 'fag' for power-conscious older boys, but did so without feeling humiliated. He had been beaten for things that he regarded as scarcely his fault, but he was not bullied or abused in any way. Looking back many years later, he conceded that he was not sexually precocious in any sense, rather the opposite, which was not unusual at that time. His energies were directed principally towards the sports field, and, as this brought success, his schooldays were exciting and satisfying, with such disappointments as there were providing a valuable insight into the world outside.

His mother continued to be the dominating influence in his life throughout his schooldays, encouraging and supporting him in work and sport. She never allowed her uncertain health to interfere with attendance at special days, plays or matches in which he took part. Happy schooldays were not by any means the only things for which he had cause to be grateful to his mother. She was difficult to be with at close quarters, but evoked sincere admiration and affection in the many she befriended from a distance and she knew how to treat people. With her immediate family, she invariably had her own agenda, expecting everyone, including her husband and later her daughters-in-law, to conform to her ideas, virtually without question.

It has to be acknowledged that Bryda Bramall was manipulative in all she did, never shrinking from using illness – sometimes of an unrecognised nature – to get her way. A favourite was temporary paralysis of the legs if thwarted in any family issue. There is no doubt that Dwin learnt a great deal from her, not least that everyone has importance, whatever their role in life. She could also see herself for what she was and recognised that in a somewhat tempestuous household her children needed an element of stability outside the family. In Dwin's case this took the form of a friend of Bryda's – Molly Neville – whom she arranged to look after him when still quite young and into adolescence. She was calm and understanding and he looked to her for support in any family or personal crisis that might prove too difficult to handle alone.

His mother also took pains to develop a cosmopolitan outlook in her children. Having been a difficult child herself, with relatively impoverished and remote parents – her father was sixty when she was born – she had been sent with her friend Molly Neville to stay with a rich and well-connected aunt who had houses in Fiesole, overlooking Florence, Montreux in Switzerland and Heidelberg in Germany. These places left a lasting impression on her, and, in consequence, Dwin and his elder brother travelled a good deal before the war to Paris and on walking tours in the Rhineland, as the Nazis were coming to power, and in Switzerland. They were taken to Madrid to view the pictures in the Prado, giving Dwin a great incentive to widen his knowledge of Europe and to take an interest in languages, not least because whenever Bryda wanted to say something to her husband she did not wish the children to hear she spoke in Italian.

Bryda had dabbled in both painting and sculpture and this had stimulated Dwin to try his hand and, from preparatory school onwards, he practised in oils and watercolours whenever time allowed. Success came early with the acceptance of two of his oils, *Sloane Square* and *The Ballet*, by the Royal Academy of Arts for the Summer Exhibition of 1940, when he was sixteen. For him, painting was a relaxation rather than a need to capture a scene or a particular moment in his own hand. He continued to paint throughout his life, exhibiting occasionally but never again at the Royal Academy. He was always intensely interested in other people's paintings, whether their own work or just owned, and his eye would be scanning the walls of a house he entered for the first time from immediately after his hostess's greeting and, given half a chance, he would tuck her arm in his, leaving other guests to look after themselves, while he walked her round her own drawing room to view the pictures.

As his time at Eton drew to a close in July 1942, the question of a career came into family discussion. Murmurings about the military met with no maternal enthusiasm whatsoever. His mother hated the war and would have liked him to become a physician, to which he was not averse, yet, other than postponing it for six months by taking a short wartime course at university, there was really no immediate alternative to military service. In view of his artistic and musical interests, it is perhaps surprising that the young Bramall should hanker after a military career. Nor was it possible to attribute his enthusiasm only to the current national and international situation or to the very obvious presence of the military all over the country. It went back to nursery days when he and his brother would work out systems for the tactical deployment and use of their model infantry and cavalry soldiers.

The solution to the problem of not causing his mother needless distress lay at hand in the form of allowing his name to go forward for the place at Christ Church College, Oxford which he had earned at school, to be taken up at the end of hostilities, in the meantime volunteering for the military service for which he would be very shortly called up in any case. Bryda was fully alert to this situation, as when war came her husband had rejoined the Royal Artillery and served in England in various gunner regiments, including a coastal artillery battery on the Lincolnshire coast during the invasion scare. She had followed wherever he was posted, living in rented accommodation, boarding houses or small hotels, where she was joined by Dwin from Eton during school holidays or breaks when not required for Home Guard or air-raid precaution duties or voluntary shifts in an aircraft-manufacturing factory in Slough. Temporary stability was achieved only when Major Edmund Bramall was appointed personal assistant to the Commandant of the School of Artillery at Larkhill.

July 1942, when Dwin Bramall left Eton to enlist, was one of the lowest points in the war for Britain. On Christmas Day of the previous year, Hong Kong had fallen to the Japanese, followed by the much graver strategic loss of Singapore in February. The German 6th Army was a mere forty miles from Stalingrad, U-boats were masters of the Atlantic and, in August, the unreadiness of the Allies to return to the Continent would be revealed by the severe losses sustained in the Dieppe Raid. The turning point of El Alamein was still three months away and even then, as Winston Churchill put it in his Mansion House speech, 'This is not the end. It is not even the beginning of the end. But it is, perhaps, the end of the beginning.'

3

The Road through Goirle

D win Bramall first experienced the ferocity of German retaliatory action in the Normandy beachhead in June 1944. He was spared the nerve-racking run-in through the mined breakers on the early morning of D-Day, but saw the dead and wounded from the first wave of the assault being carried from the landing craft into which he and his platoon were about to embark.

He had volunteered for military service immediately after leaving Eton, having already shown military aptitude by becoming a cadet under-officer in the school Officer Training Corps. But this gave no advantage on enlistment, beyond a fundamental grasp of the army system, infantry weapons and the tactical use of ground; as for everyone, his training had to begin afresh.

Although accepted at interview as suitable for a commission in the King's Royal Rifle Corps (60th Rifles), he joined the regiment as a rifleman. This was something he was to value all his service, as it provided his first insight into the world of young men from all parts of British society and the harsh realities of army life. He found himself one of a small band of cloistered public schoolboys thrust into the midst of a larger bunch of very street-wise cockney lads communicating in a cacophony of four-letter words, but whose worth they quickly learned to appreciate and who became their mates. He also learnt that life was not always fair and what it was like to be on the receiving end of what sometimes appeared to be bloody silly orders that had to be obeyed if discipline was to be maintained.

Raised in 1755 on Governor's Island, New York, from American settlers of Maryland, Pennsylvania and Virginia, together with Hanoverian and Swiss mercenaries, initially as the '62nd Royal

Americans', the regiment had an unorthodox approach to soldiering. Its original role was to fight the French and indigenous Indians along the banks of the Ohio river. Forsaking the traditional red coats and close-quarter drill in battle, which had contributed to General Braddock's defeat at Fort Duquesne in 1755, they moved quickly in loose formation, concentrating on accurate shooting. When working with other units, the 60th – as their number later became – operated in front and on the flanks of the infantry columns, from where they could bring rapid fire to bear on the enemy's closely packed formations. They provided mounted infantry in the late-nineteenth-century wars in Egypt and during the South African War, 1899–1902. The 60th attracted officers of individuality and original thought, while its system of operations developed empathy and speed of reaction with close, confident relationships between all ranks. Its record for producing generals became formidable, making it widely – if sometimes grudgingly – respected.

Bramall did his basic training in Fulford Barracks, York, and was then taught to drive trucks, ride a motorcycle and operate radios with 148 Training Brigade in Wrotham, Kent. After return to the Officer Cadet Training Unit in York, he was commissioned into the 60th Rifles in May 1943 and joined the 10th Motor Training Battalion at Strensall, north of York, where new officers and soldiers were taught the tactics of a motor battalion. A fellow subaltern serving with him then and later in Normandy, Robin Lewin, recalls that while most of the young officers took any opportunity to go to London for the weekend, Bramall had little interest in night life.

It is a measure of the potential he had already shown that he was made the commander of the demonstration platoon. His company commander allowed him almost complete autonomy to teach all he had so far learned, often using his platoon as 'enemy' on battalion exercises. Bramall's interest in minor tactics was given full leash, permitting him to set the standards that the trainees had to achieve and subsequently maintain in action. For the second half of the year he was with the 10th Battalion, he was given charge of the potential officers' platoon. A system had developed since he had enlisted as a rifleman whereby those identified as potential officers were trained together. Many of these young men later served with him in action, having acquired much from his professional skill and, in the form of audacious field-firing exercises, something akin to a baptism of fire.

This period involved him in a traumatic experience, an incident that subaltern officers dread – a casualty on the grenade range, in this case a doubly fatal one. While simple enough, the technique of preparing and throwing a Number 36 grenade has an unnerving effect on the military novice. The principal danger is that the thrower, having pulled out the pin holding the firing lever in place, drops the grenade, releasing the lever. The fuse will then start burning and, unless they get out of the throwing bay in five seconds, both thrower and the supervising officer will be blown to pieces.

There is another risk when the grenade is thrown. Fragmentation ridges in the surface of the grenade, like that of a pineapple, tempt the thrower to apply a spin. Rather than a clean lob to the front, this almost invariably results in a shallow trajectory to one side. This is probably what happened when Bramall was supervising. The grenade went wide to the right, over the top of the adjacent throwing bay, rolled along the roof of the waiting bay and fell through a gap onto the soldiers below. Two men were killed outright and two others seriously wounded. The inquiry exonerated Bramall, finding fault with the siting and construction of the 'waiting bay', but dealing with the dead and wounded on the spot gave him experience of the sudden and violent death he would later encounter in Normandy.

In May 1944, he joined 2nd/60th at Worthing. This was a regular battalion, experienced and hardened by Western Desert battles and the Italian campaign, from which it had been withdrawn with the rest of 4th Armoured Brigade to prepare for the invasion of Normandy. Veterans were readily identifiable by the 60th's red 'cherries' on their berets being bleached almost white by the sun. Reinforcement, re-equipping and reorganisation were essential before D-Day, so he found himself with a mixture of veterans and newly trained men in 'A' Company, commanded by Major Billy

Morris, under the overall command of Lieutenant-Colonel Bill Heathcoat Amory, who had led the battalion since Alamein.

Battalions of the 60th Rifles and the Rifle Brigade were responsible for close support in action and protection at night of the tank regiments of the armoured brigades. Close support demanded manoeuvrability and speed comparable to those of the armoured regiments, including ability to think at the pace of the armoured battle, receive orders on the move and deploy swiftly off the line of advance to close with the enemy. Protection from enemy fire was far below the level provided for tank crews, at least until 'Kangaroos' – Sherman tanks stripped of their turrets – appeared in the final months of the war.

Motor battalions, as these units were known, had earlier been mounted in tracked, thinly armoured Bren gun carriers and wheeled 15-cwt trucks. By 1944, they were receiving the robust and more strongly armoured United States 'International' half-tracks. Scout cars and Willys jeeps were used for command and communications, while the Bren carriers were retained to carry mortars and medium machine-guns. Each battalion had three motor companies, one to support each armoured regiment in the brigade, and a support company with 3-inch mortars, medium machine-guns and 6-pounder anti-tank guns. Each motor company also had a 'scout' or reconnaissance platoon mounted in Bren gun carriers. Although a motor battalion's dismounted strength was barely more than half that of a marching battalion, its vehicles and longer-range radios were valuable observation and reporting assets when it was required to hold ground.

Tactical headquarters and 'A' Company of 2nd/60th went ashore on 'Juno' beach with the leading elements of 4th Armoured Brigade on the evening of D+1 (7 June). Congestion on the beach was exacerbated by a German air raid, a rare event because of Allied air superiority, but 'A' Company was able to leaguer up for the night in an orchard clear of the beach. The following morning, 8 June, the company went into action. The 4th Armoured Brigade had been allocated a counter-penetration role between 3rd (British) and 3rd (Canadian) Divisions on their left and right respectively. This boundary proved to be the same as that between the 12th SS Panzer and 21st Panzer Divisions to the south. Almost immediately, the brigade had to prepare itself to repel an anticipated counter-attack by 12th SS Panzer Division in the area of the Villons-les-Buissons, a village on the western flank of the 3rd (British) Division's salient overlooking a secondary road running in from the coast towards Caen. The attack came in with great force on the Canadians at Buron, less than three-quarters of a mile to the south-east, providing a useful check of 4th Armoured Brigade's battle readiness and ability to call down air and artillery support.

The 3rd (British) Division had orders to capture the key communications centre of Caen before last light on D-Day. But, while the first two brigades reached their objectives without serious delay, fanatically held German positions in depth delayed the advance. Now the Allied strategy had to be confined, for the time being, to drawing the German armoured formations, which were fast arriving to join the battle, onto the British divisions holding the eastern end of the beachhead and hold them there while wearing them down with artillery fire and air attack. This was to allow the American 1st Army to break out in the west, against weaker opposition, seal off the Brittany peninsula and outflank the enemy's main force.

By 9 June, 4th Armoured Brigade was ashore complete. 'A' Company 2nd/60th, with Bramall in command of a motor platoon, was affiliated to the 3rd City of London Yeomanry (3 CLY) equipped with Sherman tanks. Speaking of events afterwards, he recalled the intense excitement of the landing and move inland, only to be followed by a sense of anti-climax. As the 2nd Army's initial aim had to be changed, 4th Armoured Brigade's counter-penetration task left its motor battalion with little to do beyond guarding the tanks and mopping up enemy stay-behind parties, of which there were quite a number.

Operation 'Epsom', beginning on 21 June, was Bramall's first major action, with 4th Armoured Brigade providing left flank protection for 15th Scottish Division's move forward to seize crossings over the River Odon and get onto the high ground south-west of Caen. For the 2nd/60th this was a dramatic introduction to the awesome effect of Allied air power and artillery, naval and flat trajectory tank gunfire, while the enemy 240-mm guns, firing shells with a lethality area the size of a football pitch, and multi-barrelled mortar bombs were dealing death and destruction from the opposite direction. As Bramall watched two riflemen cross a field behind the forward slit trenches, a 240-mm shell landed some way from them; when he looked up, one had been decapitated and the other blown to pieces.

Caen remained in German hands until 9 July and on the evening of the 7th, 2nd/60th were overlooking the town from the edge of Carpiquet airfield. The range of their radios made them well placed to observe and report on events. First came the 450 four-engine bomber raid on Caen, preliminary to the final ground assault. The need for this massive air attack using high-explosive bombs rather than incendiaries has long been questioned, as it not only destroyed most of the town but congested the streets with huge blocks of masonry, seriously impeding the forward movement of Allied troops. It also led to the deaths of many hundreds of French civilians.

Several days later, 4th Armoured Brigade was ordered to cross the Odon and pass through 43rd Infantry Division, which was to have another shot at taking the high ground south of the river, then advance into the more open country beyond with the optimistic idea of seizing a crossing over the next river, the Orne (see Map 1). Intense enemy artillery fire and the abrupt appearance of Tiger tanks, which outgunned any tank the 2nd Army had in the field, brought 43rd Division's attacks to a halt short of the high ground around point 112 and the fortified village of Maltot. The 2nd/60th waited their moment just to the north of Maltot throughout the afternoon and the early evening until they suddenly saw men of 43rd Division streaming back towards them.

As 'A' Company's orders group watched this alarming scene from the protection afforded by a reverse slope, a group of 88-mm flat trajectory guns opened fire from a flank. The bombardment was prolonged, with shells striking the ground around them. 'A' Company's headquarters half-track received a direct hit, which

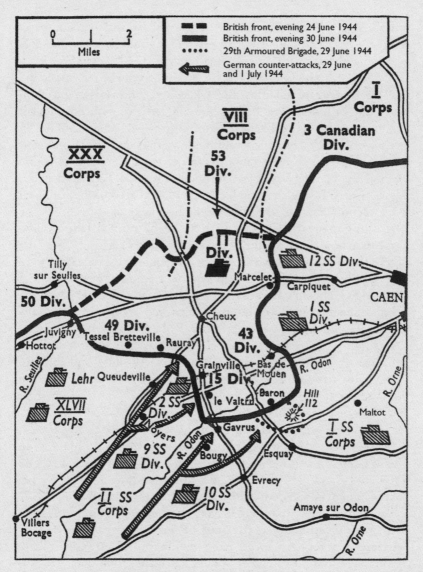

Map 1. Operation Epsom, June 1944.

killed Major Billy Morris, one of the subalterns, the company
sergeant-major and all the drivers and signallers. Of the orders
group members present, only Bramall survived.

Believing himself unharmed, he began to crawl from under the
half-track where he and others had taken cover and saw alongside him
the body of Lieutenant Bertie Jackson, an experienced platoon
commander, scorched black by the blast of the 88-mm shell. On
getting up, he felt a burning sensation down his side. Thinking himself
on fire, he rolled on the ground to put out the flames, only to realise
the sense of burning was in fact a wound in his side. At that moment,
he was joined by the commander of the scout platoon, who had been
on a reconnaissance, and, together, they were able to direct the
remaining company vehicles into a nearby sunken lane to give
protection from the direct fire of the enemy's 88mm guns.

His wound was sufficiently serious to require his evacuation from
the beachhead by hospital ship and special train from Newhaven to a
hospital in Edinburgh. He was discharged a month later and joined the
reinforcement chain for the return of recovered wounded to their units
in France. En route, he met Major Roly Gibbs, who had been
commanding 'C' Company and been wounded on the same day. He
had also recovered and, through a blend of guile and forceful
personality, the pair were able to accelerate their way through the
reinforcement and returned wounded process so as to rejoin their
battalion at the end of the battle to close the Falaise Gap in mid-
August. Their wounds had kept them out of battle for only five weeks.

Then only twenty-three, Gibbs had won the Military Cross in
the Western Desert and seen a lot of action in Italy. A fellow Old
Etonian, he and Bramall struck up a firm friendship and thirty years
later Bramall succeeded Gibbs as head of the Army. Meanwhile
command of 4th Armoured Brigade had changed after Brigadier
John Currie was killed at the start of the Epsom battle. Brigadier
Michael Carver, promoted from command of 1st Royal Tank
Regiment serving in 22nd Armoured Brigade, took over. He was
twenty-nine and had made a name for himself as an operational
staff officer with 7th Armoured Division in the desert and in
command of 1st RTR in Italy.

It is worth pausing at this point to consider the impact of the previous two months on a sensitive and perceptive twenty-year-old. As for thousands of others, transition from a mainly peaceful English setting to the turmoil and violence of the Normandy beachhead must have been severely testing to the nerves, however well individuals were prepared. The nature of a motor battalion's task necessitated a state of constant readiness to react or move. Living day after day in the open, even though the weather in June and July was warm, caused terrible tiredness and a persistent longing for sleep. Success in battle brought brief exhilaration, but the death of comrades turned thoughts to one's own mortality and the days of conflict stretching ahead.

On the first occasion Brigadier Carver visited 2nd/60th, Bramall was still in hospital recovering from his wound. Surprisingly, Carver found what he described as 'a general air of slackness' in this almost too experienced battalion and, reluctantly in view of his distinguished record, arranged for Bill Heathcoat Amory to be removed because he considered him too old for the Normandy battle. He was replaced by the second-in-command, Major Ronnie Littledale, recently awarded the DSO for his successful escape from the supposedly secure Colditz Castle in Saxony, where prisoners-of-war who persistently tried to escape were held. Consequently, the young Bramall saw something of the ruthless nature of the military system at an early stage of his career.

The scene to which he returned on the Allied closure of the Falaise Gap was one of death and desolation. In their struggle to escape the pincers formed by the Canadians and Poles in the north and Americans in the south, the German 5th Panzer and 7th Armies had left a sprawling tangle of abandoned weapons and vehicles amid thousands of corpses of men and horses. In his account of the aftermath of the fighting for the Falaise Gap, Major Dick Vernon – the new second-in-command of 2nd/60th – wrote,

The Germans were too demoralised to put up any serious resistance. Prisoners came in their thousands and were marched back to their cages – men who were hardly men; they had lived through ten days of indescribable terror; they had had loosed on them every horror of modern war, and were the comparatively few survivors of the proud German Seventh Army.

Presenting a horrific sight and appalling smell, the carnage slowed the Allies' advance to the Seine. But after crossing the river at the end of August, 2nd/60th headed north and then north-eastwards with some speed on a route roughly parallel with the coast and that of 12th/60th Rifles ten or so miles further inland. Moving with their affiliated tank regiments of 4th Armoured Brigade, they covered the 250 miles from the Seine to a point north-west of Antwerp in twelve days.

Just three days into this advance, the new commanding officer, Ronnie Littledale, was killed in action between Amiens and Abbeville. With an artillery anti-tank battery in support, the battalion was ordered to hold the village of Airaines against an enemy force reportedly approaching from the north-west. Littledale went ahead to reconnoitre in his scout car and both he and the artillery battery commander were killed by an anti-tank gun fired at point-blank range. Major Dick Vernon took over command until relieved ten days later by Lieutenant-Colonel Robin Hastings of the Rifle Brigade, who had recovered from wounds he had sustained in command of the 6th Green Howards on D-Day.

'A' Company, with Bramall again in command of his motor platoon, started for the village supported by a tank squadron of 3rd City of London Yeomanry. The enemy held tenaciously to positions in village houses and on the neighbouring high ground. As a result, entry to the village was achieved only after dark. The sense of loss of Colonel Littledale was made even more acute by the fact that Airaines had no real tactical significance. The German force had paused there by chance during its retreat eastwards across the British axis of advance and turned it into a strong point. Despite the disaster of Falaise, any idea that the German Army was defeated – as it faced the prospect of defending the Fatherland – was plainly false. Bramall was again wounded during this action, this time in the upper shoulder, but returned to the battalion after only three days in the forward field hospital.

Speaking about the Airaines action, Major Sir Hereward Wake, Bart, who commanded 'A' Company 2nd/60th from Normandy to the Rhine, said of Lieutenant Bramall, 'His Riflemen of Number 3 Platoon thought the world of him. He helped them to overcome their fear at dangerous times, as when driving the Germans out of Airaines, just south of the Somme. He was a forceful character, yet he had a kind and generous personality.'

The final stretch of this rapid advance, which averaged 80 to 90 miles per day, took 2nd/60th along the north bank of the Scheldt amid scenes of wild jubilation in the Belgian towns of Oudenarde, Dendermonder, St Nicholaas and Beverenwaas, but also encountered German units moving eastwards, trying to reach Germany from the area of the Pas de Calais. After fourteen days of intense activity, the battalion was ordered to hold a section of the Meuse–Escaut Canal at the base of the 2nd Army's thrust towards Arnhem.

In mid-October, 2nd/60th were moved to the opposite flank to relieve four battalions of 49th Division in a densely forested area on the Belgian–Dutch frontier, where the enemy had dug in only 200 yards away. This was Bramall's first experience of operating as conventional infantry. To conceal the low strength of the force from the enemy, an intense patrol programme was initiated with mortars and medium machine-guns firing, night and day.

On 20 October, Bramall led a reconnaissance patrol to gather information on enemy strengths and positions in a thick wood, which was known to be mined. The NCO with him was hit when they were engaged at close range from a German outpost and the patrol looked to be in serious trouble. Bramall attacked the position with grenades and his Sten gun, wounding two of the enemy and taking one prisoner. The remaining seven enemy soldiers abandoned the position, leaving behind a machine-gun and two anti-tank bazookas. Although still under fire from other enemy posts in the wood, he continued with his reconnaissance and returned with detailed information about German dispositions and mines.

One might be forgiven for thinking that Lieutenant Bramall was becoming over-confident at this stage of the campaign, or at least testing his luck. Shortly after midday on 27 October, two German deserters came into 'A' Company's position with information that the enemy had pulled out of the nearby village of Goirle. Bramall set off with one section of his platoon to check this report. He avoided a road block on the bridge at the outskirts by wading the stream, but the section corporal lost a foot on a Schu-mine in a ploughed field beyond. In extricating the wounded man, Bramall stepped on another Schu-mine, which miraculously failed to explode. Having sent back the wounded NCO with an escort, he continued his patrol and asked a Dutch civilian he met for a ride on the pillion of his motorcycle through the village to make sure the Germans had left. Once this was confirmed, the rest of the battalion group was called forward. He and his platoon were the first Allied troops to reach the village, their arrival bringing the long-awaited liberation to the inhabitants. (Many years later, when Bramall had become the British Chief of the Defence Staff, the Dutch General Staff laid on a special re-enactment of the clearing of Goirle for his benefit.) The towns of Tilburg and Breda were also taken, but 2nd/60th had to dismount from their half-tracks to clear the woods of snipers and bazooka parties to allow the tanks to move through. The brigade was then ordered into Corps reserve south of Breda.

October and November 1944 were devoted to clearing the Scheldt approaches to Antwerp so that the port could be brought into use for supply and reinforcement. During this time, 2nd/60th remained in Corps reserve, receiving reinforcements to replace casualties and preparing for the next push forward. But von Rundstedt's offensive in the Ardennes, beginning on 16 December, changed the situation abruptly. The 4th Armoured Brigade was put under command of 11th Armoured Division, which was without its own armoured brigade, withdrawn to Belgium to re-equip.

The 2nd/60th's task was to take over a sector facing east across the Maas, with 'A' Company based on the village of Thorn standing on rising ground half a mile back from the river. On 18 December, Dwin Bramall spent his twenty-first birthday in a slit trench on the banks of the Maas. Snow had fallen and the weather was bitterly cold; the enemy was aggressively active at night, their patrols crossing the river to shoot up British positions. A vigorous counter-patrol programme was instigated and the initiative restored. This was a grim and bleak period, quite aside from the dangers, but for Bramall the situation was lightened by his platoon presenting him with a makeshift twenty-first-birthday party and, on the following day, receiving the news that he had been awarded the Military Cross for his leadership of the patrol on 20 October.

The sector was held until von Rundstedt's offensive was defeated, albeit without any direct participation by 2nd/60th. After two months sitting back from the river in the Thorn–Wessem sector, the battalion moved to 4th Armoured Brigade concentration area at Tilburg. It was February 1945.

It was now clear that a major offensive across the Rhine into Germany was all that was required to finish the war in Europe. For this final push, 2nd/60th had just acquired a new commanding officer to replace Robin Hastings, who was evacuated with diphtheria. This was Lieutenant-Colonel Christopher Consett, a strong-willed, mercurial officer who had fought with great gallantry in the Western Desert with the 1st/60th. There was also a new intelligence officer, Dwin Bramall, who took over this post as the commanding officer's battle staff officer and right-hand man.

Although doubtless delighted by his selection, he was by then familiar enough with the army system not to attach too much weight to it. A new commanding officer needed a young man at his side who knew the battalion and its key personalities. Bramall had commanded his motor platoon with energy and competence from the Normandy beach to the Maas, twice wounded in the process. The responsibilities of intelligence officer went well beyond the receipt of intelligence from brigade headquarters and the immediate interrogation of prisoners. He ran the battalion's tactical headquarters, comprising the CO and himself with a couple of signallers, travelling in two lightly armoured scout cars. It was his job to ensure the CO had the right maps marked with the current battle situation, accompany him to brigade order groups, take down intelligence and map details, then issue any confirmatory instructions or map overlays to supplement the CO's verbal orders. It was a full-time job with not much time for sleep.

The grim fighting of the Ardennes offensive having passed them by to the south, 2nd/60th faced their stiffest test of the whole campaign in north-west Europe – the battle of the Reichswald. This was the essential prelude to crossing the Rhine north of the Ruhr and the Germans were now fighting to defend their Fatherland. Except for logging tracks unmarked on the maps, the Reichswald had few roads through the dense pine forest, gloomy and wet after the winter rain and with thick mud everywhere. This was certainly not tank country, nor could the half-tracks, carriers or scout cars advance easily in face of a resolute enemy equipped with *panzerfausts*.

This was infantry country, and 2nd/60th moved forward to its assembly area close to the western edge of the forest on 24 February. The 4th Armoured Brigade had been put under command of 11th Armoured Division, still without its own armoured brigade, which was refitting. The first operation was a brigade night advance of some 3,000 yards to pierce German positions to the south-west of the town of Udem on 27 February. Once the Royal Scots Greys and a lorried infantry battalion from 11th Armoured had forced the break in, 44th Royal Tank Regiment and 2nd/60th were to pass through and take the high ground 2,500 yards beyond.

The line of advance was already a quagmire when the 44th Royal Tanks and 2nd/60th group started their move forward; so thick was the mud that the battalion headquarters' half-tracks had to be towed through it by the tanks. This was very different from the race through Belgium. Only dismounted infantry were able to make real progress, with tank-fire support for attacks on German strong points and fortified villages. It was dangerous and exhausting work, but by last light the battalion had advanced 4,000 yards and taken 128 prisoners with only relatively light loss of killed and wounded.

Next came the northern extension of the Schlieffen Line made up of anti-tank ditches, minefields and machine-gun emplacements, which, with characteristic thoroughness and the ability to improvise with anything available, German reserve units had constructed during the winter. But the country had opened up and the scene before the battalion was one of wet, heavy going between well-defended farmsteads and woodland, all overlooked by the looming 150-feet-high Balberger Wald feature to the east.

The ensuing breakthrough of the Schlieffen Line at the beginning of March was the first in which 2nd/60th were to be mounted in 'Kangaroos' used as infantry-armoured personnel carriers. Each vehicle carried ten men under heavy armoured protection. The break-in operation was conducted by a Canadian division on the left, while 3rd (British) Division took the small but well-fortified town of Kervenheim on the right flank. The 4th Armoured Brigade was to pass through the centre in a new form of grouping, which later became known as a 'square brigade'. This comprised the Royal Scots Greys in their Sherman tanks grouped with a battalion of the King's Shropshire Light Infantry (KSLI) in Kangaroos, advancing on the left, while 44th Royal Tank Regiment and 2nd/60th, now also in Kangaroos, advanced on the right.

The outcome fell well short of a successful set-piece battle. Soft going and lack of experience of the Sherman tanks and Kangaroos operating together brought an inconclusive result on the first day, as well as a disproportionately high number of tank losses. (As their firepower was more effective on the enemy and from a much greater range, the tanks drew the deadly 88-mm flat trajectory fire rather than the Kangaroos.) A new plan was made and at 1400 hours the following day the battalion began a straightforward infantry-style advance on foot, through some deep and water-filled ditches, with strong artillery support. The objectives were reached, but this was an untidy, scrappy battle against still-determined opponents. The battalion killed 50 of the enemy and took 150 prisoners, but with a loss of 49 riflemen, all in the motor platoons.

As intelligence officer, Bramall saw this action from a radically different standpoint from that of a motor platoon commander. Invariably at the CO's side, he had to be at exposed points where the latter could see the ground and the progress of the tanks and Kangaroos across it and, concurrently, keep him in radio touch with all the tank squadrons and motor companies of the battle group. Instead of hastening to ensure his four half-tracks fitted into the battle plan as intended, he was watching anxiously to see that the squadrons and companies moved according to the CO's orders so as to detect any hold-up likely to disrupt the overall plan.

The 2nd/60th's final battle of the war was the crossing of the Rhine and subsequent advance to the Dortmund–Ems canal north of Münster, then on to Bremen and finally Hamburg. The Rhine crossing on 26 March was a classic set-piece battle with all the meticulous attention to detail that was the hallmark of Field Marshal Montgomery's success. The 4th Armoured Brigade was initially in support of 15th Scottish Division. The tanks and half-tracks were carried over the 500-yard-wide river on rafts and the Royal Scots Greys and 2nd/60th group were over by mid-morning to begin a series of advances eastwards. By last light 28 March, the group was into open country south of the town of Bocholt.

On his way to a brigade order group, the CO's two-seater scout car ran over a mine. He was temporarily deafened but otherwise unhurt, although his driver lost a foot. Bramall had been leading in his scout car and avoided the mine by telling his driver to stick to the middle of the road and keep clear of the verges, where the Germans habitually placed their mines. He had another lucky escape in mid-April when the 44th Royal Tank Regiment and 2nd/60th group were ordered to carry out a daylight attack at very short notice, and enemy shells landed near a hastily called orders group rather too close to a prominent cross-roads. More fighting followed until the battalion entered Hamburg on 5 May 1945 and celebrated VE Day on the outskirts of the city. The battalion's battle against elements of the German Marine Division took place only a few miles from where Bramall and his wife Avril were to live nearly thirty years later, when he commanded the 1st Division in the British Army of the Rhine.

Lieutenant Bramall could look back on his first campaign, the decisive one fought by the Western Allies to end the war in Europe, as a source of great experience. As well as being decorated for gallantry and twice wounded, he had experienced the carnage of war at its worst in the Falaise Gap, seen his company commander and a fellow platoon commander killed alongside him, led his motor platoon from the frustrations of the Normandy *bocage* to the Maas and finally been at his commanding officer's right hand in the Reichswald battle and the crossing of the Rhine.

He had received the ribbon of his Military Cross from Field Marshal Montgomery in February. There was a significant wait outside the tent in which the great man was decorating those who had served him so well. As Bramall reached the tent flap, an ADC explained to him, 'The Field Marshal will ask you whether you and he have ever met before. He will not mind whether you say "Yes" or "No", but he *will* mind if you say that you can't remember!'

The 2nd/60th spent the early summer of 1945 in unspoilt and gratefully hospitable Denmark. The battalion entered the country on 12 May, a few days after the German surrender, to be welcomed quite literally with open arms. This is an occasion still remembered by the Danes as the festival of the 'Coming of the Light', when candles are lit to mark the end of the German occupation.

Together with the Royal Dragoons, an armoured car regiment, the battalion had the task of organising the withdrawal of a quarter of a million German troops from the Jutland peninsula and the island of Zeeland, as well as housing and feeding displaced persons from a variety of European countries, previously overrun by Nazi Germany.

4

Getting Around

Having no knowledge of what the immediate future held for the 2nd/60th Rifles after the end of the war in Europe, Dwin Bramall with some other officers volunteered for service in the Far East. His enthusiasm to see more active service had its origins in the fact that he had been on operations for only one year, while others had served abroad and been actively engaged for up to four or even five. This desire was not all that common, many servicemen being only too thankful to emerge from the conflict with their lives. His wartime commission had already been converted to a regular one after he had attended an examining board in Brussels, which put paid to his mother's idea that he might become a doctor, and the dropping of atomic bombs on Hiroshima and Nagasaki on 6 and 8 August 1945 brought the war with Japan to an end. By then, however, Bramall was already in India. As he had volunteered for Airborne Forces, which were being concentrated there in preparation for an assault on Japanese-occupied Malaya, his first commitment was to qualify as a parachutist at Rawalpindi.

The course completed, he joined Headquarters 1st Airborne Corps at Gwalior, near Agra, as a junior staff officer (General Staff Officer Grade 3 in the terminology of the time) with responsibility for 'staff duties'. This arcane term had been introduced in 1904 when the British General Staff was first established. It was a catch-all phrase to encompass the difficult-to-define responsibilities of seeing the new staff system through its first few years. It is still going strong a century later, having assumed the functions of army organisation, manpower levels and deployment. At a Corps or other field headquarters, 'SD' was second only to the Operations staff, and responsible for planning implementation.

Following Japan's unconditional surrender, the Allies' immediate need was for an army of occupation. It was decided that the American and Australian Armies would provide the bulk of the force, but a combined British and Indian division was formed specifically to join it. The division was commanded by Major-General 'Punch' Cowan, a remarkable fighting soldier who had led the 17th Indian Division with great skill and resolution in the four-year-long Burma campaign.

Cowan's ADC, Captain John Slim – son of the illustrious commander of the 14th Army – noted the impact made by the self-confident young captain from the 60th Rifles with a Military Cross, who reported for duty at this divisional headquarters after 1st Airborne Corps was disbanded. After his very brief period with SD, Bramall was appointed Staff Captain A/Q (administration, quartering and supply) to the new 'Brindiv' Headquarters. His primary responsibilities were discipline and personnel matters, and coordination of the provision of supplies delivered under arrangements by specialist staff. Initially, discipline was not a serious problem – the Japanese were submissive after their humiliating surrender – but the occupied cities and towns soon became rife with black-market activity and prostitution, threatening both the discipline and the health of the occupying Allied troops.

After nine months as Staff Captain A/Q, he succeeded his immediate superior, Major Virendra Singh, as Deputy Assistant Adjutant-General of the division. This archaic, high-sounding title from the Victorian era carried only the rank of major, but was a significant advance for him at just twenty-two. It was unusual at that time for a British officer to report directly to an Indian officer, but Bramall had clearly impressed Virendra Singh, an exceptionally able and politically astute individual who rose to major-general in the new Indian Army. The two men got on well together, forming a friendship that lasted sixty years. While his new appointment did not call for intellectual brilliance, it required accuracy and sensitivity in the application of military law and local regulations in the unusual and difficult circumstances where the British and Indian troops in Japan were restless to get home.

This was Bramall's first experience of Gurkha soldiers, with whom he was to become closely associated in later service. The American, Australian and British troops in Japan were allowed to run on a comparatively loose rein after the tight control essential for operations. The commanding officer of the only Gurkha battalion, which included three holders of the Victoria Cross, felt so keenly for the welfare of his men, however, that he allowed them out of camp only under strict control. Inevitably, resentment developed when his men observed the freedom enjoyed by their white comrades, and stirrings of what might have become close to a mutiny began to show themselves. Bramall accompanied General Cowan to the Gurkhas' camp and watched him scotch the whole affair in less than half an hour by some straight talking in Gurkhali to soldiers whose quality he knew so well.

Around this time, General Cowan wrote to General Slim, a very old friend going back to pre-war days with the 6th Gurkha Rifles, to say – perhaps rather extraordinarily – that he had a young officer working for him whom he judged would one day be Chief of the Imperial General Staff.

While in Japan, Bramall took the opportunity to visit Hiroshima to see the scene of devastation left by the atomic bomb. Although horrific, to his mind the scale of damage was less dramatic than that he had seen in Hamburg in early 1945. Moreover, Hamburg was an ancient European city, where thousands of historic and substantial buildings of brick and stone had been razed by the fire-storms brought about by Allied bombing in July 1943 and subsequently, whereas the buildings of Hiroshima had almost all been constructed of wood and paper, leaving virtually no rubble or ruins to see.

In a letter home, Bramall described the scenery and way of life of Japan as being still that of Madame Butterfly and Lieutenant Pinkerton, devoid in the main of the excrescence of modern industry or commercialism. It held a strong attraction for him, in particular that around the British–Indian Division headquarters at

Okayama, 85 miles up the coast of Honshu from Hiroshima, with glorious views over the islands of the inland sea bordered to the south by Shikoku. He saw as much of the country as his work allowed, visiting Nikko, Kobe and Kyoto, as well as Tokyo and Mount Fuji, painting and taking photographs until his return to England on a 28-day sea voyage at the very end of 1946.

While he was still in the Far East, news came through that the place at Christ Church College, Oxford, which he had won at school, was available for him to take up. By then a major aged twenty-two, he did not feel inclined to accept it, even as a 'mature student', and so gave it up. Leave followed but not return to 2nd/60th Rifles, who were then in Tripoli. Instead he reverted to his war-substantive rank of captain – his basic rank was still lieutenant – to take up an appointment in the Military Operations Directorate of the War Office. One might reasonably ask why the ministry for the Army needs such a thing when operations are the responsibility of the generals commanding the theatres abroad. This relatively small and always carefully chosen staff acts as the interface between politico/military policy-makers in London and commanders and their staffs abroad. They work closely, but not always in agreement, with the Military Intelligence Staff and the Foreign Office to determine the wider operational policy to be recommended to Ministers, through the Chief of the General Staff.

Bramall was a member of Military Operations 4 (MO 4) responsible for operations in the Middle East. Head of the branch was Lieutenant-Colonel Martin Charteris, 60th Rifles and later Lord Charteris of Amisfield, Private Secretary to The Queen, 1972–7. At that stage of his career, Bramall had no first-hand knowledge of the Middle East, then enduring its early postwar turmoil. The central point of trouble was the Jewish insurrection in Palestine, where, in conformity with the 1922 League of Nations Mandate, Britain was struggling to govern the country while maintaining a balance between Jewish national aspirations for land and influence there and the Palestinian Arabs' implacable opposition to any increased Jewish hold on either. Egypt fretted under British control of the Suez Canal Zone, Iraq resented the

British military and air force presence watching over the Iraqi oil fields and the Libyans had begun to slaughter the Jewish population with whom they had lived in peace for five hundred years.

Sixteen years later, Bramall was to have a not insignificant hand in the reorganisation of the Ministry of Defence following its incorporation of the three single Service Ministries, but the functions and organisation of the Military Operations Directorate remain much the same today. The prompt provision of accurate briefs on operational situations abroad and their implications, and assimilating the Intelligence Staff assessments and Foreign Office opinions, was the bread-and-butter work at Military Operations, but quickly made calculations of what could be done in a crisis – and by what forces – was also the routine. Bramall thrived in this atmosphere, enquiring, weighing up the options and trying to distil a course to recommend. This was not the strategy and tactics that he later found to be the most stimulating aspects of his military thinking, but it was acutely interesting just the same.

Still a bachelor, he lived at home with his parents in Symons Street, off Sloane Square, just behind Peter Jones. This provided a perfect base for night-clubbing with friends, playing cricket at Winchester in the summer and even the occasional hunt ball, although he never hunted or aspired to do so. During the winter of 1948, he met Avril Vernon, sister of Dick Vernon, who had been second-in-command of 2nd/60th during much of the north-west European campaign, and only daughter of the late Brigadier-General Henry Vernon, DSO, also of the 60th. Her mother, 'Bunde', had remarried and lived with her second husband, Brigadier-General Godfrey Willan, another former 60th officer, at Number 8, The Close, Winchester.

Bramall was twenty-five, she a few months older and, if photographs of the time are any guide, the rather more poised. His pensive and rather serious expression had given way to youthful exuberance and the ease and laughter of romantic but secret-seeming camaraderie. She wears a serene half-smile, but with the hint of a question about to be asked, that became so familiar to their friends. A photograph of them together at a dance catches him looking distinctly raffish and she – well, just lovely. Whoever took it has written on the back, 'Dwyn – some day a General – and Avril Bramall', so it was taken shortly after they were married, probably in the winter of 1949.

Swift and bold as his regimental motto demanded, Bramall made certain the romance was not slow to blossom. Introducing his future bride to his parents presented some difficulty, at least in the eyes of his mother, ever conscious of keeping up appearances. After demobilisation, his father was again without any civilian occupation, something that Bryda Bramall judged Miss Vernon might consider strange. So she sent her husband out, complete with bowler hat and umbrella, with instructions to return to their house in Symons Street around 6 p.m., by which time the young couple would have enjoyed afternoon tea and he would give the impression of having had another 'hard day at the office'. This subterfuge required some careful explanation to Avril, once she and Dwin had come to know each other rather better.

Announcement of their engagement on 12 May 1949 brought a letter from his wartime commanding officer, Colonel Robin Hastings. After expressing his delight at this turn of events, he went on,

It will be a relief to your Sergeant-Major, Adjutant or Chief of Staff, or whatever you have now, in that you will let them off five minutes earlier on Saturday mornings than you generally do. I shall expect it to make a great difference to your appearance and character, that you will give up the studied Prussianism of your coiffeur, allow the lines already graven on your Montgomery brow to soften, that you will sometimes put down the Field Service Pocket Book for Marie Stopes on 'How to Wash the Baby'.

They attended their first engagement as a couple at a dance given by Lady Barker, wife of General Sir Evelyn 'Bubbles' Barker, Colonel-Commandant of the 60th Rifles, at Walton-on-Thames on 20 May. Marriage with full pomp and circumstance in Winchester Cathedral followed on 16 July 1949. The ceremony was performed by the Lord Bishop of Winchester, the Right Reverend Dr Mervyn

Haigh, assisted by the Dean. The bride was given away by her brother, by then a lieutenant-colonel, and the best man was Major Roger Nixon, former Adjutant of the bridegroom's wartime battalion. The bride wore gold brocade with a train of old Honiton lace and matching veil – an heirloom lent by a friend, Mrs St Maur of Hampton Hill House, Hampshire. They spent their first night in an apartment at Claridge's, for which the bill, including dinner and breakfast, amounted to £9 12s 4d. One might marvel, but this represented around one-third of a captain's monthly pay in 1949.

The honeymoon was divided between the Hotel Splendide at Bellagio, on the very tip of the peninsula jutting into Lake Como, the Hotel Regina on the Grand Canal in Venice and a hot and noisy hotel near the station in Florence. They did all the sights, and one photograph of the future field marshal suggests that he drank what looks suspiciously like lemonade in the Piazza San Marco outside Florians.

This was the start of a long, successful and very happy marriage, each partner providing the perfect foil for the other. Dwin, however clever and strong-minded, could be over-particular, even fussy – especially if someone else's comfort was involved – injecting an air of anxiety into a situation when it was not really necessary. Avril, calm and serenely at ease, would be quietly confident that all would be well or, even if a catastrophe might occur, certain that they could handle it with assurance. Although daughter of a soldier and married to another, she was far from the archetypal 'army wife'. She was elegant, most certainly, and a gracious and welcoming hostess, but her quiet humour and occasional quizzically raised eyebrow were enough to win everyone's loyalty and affection.

The immediate postwar years saw the size of the British Army drastically reduced. Infantry of the line and the rifle regiments were reduced from two to one battalion each and grouped so that, when necessary, one or perhaps two in each group could be reinforced by the others. Within each group, one regiment became a cadre of officers and NCOs responsible for training National Service recruits for the remainder. The 60th Rifles and Rifle Brigade were reduced to a single battalion each, with 1st/60th becoming the Rifle Group's training battalion at Bushfield Camp above St Cross in Winchester. This was the unit to which Bramall made his return to regimental duty after his various staff appointments abroad and at the War Office.

The disappointment of professional soldiers, on finding their careers and overseas service prospects curtailed by the reduced army structure and deployment, was to a large extent mollified by the fine quality of the National Servicemen it was their task to train. Bramall was especially fortunate to be appointed to command the potential officers' company. This was not only an important job, but one in which his talent for getting the best out of people, and spotting the more talented, could be put to good use. The care he took over the development of the potential officers under his care soon became known outside the Rifle Group; recruits with university degrees selected to be officers or sergeant instructors in the Royal Army Education Corps were also sent to him for training. It was during this period that a fellow officer with the training regiment gave him the nickname 'Field Marshal Lord Bramall of Bushfield', which was quickly picked up and jokingly used behind his back by the senior NCOs. When, some thirty years later, he had retired as Chief of the Defence Staff, was about to receive a peerage and needed a geographical location for it, he rang one of the officers who had served in the training battalion and asked, 'It has to be "Bushfield" hasn't it?' And so the title was adopted.

But that was a very long way off. Promotion prospects were low for everyone, as many wartime officers had elected to stay on, while the number of units had been reduced. Although the chance of commanding even an operational company at that stage was some way ahead, in early 1949 Bramall was sent on a company commanders' course at the School of Infantry, Warminster. His operational experience allowed him to take the content of the course in his stride, while his ability to express himself in an articulate and engaging manner brought him to the attention of the directing staff. In consequence, he was called back to the School as an instructor in August that year.

For the following two years, Bramall was in his element teaching infantry tactics and operational techniques – cooperation with armour and supporting artillery, all matters he understood clearly – to subalterns on the platoon commanders' course, who for the most part had no operational experience whatever. A measure of the School Commandant's confidence in him became apparent during a visit to Warminster by the Army Council, as it was then known. There was to be a demonstration of directing artillery supporting fire by an infantry officer remote from the guns. The system for this using radio is simple enough in theory, but it can go quite dramatically wrong in practice. Captain Bramall was in charge.

It was one of those days on Salisbury Plain with which every British soldier is familiar. Rain drained fitfully from a leaden sky, the ground was sodden, and visibility, if one could keep the rain off one's binocular lenses, was what is termed 'limited', but real guns were about to fire real shells. As the Army Council viewed this depressing scene, the lively voice of Captain Bramall could be heard competing with the 'feed-back' on the public address system, 'Great privilege to have the Army Council here to watch this – crackle crackle. Just to show how easy it is for the infantry to direct artillery fire – crackle crackle – I am going to select a member of the platoon commanders' course – crackle crackle – to give the fire directions.'

Forty-five blood-flow systems ran ice-cold and as many pairs of eyes were raised to the sullen heavens with prayers more fervent than any since childhood. The name was called out and forty-four young men relaxed to enjoy the fun. 'There's the target,' said Bramall, dabbing a wet forefinger on a wet, crumpled map. 'You can see it quite clearly over there', pointing encouragingly towards Andover. 'So we can follow what is happening, your orders to the guns will be broadcast over the tannoy.'

The method for infantry giving artillery fire directions is based on the not unreasonable assumption that the infantryman, very probably uncertain of his own position, will give an incorrect map reference for the target. Therefore the first ranging shot is directed *beyond* where he thinks the target lies. This, in nine cases out of ten, will give the gunners an indication of the maximum range. Then, using the plume of smoke as his reference point, the infantryman brings the next ranging shot closer towards him, by ordering over the radio, 'Drop four hundred', or as many hundreds of yards he judges are required to bring the next shot to *his* side of the target. Ideally, the adjustment should be given in an even number of hundreds of yards to save the gunners stress in dividing it by two to 'bracket' the target more closely. Once it is 'bracketed', the infantryman orders add or drop half the distance and then 'Fire for effect'.

The quavering voice of the wretched subaltern selected to demonstrate the technique broke the silence over the tannoy, but he wisely paused with 'Wait', blew his nose, wiped his eyes and binocular lenses and began again. The first shot was heard and the shell whistled if not actually overhead, somewhere to a flank, to explode just beyond a ragged line of trees, which everyone from the Chief of the Imperial General Staff downwards was then able to identify as the target. From then on it was plain sailing. The next order was given and it came as a surprise to only a few of those watching that the shot fell a neat 200 yards on the observers' side of the target. 'Add 200, five rounds gunfire', ordered a newly confident voice over the tannoy. Twenty shells struck the target in five tight groups of four and the Army Council led the applause. These were experienced gunners!

Dwin Bramall made best use of the stimulating comradeship of like minds among the instructional staff and steady training routine at Warminster to study for and take the Staff College entrance examination. In those days, this entailed three tactics papers, military law, a paper on administration and morale, a military history paper based on knowledge of seven major campaigns from Roman times to the Second World War and perhaps most formidable of all, a wide-ranging paper on current affairs. Even if one passed the examination, there was still a hurdle of selection based on the individual's confidential reports to date. Between 15 and 20 per cent of those who passed the examination would be disappointed when the selections were announced in *The Times*. Captain Bramall passed first time and was selected to attend the command and staff course at Camberley in 1952. At only just twenty-nine, he was the youngest man of his year.

Predictably perhaps, instruction at Camberley in 1952 focused on methods used when things had gone well for the British Army during the Second World War. Reasons for a battle having gone wrong or a defeat inflicted received markedly less emphasis. This was a serious omission, but the war experience of the members of the Directing Staff at that time would, consciously or otherwise, bridge the gap in the form of their often vivid recollections of military disasters and their assessment of why they had occurred. An atmosphere of victory still hung about and success and failure could be discussed with wry humour. This came as a surprise to foreign students, in particular those from continental Europe or the United States, where military instruction and witticisms seldom went hand in hand.

Bramall greatly enjoyed the camaraderie and the intellectual challenge of Camberley, speaking his mind frankly during debate in the ten-strong syndicate groups and also in Rawlinson Hall, where visiting lecturers, Cabinet ministers and senior generals among them, gave their talks and invited student questions. He did well on the year-long course and formed a sound platform for the development of his wider career in the Army.

There was a rather eccentrically English custom for the student not to see his report at the end of the course or to be told specifically how well he was considered to have done. Some degree of revelation came at the end of the first week in December, when each student received in his pigeonhole notification of his next appointment. Except for those who were returning to their regiments or corps, for whom no such revelation was available, the measure of how well you had done became evident from the appointment you received. Brigade majors of regular brigades were generally regarded as the 'top dogs', closely followed by General Staff Officers Grade 2 (GSO 2s) at the War Office or on the headquarters of a regular division. It was a cruel form of amusement, not untypical of the Army, to watch the faces of those who thought they had done well, but actually had not, when they opened their envelopes. Bramall was appointed GSO 2 (Operations) at Headquarters 3rd Infantry Division, which had just left the United Kingdom for Egypt, where the new Arab–Socialist regime was confronting the British presence on the Suez Canal.

Experience as a member of the Military Operations staff in the War Office in 1947–8 had given him some background on Egypt. But the situation there had worsened abruptly when King Farouk was deposed in 1953 and a republic proclaimed. Initially, this was presided over by General Mohamed Neguib, soon to be superseded by Lieutenant-Colonel Gamal Abdul Nasser, previously his right-hand man. There were some 80,000 British troops in Egypt, but, while the political and security situation was tense, the operational tempo was relatively low. The period reflected the closing years of Britain as an imperial power. The Korean War had demonstrated that not only the United Kingdom but also the Commonwealth had to rely on American air power, technology and finance in any future medium or large-scale conflict; yet many senior British officers either remained oblivious of this or chose to ignore the facts before them. The Suez Canal in particular was regarded as a vital and therefore sacrosanct stone in the arch of empire, as it provided the shortest sea route to the Far East. The 1st and 3rd Divisions were situated in the south and north of the Canal Zone respectively, with the task of ensuring its security.

Contingency plans for advances on Cairo and Alexandria had been prepared against the possibility of Egyptian opposition to the British presence taking some form that might threaten safe passage through the Suez Canal. Major Bramall was responsible for planning the 3rd Division's part in all this, but it was not long before the style of command exercised by the General Officer Commanding 3rd Division, Major-General Nigel Poett, began to give his GSO 2 (Operations) some difficulties. Poett was a brave, enthusiastic and friendly commander who had distinguished himself commanding a parachute brigade in the invasion of Normandy. He was always to be found where the fighting and shelling were heaviest, encouraging his troops with his unconcerned demeanour and cheerful chat. Unfortunately, although he had a detailed knowledge of his profession and was good on paper, his habit of speaking before he had really thought through a problem did not lead to crisp and unambiguous decision-making. Indeed it was sometimes difficult to know exactly what he had in mind. This gave the Commander of

32nd Guards Brigade frequent opportunity to put his own interpretation on what he had been instructed to do. There was also another reason for the brigadier to be difficult. The two senior officers did not like each other, having previously been rivals for a lady's hand in marriage, which General Poett had won. Luckily, Bramall's friendly relationship with the brigade major of the Guards Brigade, Major Ronald Taylor, helped to smooth over the military differences.

Fifty years later, interest was again briefly focused on what had become known among the veterans as the 'Forgotten Egyptian Campaign'. During what he judged to be the most dangerous phase of the emergency, General Sir Brian Robertson, Commander-in-Chief British Troops in Egypt, had recommended that a medal should be awarded for service in Egypt at the time. Anti-British demonstrations had given way to the ambushing of military vehicles travelling between the various barracks and camps and, in January 1952, a pitched battle had been fought with 1,000 Egyptian armed police in Ismailia. In all, thirty British servicemen had been killed and another sixty-nine wounded. Because of 'political considerations' General Robertson's recommendation was ignored, but, in 2003, it was announced that the surviving veterans of the emergency were entitled to the General Service Medal 1918 (still extant in 1954–5) bearing the clasp 'Canal Zone'. (Bramall played a part in this decision by persuading the Cabinet Secretary, and through him the Prime Minister, that an injustice had been done.)

In addition to his responsibilities in Egypt in the early 1950s, Bramall was instructed by General Poett to make a theoretical study of how 3rd Division might operate in battle under the threat of nuclear weapons. Having done this, as far as information available allowed, Bramall concluded that the most likely outcome would be that all movement and deployment by the antagonists would come to a halt, with no perceptible advantage to either.

In the autumn of 1954, agreement was reached between the British and Egyptian Governments whereby British forces would evacuate the Canal Zone, but leave Anglo-French pilots to guide the vessels using the Canal. The 3rd Division returned to Colchester shortly before Christmas 1954 and, coincidentally,

Bramall returned to regimental duty, going for the first time to the Rifle Depot at Winchester to command the Training Company.

This assignment suited him very well, as it gave him full rein to exercise his flair for training young soldiers, as well as officers, but it was to last only eighteen months. In mid-1956 he was posted to command a motor company, with 1st/60th, now reconstituted as a motor battalion and serving with 10th Armoured Division in Libya, under treaty arrangements with Britain following the emergence of Libya as an independent state in 1949.

Hardly had Major Bramall completed arrangements for his move abroad when he was ordered to report instead to the War Office, where his old divisional commander, General Nigel Poett, had recently become Director of Military Operations. Curious though they undoubtedly were, the events that then unfolded gave him a useful insight into how things worked, or sometimes didn't, in Whitehall during a crisis.

5

Acquiring a Reputation

On taking up his new appointment in the War Office, General Poett found his staff severely stretched in planning how to react to the situation in the Middle East brought about by Nasser's nationalisation of the Suez Canal Company in July 1956. Having formed a high opinion of Bramall while on his staff in Egypt, he called him in to help. This was just the sort of predicament in which officers of ability can find themselves and against which it would be both graceless and pointless to complain. In London, Bramall found that a large planning staff had been set up in the War Office basement under Lieutenant-General Sir Hugh Stockwell, a charismatic and popular leader whose proud boast was that he had not attended the Staff College and, until recently, had been the Commander of 1st (British) Corps in Germany. It was his responsibility and that of his staff to plan for any military intervention in Egypt, and, for a few weeks, Bramall acted as a liaison officer between Military Operations 4 (MO 4) and those toiling in the basement.

In the early stages of contingency planning, thinking in the War Office centred round regaining control over the Canal by a landing at Alexandria in order to advance on Cairo and bring about Nasser's downfall. Bramall was horrified by this proposal (as was the Foreign Office), by the exaggerated nature of the threat Nasser was purported to present to British interests and, most serious of all, the complete lack of awareness of the new sensitivity of the Arab world towards western interference in its affairs. He was equally appalled by the ponderous nature of the operations, as planned, which would expose Britain to criticism and censure on the wider stage long before the proposed operations could be concluded. As an example, one element of the basement staff was busying itself over the stores and vehicles to be unloaded at Alexandria up to D+62 – nine weeks after the opening of hostilities!

The Chiefs of Staff were deeply divided over whether an intervention was feasible, politically or militarily. Mountbatten, First Sea Lord and Chief of Naval Staff, opposed any military intervention and threatened to resign. The Chief of the Imperial General Staff, General Sir Gerald Templer – not a man to hesitate about 'having a go' – summed up the situation with the words, 'Of course we can get to Cairo, but what I want to know is what the bloody hell do we do when we get there?' Bramall was to recall these words forty-six years later in a letter he wrote to *The Times*, pointing out the grave risks to stability in the Middle East of the proposed US–UK intervention in Iraq.

After a few weeks in London, Bramall was greatly relieved when, after a certain amount of badgering, General Poett allowed him to join the 1st/60th in Libya. He set off, not only with a personal sense of release, but hoping the Suez crisis would blow over so that the contingency plans would not be put to the test. On arrival in Derna, he was to take over command of 'D' Company from his old friend of Normandy days, Major Roly Gibbs.

Gibbs and his company had recently returned to Libya from the Persian Gulf, where they had been on standby to assist with a series of threatening local emergencies. Soon after Bramall took over 'D' Company in October 1956, the Battalion came to 24 hours' notice to move. Although it had been rather belatedly discovered that the 10th Armoured Division was precluded by the Libyan treaty from taking part in any intervention in Egypt, its units could be used to meet emergency situations arising elsewhere. Therefore, in common with others, the battalion was reinforced by regular reservists recalled from their jobs and homes because of the Suez crisis.

A total of 300 reservists from the 60th Rifles, the Rifle Brigade, the Duke of Cornwall's Light Infantry and the Durham Light Infantry were sent from England to join the battalion. The realisation that they would not be used on any operation against Nasser, who had become something of a hate figure at home, did not improve their state of mind nor calm their impatience at being kept in poor accommodation on the outskirts of a town virtually bereft of amenities. After a beer-drinking marathon in a leaking NAAFI canteen on a wet night, this situation finally resulted in a rampage in which windows were smashed and other damage caused to one of the battalion's two barracks. Bramall came back from Benghazi, where he had been to collect a new car, to find East Barracks, in which his company was housed, looking like a battlefield. Order was quickly restored and the Commanding Officer punished the ringleaders severely. Even so, much was learnt about man management and everyday communication with soldiers. The 1st/60th was not the only battalion to suffer such disturbances; they had also occurred elsewhere in the Mediterranean theatre, where reservists had been recalled.

Although his battalion was not involved in the Anglo-French operations at Port Said in November 1956, ostensibly to separate the two sides following Israel's thrusts to the Suez Canal across the Sinai Desert, Bramall was ordered to take his company to the Libyan–Egyptian frontier to show solidarity with the Libyan border force. Once the situation on the Canal had stabilised and control had been handed over to a United Nations' force, the reservists were sent home and the implications of the Suez venture for the Army as a whole began to filter through to Libya. The 10th Armoured Division was to be broken up and, after twenty-five years in the motor battalion role, 1st/60th was to revert to being a marching infantry battalion. Having lost the reservists and National Servicemen due for release, the battalion was down to little more than half its establishment strength, but still with the full scale of weapons, vehicles and equipment to look after. In these less than ideal circumstances in a station devoid of entertainment facilities, Bramall devised an interesting diversion.

After a good deal of planning and training in desert navigation and travel, he organised and led an expedition of five officers and sixteen NCOs and riflemen chosen from volunteers from the battalion as a whole. The plan was to travel in a total of eight vehicles across the neck of the Great Sand Sea south-west of Siwa

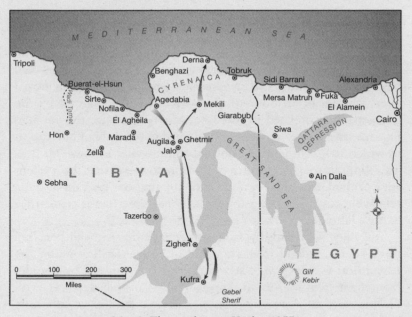

Map 2. The expedition to Kurfra, 1957.

to the Kufra oasis. This was more than just a long drive in the desert, as, in many respects, the chosen route represented making the journey the hard way. Kufra lies some 650 miles south of the coast of Cyrenaica and, in the days before oil exploration had opened up communications, was isolated from the rest of the country. Rightly insistent that the expedition should not depend on guides, Bramall turned to the navigational skills developed by the Long Range Desert Group (LRDG) from the experiences of Ralph Bagnold, Rupert Harding-Newman and Bill Kennedy-Shaw in the years before the Second World War. Their work had paved the way for operations by the LRDG and 1st Special Air Service Regiment against the open flank and rear airfields supporting Rommel's Afrika Korps during the Western Desert campaign of 1941–3. Kufra had been the LRDG and SAS desert base until moving to Siwa, after the enemy had been cleared from there.

Lieutenant Guy Crossman was sent to RAF El Adem to learn the skills of desert navigation from the RAF Regiment desert rescue section. This system works on dead reckoning by prismatic and sun compass combined with solar and star fixes. The sun compass used by Bagnold was rather like an adjustable sundial with an arm moved every quarter of an hour to align with the shadow cast by the gnomon. When related to the distance covered since the previous fix, this gave a dead-reckoning position limited only by the extent to which rough ground had obliged the traveller to move off line. Travelling in roughly a north–south direction skirting the western edge of the Great Sand Sea made calculating the position at noon relatively easy, as setting the exact local time is not critical for fixing a latitude.

Travelling westwards by the coast from Derna, through Benghazi to Agedebia, inland from the Gulf of Sirte, the first leg of the expedition was relatively straightforward. A forward base under Lieutenant John Mason, an imperturbable Australian officer, with Colour Sergeant Fowley and six men was established at Jalo, from where the main body began the 350-mile journey south-eastwards and then south to cross the Great Sand Sea. Before the northern edge was reached, however, soft going leading to heavy petrol consumption persuaded the expedition leader that he must reduce the size of the group to go on to Kufra. After establishing another advance base on the northern edge of the Sand Sea at Zighen, Bramall continued with just five landrovers. The party comprised Lieutenants Guy Crossman and Charles Williams – later the Labour Peer Lord Williams of Elvel – and two expert vehicle fitters – Warrant Officer Rodigan of the Royal Electrical and Mechanical Engineers and Sergeant Lew Fee of the 60th. Mr Marsaud from the Derna YMCA accompanied them as their Arabic interpreter.

The two fitters worked miracles keeping the vehicles in running order until Kufra was reached two and a half days after crossing the Sand Sea in a sandstorm (see Map 2). On the way out, a Lanner falcon's eggs were found in a rusty tin in the middle of nowhere; the laying was thought probably timed to hatch during the bird migration, which provides most of the prey for the Lanner and her chicks. On arrival at the oasis, the party was greeted by a local official with a handsome flywhisk. Before Guy Crossman could warn him, Bramall expressed admiration for the object, thereby obliging its owner to present it to him on leaving. When the gift was presented, he risked giving offence by attempting to decline. Years later he described the incident in a book of personal reminiscences by members of the Travellers' Club under the title *Don't look a gift horse in the mouth!* After a reception by the Mudir and his committee, the cool waters of the oasis were enjoyed and Charles Williams joined in with the Tebu dancers late into the night, before the party set off for Jalo, then over the open desert for Mechili and through the coastal range of hills to Derna.

In addition to making the difficult choice of who would remain behind at the forward base at Jalo, Bramall was faced with problems of which route to take and other difficulties. Undoubtedly his most difficult decision was to leave the jovial and unflappable Captain Christopher Adami and two members of the expedition at the bleak and featureless spot at the Zighen Gap, in order to cut down on the group to make the final dash for Kufra. The return journey proved no easier than the outward one. The steering of Guy Crossman's land rover was wrecked by a plunge down a sand slope, but repaired by the indefatigable Warrant Officer Rodigan. Guy Crossman recalled that Bramall had a seemingly effortless air of command, bordering on familiarity, which made everyone want to give of his best. The two advance base parties were picked up at Zighen and Jalo, so that everyone returned together. The expedition gathered much useful information for others who planned a similar, later expedition. This led to discovery of a route twenty miles west of the one Bramall took, with firmer going that saved time.

In October 1957, 1st/60th was moved into barracks in Tripoli. Bramall was left with a rear party at Derna until the base there could be handed over to the Cyrenaica Defence Force. He had commanded a motor company for just over one year, when the principal challenge was leadership: first in dealing with the reservists, understandably resentful at their recall and at not being sent on active service, and National Servicemen far from home engaged in duties in which they could seldom see much point. In November 1957, the battalion sailed from Tripoli, destined for Ballykinler in Northern Ireland, but Bramall had already received notice that he was to return to the Staff College, Camberley, as a member of the Directing Staff.

Then, as now, this was a prestigious and encouraging appointment for any officer who was perceived as a rising star. In terms of workload, it is difficult to think of any heavier in peacetime. The appointment then carried the *local*, that is unpaid, rank of lieutenant-colonel for its duration only, but, despite these drawbacks, the incumbent knew that he had been talent-spotted and given an opportunity to demonstrate his worth and potential.

The Staff College had changed little in the five years since Bramall had left as a student, except in one significant regard. The year he re-joined (1958) marked the introduction of study and exercises in the use of tactical nuclear weapons on a future European battlefield. This called for much fresh thought and discussion by the Directing Staff, as, of course, there was no experience of any kind on which to draw for the development of tactics – only the record of the devastation and residual effects of the high-yield atomic bombs dropped on Hiroshima and Nagasaki in 1945 to set the scene.

Bramall had several friends among the Directing Staff, including three Rifle Brigade officers, the 60th Rifles' sister regiment. The Commandant was his old Divisional Commander from the Middle East, Major-General Nigel Poett, who may have had a hand in his return to Camberley to teach while so young. He was thirty-four and, although a local lieutenant-colonel, confirmed in his substantive rank of major only as recently as his birthday the previous December. While it had been commonplace to have young instructors at the Staff Colleges during the war, when recent operational experience was in prime demand, thirty-six or thirty-seven years of age had become the norm, with expectation of command of one's regiment or a lieutenant-colonel's staff appointment in two or three years' time. His youth precluded Bramall from hoping for command or a Grade 1 staff post in three years, but the prospect of teaching the new generation of officers greatly appealed to him. Many were postwar Sandhurst graduates with little or no active service experience.

The Camberley ethos, at least since the Edwardian period, demanded exacting work, and there was no sympathy for any student who failed to match up. Other than the few instructors who were not up to *their* jobs, the Directing Staff came over to the student body as a fierce and ruthless lot, especially in terms of verbal criticism during syndicate discussion and searing comment on written work. This was all designed to develop an ability to work accurately and quickly under intense pressure and build up the student's confidence in the face of criticism, whether justified or not. The more robust students found it quite entertaining.

As an instructor, Bramall had the advantage of an ability to absorb a mass of detail quickly and select the key points, together with a manner that won students' confidence. His short, almost self-deprecatory laugh before any comment would take the sting out of even the most swingeing criticism and be followed by a constructive, 'Don't you think it would be a better idea to try so and so.' He was no slave to the 'pink', as the solution to any exercise or problem was known, but able to listen to a student's alternative ideas and, when appropriate, commend him for them. Word soon got around, just as it did about any member of the Directing Staff given to being gratuitously offensive in his censure, and soon the students in his Division were hoping that they would have the luck to be in his syndicate in one of the subsequent terms.

The work of the Directing Staff was not confined to teaching. Every now and then one would be awarded what was euphemistically called a 'resting term'. This forecast not a relaxing time, only freedom from teaching so as to write a new exercise, revise a previous one incorporating new ideas or, rather more challenging, develop techniques for a new form of operation, such as defence against massive armoured attack in central Europe, use of helicopters or counter-urban guerrilla tactics in an environment where the insurgents would not be intimidated by the infliction of a handful of casualties.

Study of the use of tactical nuclear weapons against Warsaw Pact forces on the NATO Central Front in Europe was the chief innovation in 1958. A theoretical technique was put forward for discussion termed 'the nuclear defence of the river line'. This stemmed from early NATO defensive plans based on the Rhine and later, after West Germany had joined the Alliance, the Weser. In essence, the infantry was to observe and hold the river line to force an enemy concentration on the opposite bank; this would then be destroyed by a tactical nuclear strike. The fate of the infantry was possible survival under four feet of overhead cover and on-the-spot decontamination from the inevitable nuclear fallout.

This was an example of that well-known British facility for self-delusion when no practical option is apparent, something the military usually flatter themselves they resort to less frequently than their political masters. It was received with ill-concealed astonishment by the students, other than those ready to accept anything rather than risk disapproval. General Poett therefore decided to call the Directing Staff and the students together to explain why he disagreed with the tactics proposed. Unfortunately, and this was a burden under which this gallant and courteous officer constantly laboured, his explanation was so extensive that no one carried away any clear impression of the alternative he suggested.

As it was by then decided that the 1st (British) Corps in Germany would adopt 'nuclear defence of the river line' as its mantra in the event of a Warsaw Pact attack, the Directing Staff at Camberley had no option but to teach it. Some of the more independently minded, Bramall among them, privately ridiculed it in syndicate discussion; he recalled the conclusions he had reached when having a first look at such issues while on the staff of Headquarters 3rd Division in Egypt. At the same time he recognised that some form of 'trip-wire' deployment for the release of battlefield nuclear weapons would have to be adopted, until closer parity between NATO and Warsaw Pact conventional forces in central Europe could be achieved.

In 1961, at the age of thirty-seven, Bramall was made a brevet lieutenant-colonel. This gave him the rank of lieutenant-colonel in the Army without changing his seniority as a major in his regiment. This curious and difficult-to-comprehend arrangement had been introduced in earlier times to reward gallantry before honours below Companion of the Bath were introduced. After the Second World War, brevets for lieutenant-colonel only were reintroduced as a means of giving a 'leg-up' to majors of unusual promise to allow them to compete for Grade 1 (lieutenant-colonel) staff appointments with their slightly older and more senior contemporaries.

There is an apocryphal story of a battalion second-in-command who was a brevet lieutenant-colonel and, by date, senior in the Army to his own commanding officer and to the others in the brigade. The crunch came when the brigadier went on leave, leaving the brevet lieutenant-colonel in command of the brigade and able to take advantage of the opportunity to subject his own CO to a thoroughly testing time. When he had completed his time at Camberley, Bramall left to join 2nd Green Jackets (The King's Royal Rifle Corps), as the 1st/60th Rifles had become, in Berlin as battalion second-in-command. There were three lieutenant-colonels in the battalion, the CO, the second-in-command and one of the company commanders.

Before then, for his last six months at Camberley he was appointed GSO 2 for tactical coordination. This carried responsibility for re-examination of all the Staff College tactical training and introducing changes consequent on lessons learned by the British and other armies in limited war and counter-insurgency operations since 1945, in addition to tactics with which to confront the Warsaw Pact in central Europe. Unknown to him at the time, this experience provided a useful foretaste of the job he would do after his regimental command when, returning once again to the Staff College, he would serve as the Army's author of tactical training manuals.

Until the 1970s, officers who had served in key command and staff posts in the North-West European campaign were available to describe their wartime experiences during battlefield tours conducted each Staff College year. It is hard to overestimate the value of this to students who had little or no active service behind them. The 'Epsom' and 'Goodwood' battles of 1944, neither of which could be counted as a real success, were ideal vehicles for bringing home to students the realities and tempo of battle, as well as providing valuable lessons for the future in different circumstances.

Epsom, in which Bramall had taken part and as described in Chapter 3, was an attack by VIII Corps in June 1944 to secure crossings over the Rivers Odon and the Orne, south-west and south of Caen. The operation also had the purpose of putting pressure on the Caen defences from the western flank, in preparation for an attack on the town and an armoured advance on the eastern flank towards Falaise. Epsom became so extended and confused that VIII Corps had to settle for achieving only crossings over the Odon. A month later, Operation Goodwood – launched while Bramall was in hospital recovering from his first wound – entailed an armoured thrust on the eastern side of Caen to seize the high ground south of the Bourguebus Ridge (see Map 3). Because of the shortage of infantry, this assault was made by three armoured divisions following a massive air bombardment.

The most important lesson to emerge from both battles was the degree of success the Germans achieved, despite the British superiority in numbers and fire-power, with their well-sited defences in considerable depth and taking advantage of the close Bocage country. In the case of Epsom, the Germans maintained a lightly held forward screen with three or even four strong defensive positions echeloned back to a depth of several miles. There was nothing new in this. Similar dispositions had been used by the German Army on the Western Front in 1917–18, so that each time there was a breakthrough by the Allies in one belt of defences, their reserves were regrouped to form a new line, making best use of ground and obstacles. During Goodwood, once the British bombardment had lifted, the resolute German use of flat trajectory anti-tank weapons fired from interlocking positions in the farms and villages, with which the countryside was liberally dotted, proved highly effective. Such tactics used against the British Second Army during Operations Epsom and Goodwood clearly had relevance to

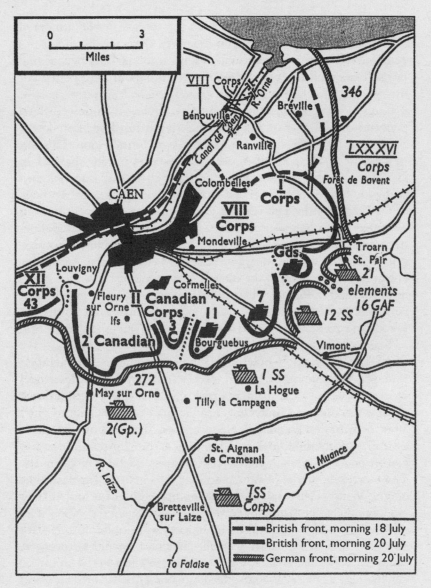

Map 3. Operation Goodwood, July 1944.

those that NATO forces would have to use against the armoured formations of the Warsaw Pact on the north German Plain.

There were also other valuable lessons to be learned by studying British tactics in these two battles, notably, in Epsom, the potential of the quickly launched and almost entirely silent infiltration attack, making best use of ground and natural cover, to achieve a deep penetration. This was done by 2nd Battalion The Argyll and Sutherland Highlanders to seize two bridges over the Odon. This was in contrast to the ponderous, set-piece infantry assaults behind an artillery barrage, thereby forfeiting any chance of surprise and attracting heavy defensive fire, which had marred the opening stages of the Epsom battle. The value of flexible artillery support in holding ground won was demonstrated in the fighting around Caen, as was the need for infantry in support of armour – both working closely together – in Operation Goodwood. The difficulties encountered during this operation were to lead to the use of a new grouping of two armoured regiments and two infantry battalions, the latter mounted in armoured personnel carriers, in the later stages of the campaign in north-west Europe and eventually adopted in the Army as a whole, under the title of 'Square Brigades' after trials in the 1970s.

All these lessons of how attacks by a seemingly overwhelming force of armour might be delayed, halted and then destroyed piecemeal were not lost on Bramall, either as the coordinator of tactical teaching at Camberley or later when the GSO 1 (Author) after his battalion command. He would also experiment with them as a brigade commander and introduce them into his tactical contingency plans when GOC 1st Armoured Division in Germany. The more flexible use of British armoured formations on the flanks of any Warsaw Pact advance, between fortified hamlets and villages predominately held by infantry, was also taken up and developed by others determined to introduce more modern thinking into NATO defence. General Sir Nigel Bagnall, later professional head of the Army himself, Lieutenant-General Sir Robin Carnegie, who earlier commanded 11th Armoured Brigade in Bramall's 1st Division, and Major-General Peter Reid, Director Royal Armoured Corps 1981–3, were prominent among these.

By the time Bramall left Camberley at the end of 1961 to rejoin 2nd Green Jackets (KRRC) in Berlin as battalion second-in-command, the post of '2 i/c', sometimes derided as 'Too Idle Charlie', had become a key driving cog in any well-run unit machine. His principal task was planning and organising exercises and training, but any new commitment almost invariably would come his way to study and implement. Political tension was high in the city, following the building of the hated wall dividing the western part occupied by American, British and French brigades from the eastern part controlled by the Russians. Consequently, readiness and hard training were important features in the lives of the western military garrisons, even though ground suitable for training in any realistic fashion above company level was hard to find. Unfortunately the goldfish-bowl situation led the staff of the Headquarters British Sector to consider the appearance and discipline of British units above all other considerations. The sporting opportunities were outstanding, but it was not an easy place in which to train for war.

War was always on everyone's mind, with the Group of Soviet Forces in (East) Germany surrounding the city and the nearby Russian 10th Guards Tank Division reputedly ready to lead any Soviet venture to overwhelm the Western Powers garrison. Contingency plans to counter a Soviet takeover of the city were essentially theoretical, and, to avoid giving alarm to the civilian population, anything beyond reconnaissance in plain clothes down to company and specialist platoon commanders was out of the question. Berlin had the high-octane atmosphere of an international competition in military expertise and sporting skills, with no holds barred.

Largely because of their former motor battalion role, no battalion of the 60th Rifles or Rifle Brigade had previously served in Berlin. The commanding officer for the first year, Lieutenant-Colonel Tom Acton, was a fastidious and punctilious bachelor who had spent most of the war as a prisoner after being captured at Calais in 1940, and ensured that duties such as ceremonial guards at Spandau prison, Guards of Honour for visiting dignitaries or other presentational military tasks were take in the battalion's stride. Lieutenant-Colonel Peter Curtis, who succeeded Acton, was keener on the regiment's traditional role as skirmishers, and therefore less enthusiastic about the ceremonial and other peacetime demands, which led to conflict with the brigade commander, a Grenadier Guardsman, who – although highly intelligent – had more of an eye for ceremonial detail. In consequence, Bramall found he had a few fences to mend with the brigade staff when he took over as battalion second-in-command. He also had a more active role to which to look forward when the battalion joined the 3rd Division in the UK-based Strategic Reserve in mid-1962.

In the eight months with 2nd Green Jackets in Colchester, before returning to the staff, Bramall mastered the intricacies of emergency air movement to trouble spots abroad, the *raison d'être* of a Strategic Reserve battalion. A distinct change of mental attitude from Berlin was essential, as the Air Movement's staff was dependent on units arriving at departure airfields with their weapons and equipment packed in accordance with strict standing operating procedures if they were to be despatched on time. These techniques could not be improvised 'on the night', but had to be learned, practised and endlessly improved. They were tested during the winter of 1962–3 on Exercise Desert Storm.

The exercise was conducted in Libya, together with 'M' Battery (Eagle Troop) Royal Artillery, an engineer troop and an enemy force provided by the Queen's Royal Rifles TA. The ground was very familiar to Bramall and to many of the more senior officers and NCOs. The battalion was flown to El Adem airfield, collected vehicles from the emergency stockpile at Tobruk and, following several days' acclimatisation and practice in desert navigation, advanced westwards over the ground of General Sir Richard O'Connor's lightning campaign against the Italians in the winter of 1940–1. For the final advance towards his old camp at Derna, Bramall was put in command of the battalion. The assault was made at night by two rifle companies, while he sent the third at dawn round the back by helicopters to cut off the enemy's withdrawal. The exercise concluded with that Libyan phenomenon in which few believe – a flash flood. The normally dust-dry wadis were swamped by swirling brown water up to 5 feet deep and the Mediterranean winter sun brought out a crop of tiny multi-coloured flowers wherever water had briefly gathered on the desert floor.

It was a satisfactory and in many ways stimulating end to Dwin Bramall's brief return to regimental service, before he began his next stint on the staff, this time at the War Office now as a *paid* lieutenant-colonel.

6

The Sorcerer's Apprentice

Convinced of the urgent need to modernise the decision-making process in matters of defence policy, in 1962 Prime Minister Harold Macmillan extended the tenure of Earl Mountbatten as Chief of the Defence Staff from three years to five. The former Viceroy of India was only the second holder of the most senior Service post and, in the words of his biographer Philip Ziegler, 'He was resolved that the office would be vastly different when he left it to what it was when he took it over.' He envisaged an overhaul of the whole structure of defence, in which the machinery of Whitehall would be radically reorganised and the relationship between the three Services reconsidered. Whatever it took, Mountbatten was utterly determined that he would bring about what he perceived as the essential changes.

When Lieutenant-Colonel Dwin Bramall reported for duty at the War Office on 29 April 1963, he had no inkling that he was to become the Joint-Services Secretary of the Centralisation Steering Committee. In effect, he was to be the staff officer responsible for planning the implementation of the whole reorganisation to which Mountbatten was committed.

On promotion to acting, and therefore *paid* lieutenant-colonel, he had been posted from 2nd Green Jackets to join the Combat Development staff at the War Office, probably with a view to brightening it up. The subject was a logical continuation of the work on which he had been engaged at the Staff College, but he had scarcely set foot inside the Combat Development Directorate before he was sent for by Mountbatten and told of his future role.

There was no question of 'Would he like the job?' Mountbatten had demanded the best man available and it was Bramall's name that came up. The career potential was obvious, even though he knew of the acrimony Mountbatten's policies on Whitehall centralisation and his means of achieving his aims were already generating among the Naval, Army and Air Force Chiefs of Staff and their still separate ministries.

Mountbatten's theme of 'more power to the centre' was not centralisation for its own sake, or wish for further personal aggrandisement, even though he was to prove utterly ruthless in his ambition to bring about reform. Closer coordination of single Service capabilities and consequently of their budgets had become inescapable with the ending of National Service and a beginning of withdrawal from stations overseas, although with very little reduction in defence commitments. The single Service Chiefs of Staff knew closer cooperation was essential, but, to their minds, this did not predicate any reduction in their individual freedom of opinion or the right to tender it directly to the Cabinet. This remained the key difference of view between the Chief of the Defence Staff and Service Chiefs throughout Bramall's time as Mountbatten's personal Staff Officer on reorganisation and later as his representative on the Centralisation Steering Committee. It gave him close insight into the mechanisms and difficulties he would encounter as CDS twenty years later.

Behind this unseemly management struggle lay the infinitely more serious issue of the place of nuclear weapons in the overall shape of defence policy. During the period when Duncan Sandys was Minister of Defence (1957–9), Britain's nuclear capability was perceived as the panacea for every awkward problem, extending even to such absurd comments as 'If they don't behave, we'll get the RAF to deal with them.' But the Suez Crisis obliged even the most fervent enthusiasts of nuclear weapons to recognise their limitations as a *deterrent*; and Britain's successful defence of Kuwait against the threat of invasion by Iraq's revolutionary General Abdul Kassem, in 1961, demonstrated the country's continued need for an effective conventional capability.

The nuclear/conventional forces debate had been candidly addressed in the Conservative government's Defence White Paper of February 1962, which stated, 'Our policy of deterring war has been severely tested in the past twelve months. If we had nothing but nuclear forces, this would not be credible. A balance must be maintained, therefore, between conventional and nuclear strength.' So when Dwin Bramall set up his desk in a small office in the embryo Ministry of Defence in Storey's Gate just along the corridor from that of the CDS, the main strategic priorities were settled; but the struggle for power and influence between Mountbatten and the single Service Chiefs had yet to be engaged and fought to the finish.

Much of the problem lay with the personalities concerned, not least with Mountbatten himself. His war experience first as Chief of Combined Operations (in truth something of an over-statement of his responsibilities) and then as Allied Commander-in-Chief South East Asia gave him claim to know more than most about how the three Services should work together. Unfortunately he was inherently incapable of maintaining a straightforward approach and, such was his personal vanity, he could not resist the petty triumphs to be gained by deliberately wrong-footing the single Service Chiefs, collectively or individually, by trading on his special relationship with Prime Ministers Harold Macmillan and later Harold Wilson and, above all, with the Palace, often improperly and misleadingly quoting the Queen's support for what he wanted to do. This inevitably increased the mistrust in which they already held both him and his efforts to enhance his authority.

The Chief of the General Staff, General Sir Gerald Templer, the highly strung and belligerent 'Tiger of Malaya', had been Mountbatten's strongest opponent when, as the First Sea Lord, he had initially put forward arguments for greater centralisation of the Whitehall staffs. Templer's immediate successor, General Sir Frank Festing, a large, untidy Wykehamist and Green Jacket with a sharp mind, inclined more towards Mountbatten's views, but his successor, the much more conservative General Sir Richard Hull – who was Chief of the General Staff when Bramall arrived at the War Office – not only opposed them but had a deep-seated dislike and mistrust of

Mountbatten as a person. The Chiefs of Naval and Air Staffs, Admiral Sir Caspar John and Air Chief-Marshal Sir Thomas Pike, opposed any erosion of their authority or access to ministers and were consequently suspicious of any proposal emanating from Mountbatten. As the youngest Service, the Royal Air Force was alert to potential threats to its operational capability through the machinations either of Mountbatten or of the other two Services, while the Army, fearful of being outwitted, maintained an obdurately conservative attitude.

Although at the bottom of the heap of those involved in the consultative process, Bramall saw all the papers, picked up the gossip and was all too well aware of the personal animosities and professional tensions between the protagonists. These included junior ministers standing to lose their prestigious single Service responsibilities in exchange for some more challenging functional task – across-the-board procurement, for example. He also knew that, on appointment as Minister of Defence in 1957, Duncan Sandys had been given a remit by Macmillan 'to decide all questions on the size, shape, organisation and disposition of the forces, as well as their equipment and supply, their pay and conditions of service'. This mandate still stood and Bramall appreciated that no defence minister, whatever his authority, could carry it out without a much more centralised organisation for defence with real power at the centre to formulate policy and to take decisions on these matters. In essence, the Minister for Defence needed an Armed Forces and Civil Service structure answerable to him through one paramount Service Chief and one Permanent Under-Secretary.

Determined though he was to bring about far greater centralisation, Mountbatten knew it would be a mistake to put forward proposals in his name alone, as that would further exacerbate the already fierce antagonism of the single Service Chiefs. Yet he had to get the thrust of his argument across to ministers, and win at least tacit Cabinet support, without allowing the single Service Chiefs opportunity to distort his arguments or water down his proposals. Macmillan recognised this problem and so asked the Chief of the Defence Staff to put forward his *personal* views through the Minister of Defence.

Within two months of extension of his tenure as CDS, Mountbatten had submitted a memorandum to the new quick-witted and able minister, Peter Thorneycroft, explaining how the faults of the current structure and system hindered sound decision-making and budgetary procedures. Then he outlined his conclusions and recommendations, which, in essence, would lead to the abolition of the single Service Ministries and their replacement by a Ministry of Defence, with one Secretary of State and integrated Service staffs reporting to the Minister of Defence through the CDS. He could have had no doubt that this would be strenuously opposed by the single Service Chiefs, who would be reduced to little more than the titular heads of their Services without the right of direct ministerial access.

Bramall had not started work in the Ministry of Defence when Mountbatten's memorandum was being written, but it eventually fell to him to act as coordinating secretary of the main military sub-committee formed to discuss, under the Steering Committee, the detailed implementation of the merger, particularly of the then small defence staff with those of the three single Services. The major decisions on this came not directly from Mountbatten's memorandum, but from a report resulting from it. Once completed, Mountbatten's memorandum had found favour with Macmillan but, as anticipated, drew fury from the single Service Chiefs. Although they accepted the proven worth of combined Service headquarters overseas and the economic advantages of closer coordination of procurement, they could not stomach the obvious threat to their positions as heads of their respective Services and right of direct access to Cabinet Ministers. The very vehemence of their objections and the extent to which these became known in the defence community, as well as to the public at large, indirectly played into Mountbatten's hands. The single Service Chiefs distilled their objections into a paper of their own, which, in time-honoured fashion, Macmillan referred to an independent inquiry together with Mountbatten's own memorandum.

This tactic might have resulted in the whole dispute being kicked well beyond the touch-line for a decade but for Macmillan's skilful choice of the inquiry members. Both were ex-soldiers but each had profound experience of working with all three Services and of political sensitivities. They were Winston Churchill's wartime Chief Staff Officer, General Lord Ismay, and Lieutenant-General Sir Ian Jacob, former Deputy Secretary of the wartime Chiefs of Staff Committee, author of the 1946 White Paper on the Central Organisation of Defence and famed for his clarity of thought. The two were instructed to examine both Mountbatten's memorandum and the single Service Chiefs' combined rebuttal and report to the Cabinet without delay.

They made no attempt to compare Mountbatten's memorandum with the single Service Chiefs' objections, still less to reconcile them. Instead they put forward three suggestions of their own. It took Jacob just six weeks to write the Report containing their three options:

1. Minor modifications of the status quo as a very tentative step towards a closer integration of the three Service Ministries.
2. Co-location of the three Ministries in one building, with a strengthened Central Staff and the Minister of Defence in overall charge; and the three Service Ministries downgraded to 'Departments' of the MoD. The single Service Chiefs would retain corporate responsibility for their own Service and status of professional Head of Service.
3. A fully integrated functional Ministry of Defence with all officers of two-star rank and above merged into an Armed Forces Staff and wearing the same uniform.

Having set out the options, the report recommended that the Cabinet should adopt Option 2, while regarding Option 3 as a possible longer-term objective.

The Cabinet decision was announced in March 1963, just two months before Bramall reported for duty at the War Office. The Cabinet had called for a White Paper by July explaining the decision that had been taken, the reasons for it and the outline means of its implementation, so there was not a moment to be lost. The Steering Committee set up to execute the Cabinet decision was chaired by the Deputy Under-Secretary of the embryo Ministry of Defence in Storey's Gate, Sir Frank Wood, and included three two-star officers, each of whom would eventually achieve four-star rank and, in one case, five-star rank as CDS. They were Rear-Admiral Peter Hill-Norton, Major-General Desmond Fitzpatrick and Air Vice-Marshal Thomas Prickett, all with quick brains and the former two with imperious manners. There was also a two-star officer as the CDS's personal representative on the Committee, Air Vice-Marshal Donald Evans – who also rose to four-star rank, but was in indifferent health at the time, so the bulk of his work fell to Bramall. Later, Bramall was to recall that Admiral Hill-Norton never addressed a civil word to him, but invariably opened proceedings by glaring round the table and demanding, 'Where are the f—— ginger biscuits?'

As Bramall set about gathering information in preparation for the merging of the Ministries, it was not long before he came under suspicion as 'Mountbatten's man', in particular with members of his own Service, who thought he might be engaged in selling them down the river. It was a difficult and testing time for him, but nothing that he had to do went against his own convictions. He could not help but be impressed by Mountbatten's openness with him and the rest of his staff. Each day began with 'morning prayers', when everyone was at liberty to express his opinion on current issues, could expect to be heard and was seldom disappointed. Bramall described this technique as the 'philosophy of the hive', which led everyone to connect with the key issues and his personal role in overcoming the problems.

The single Services' perception of their side of the merger soon became apparent to Bramall, through his discreet soundings for information. Consequently, his ability to feed this into the 'hive' debates, with suggestions of how unhelpful perceptions might be ameliorated, made a significant contribution to the preparation of the merger plan. He was of course subjected to single Service pressure, some positively threatening. The Army's Director of Staff Duties asked, 'You would not want your battalion to be taken away Colonel, would you?' (meaning the impending command of a battalion). Coming from probably the most influential major-general in the War Office, such a thinly veiled threat could be intimidating, but Bramall was able to deflect it with his characteristic half-apologetic laugh and reply, 'No, I certainly wouldn't, but I am sure you are not being serious!' and then not give an inch on the point under discussion.

The Ismay–Jacob Report had been sent to the single Service Chiefs, and battle was immediately joined on the precise interpretation of Option 2. Bramall became aware of a fundamental difference in philosophy between Mountbatten's ideas at the centre and those of the single Service Chiefs. Whereas Mountbatten was seeking *flexibility* in defence planning and in dealing with the unexpected, the single Service Chiefs put their reliance on a 'fail-safe' system of not venturing down any road where the end was anything but absolutely clear and had not been given the fullest scrutiny by the single Service staffs, so that power and responsibility for each Service did not get for a moment out of step. To Bramall, young and standing on the brink of a potentially brilliant career, the single Service Chiefs appeared reactionary, but the time would come when responsibility for his Service would weigh on his own shoulders as Chief of the General Staff. This is a quite different situation from that of the Chief of the Defence Staff, with responsibility to no Service in particular but to the Cabinet and the nation.

He was also able to observe at close hand how Mountbatten dealt, or tried to deal, with the attempts by the Service Chiefs to turn the Option 2 plan into a compromise closer to their wishes. Broadly speaking, there were two ways in which the CDS might have handled this situation: he could have got the three Service Chiefs round the table and said, 'Well Gentlemen, this is the situation we face and our task is to work together to bring out the best solution,' or he could pick off their arguments individually, while working to swing the interpretation – and eventually the implementation of Option 2 – ever closer to his own objective of complete integration. He chose the latter and used every trick in the book to achieve his aims, often pushing his junior staff out in front to draw the fire, so that he could operate an outflanking movement when he knew the exact strength and direction of the opposition.

The power of patronage played a large part in the reservations that the single Service Chiefs held about closer integration of the upper echelons of the three Services. Except for the nomination of their successors, which required the Prime Minister's approval, they and they alone chose the men to be promoted above two-star rank. They would usually consult their near contemporaries on the more senior or sensitive appointments, but the ultimate choice was theirs, and every two-star officer who had further ambitions knew full well that he crossed his head of Service's path at his peril. Loss of such powerful patronage would significantly weaken the authority of each Chief of Staff and his ability to run his Service.

Mountbatten recognised this reservation and, as Bramall was later to relate, chose to play on the single Service Chiefs' fears rather than to allay them. Each Service had a three- or two-star officer responsible to his Chief for drawing up short-lists of candidates for senior appointments. These men were powerful but not ultimately so. In a move to cut back such influence as they had, Mountbatten proposed the establishment of a four-star 'Defence Services Secretary' who would make recommendations to *him* on appointments to and promotions within the Central Staffs. To rub salt in this wound, he opened a Chiefs' of Staff meeting one morning with the remark that he had spent the weekend at Windsor and, 'I am pleased to say that the Queen was delighted by this innovation.' None of the Chiefs believed him for a second and Mounbatten knew that they didn't, but somehow it pleased him to torment them a little.

Co-location of the then tiny Ministry of Defence Staff into one building together with the core policy staffs of the three Service Ministries, something with which Bramall would shortly become intimately involved, exercised the Navy and Army Chiefs to an exceptional degree. The Admiralty, on the west side of Whitehall and flanking Horse Guards Parade, had controlled Her Majesty's ships at sea since before Nelson's time and had become a shrine to his traditions. How could the Navy be asked to move from it? There was certainly no room for anyone else. With rather less justification, the Army drummed up a case for remaining in the pretentious Victorian 'War Office' obliquely opposite, while the RAF sat tight in the new, green-tiled-roofed 'Whitehall Gardens' building it shared with the Board of Trade, which had been chosen to be the combined Ministry of Defence.

This purely administrative and organisational matter quickly became a highly charged emotional issue. Bramall made his way doggedly round the corridors of the Admiralty and War Office seeking a solution that would allow the Navy and Army either to settle for some kind of representational presence in their historic buildings or, preferably, accept a formula that would save face in their acceptance of a seemly section of Whitehall Gardens. In this instance the Bramall persuasive charm did not work and he had to report to the Chief of the Defence Staff that the Navy and Army were adamantly against moving. Mountbatten dealt with the matter with duplicitous ruthlessness. After informing the Naval and Army Chiefs that he would support their positions at a meeting to be arranged with the Minister of Defence (Peter Thorneycroft), he made an appointment for the following Monday but sent an eleventh-hour message crying off the meeting on 'doctor's orders', having earlier advised Thorneycroft to reject their objections out of hand, which he did.

Co-location in the Whitehall Gardens building having been decided, it fell to Bramall to plan and negotiate its occupation. This demanded much ingenuity. The essence of the plan was for the small briefing staffs at the embryo Ministry of Defence in Storey's Gate to be expanded into several Defence Planning Staffs (DPS), each with an equal balance of middle-ranking staff officers from each Service, to become the core of the Defence Staff. Round this core would be situated the sections of the single Service staffs who had the expertise and detailed knowledge essential for the DPS groups to do their work. Further out, in what was intended to be a concentric staff structure, would lie the administrative and specialist staffs on which the single Service elements would depend for that type of information and for the implementation of relevant aspects of plans, directives or operational orders conceived at the centre.

On the face of it, there was nothing more difficult to do than fit the staff structure into that of the building, but its internal layout had been designed for a different purpose. Moreover, once it had been decided that the hierarchy and key staffs of the former Navy, Army and Air Force Ministries would move into the Ministry of Defence 'Main Building', as Whitehall Gardens was renamed, prestige raised its unhelpful head. The sixth floor was allocated to the Chiefs, their immediate staffs and the DPS, while the other staffs moving in – perceiving themselves of a significance which demanded that they should be not more than one floor below – fought for space there. Lateral location also came into play, as everyone wanted to be near the people with whom they usually worked. But these arguments were puny in comparison with those about who should be left behind in the Old Admiralty and Old War Office, as the venerable buildings were retitled.

In parallel with his decision about co-location in the Main Building, the Secretary of State ruled that, to avoid the Old Admiralty and Old War Office buildings becoming reactionary coverts, members of all three former Ministries who could not be accommodated in the Main Building would be distributed equally between them. One outcome of this policy was that the Naval Hydrography staff eventually found themselves hanging their exquisite nineteenth-century survey drawings of foreign anchorages on the drab walls of the Old War Office basement. Such detail was not of Bramall's doing. His primary task was to devise the Main Building layout so that the Central and Service Departments staffs could function efficiently and allocate accommodation to the Navy, Army and Air Force Departments to fill as they judged appropriate. The Board of Trade had to be moved into a building in Victoria Street that Bramall had discovered was under-used.

The day designated for the move was 1 April 1964, and inevitably much play was made of it being April Fool's Day. This gave Bramall less than six months to complete the plan, but it also familiarised him with the functioning of the Ministry, which was to be so valuable to him twenty years later. The Steering Committee plan, in which Bramall had a hand, was based on the structure of a layered cake: each Service took over a vertical slice of the building, the Air Force remaining where it was in the Parliament Square end, the Central Staffs and the Army occupying the middle and the Naval Staff moving into the Charing Cross end. Mountbatten's functional demands were met in the horizontal layers, with all personnel and logistic *policy* staffs on the seventh floor, Ministers, Chiefs of Staff, Chief Scientist, the most senior civil servants and their personal staffs on the sixth floor, operations staffs next below and then the intelligence staffs (shortly to be fully integrated) below them and so on down to ground level. Not everyone was satisfied.

The plan made and the move accomplished, Bramall took the opportunity to have some leave with his son Nicolas in Normandy, taking him to where he was first wounded in 1944, to Paris and the valley of the Loire. This had not been suggested by Mountbatten, who, although complimentary about what he had achieved, never made even the most casual enquiry about his private life or family. This omission was not uncommon at the higher levels of the affairs of state. Bramall once asked General Sir Ian Jacob how he was regarded by Winston Churchill during the Second World War, when he served in the Cabinet Secretariat's military wing under Lord Ismay. 'Oh, just as part of the furniture,' Jacob replied.

Not surprisingly, the press had taken the opportunity to lampoon the move of the single Service staffs into the Main Building whenever possible. The shifting of the furniture was likened to a recent occasion when the country's two major circuses met while travelling in opposite directions through the already congested traffic system of Salisbury. On 1 April 1964, *The Times* – one suspects with editorial tongue in cheek – described Peter Thorneycroft as 'one of the most powerful men in Britain' after summarising, unkindly and unfairly, his previous political career and crediting him with 'putting 100 years of thought about the unified command for Britain's forces into action'. The same article criticised the continued employment of 26,000 people in the combined Ministry, one of the arguments for which had been saving manpower. Another press article denied Bramall any credit for the division of the Main Building, presenting the arrangement as simply a means of giving all the Service Chiefs an equal level view across the Thames.

Bramall remained in post for eight months after vesting day of the new Ministry, during which he was given responsibility for explaining to subordinate headquarters and Service agencies outside the Ministry how the new structure would function and their relationship to it. Although by that stage he had probably the best understanding of the subject of anyone around, this was not a straightforward undertaking. The well-known opposition of the single Service Chiefs to the merger made it impossible for him to touch that nerve and widespread scepticism remained as to what it was all about and what future misfortunes were foretold for the careers of those manning the stations and units he visited.

Consequently, while he had begun to develop his own public speaking technique when instructing at the Staff College, this was the point in his career when Dwin Bramall began to make his mark in that difficult accomplishment. In some ways his subject matter and the manner in which he knew it was perceived were a help to him. As he would throughout his subsequent career, he conveyed a slight suggestion, by tone of voice and choice of words, of just a sliver of doubt about the validity of his theme – as if musing aloud – which would catch his listeners' mood exactly and engage their interest. It may have been an extension of the easy discussions he had enjoyed in Mountbatten's 'hive' or just a perfectly natural approach to a tricky topic. He took care never to appear in the least bombastic or over-confident of his subject and, perhaps above all, handled questions with reflective interest, where appropriate giving the questioner credit for a new angle worth examining.

His lecture tour brought him into closer touch with the other Services than previously, as well as enhancing his reputation as a rising star in the Army. As early as 8 May 1964 a letter from Major-General David Price on behalf of the Commonwealth Relations

Office to Air Vice-Marshal Donald Evans read, 'Lieutenant-Colonel Bramall's lecture to the Commonwealth Defence Advisors (who would report it to their respective Governments) on Wednesday was an outstanding success. He managed to give a very clear picture in a short space of time and answered some very "googly" questions admirably. Altogether a brilliant performance.'

Demands for his expertise also arrived from abroad. In what must have been his final assignment before ending his appointment in December 1964, he visited Ghana to advise the government in Accra on the integration of its own Service staffs. Such was Mountbatten's reputation abroad that Lieutenant-Colonel Bramall was taken at once to see Kwame Nkrumah, who, living almost as a recluse, had declined to receive the British High Commissioner for several months. The head of the British Joint Services Training Team to the Ghanaian armed forces wrote to Mountbatten,

After a most thorough investigation and study, he has produced proposals which I am sure will not only please the President and Minister of Defence, but will also be readily accepted by all those who will have to put them into practice. I am sure, too, that a well integrated and more efficient Ministry of Defence will in consequence emerge.

The ultimate test of his work for Mountbatten was whether the new-style Ministry would work. There were some inevitable creaks and groans at the outset, but four fully integrated staffs had been formed: the Defence Operations Executive for crisis management; Defence Operations Requirements for weapons and equipment specification; the Defence Signals staff and the Defence Intelligence staff. Cooperation in other key policy areas was between *joint* staffs comprising relevant experts from the single Service Departments.

So in the interim analysis, for that was what it was to prove to be, Mountbatten had not achieved the degree of integration he had sought. But a far smoother way of working had undoubtedly resulted from the merger of the Ministries. Planners engaged on the same enterprise had no longer to ring up to make an appointment, then cross the street to consult a colleague in another Service; they could just walk down the corridor to his office. It was a formula for confidence and friendships rather than rivalry and distrust. The civil servants working in the Central Staff also gained an enhanced grasp of defence issues through day-to-day contacts with all three Services, leading to their greater self-confidence and hence cooperation.

Mountbatten had not been able to strengthen his position as CDS *vis-à-vis* the single Service Chiefs to the extent he had hoped. His authority had been increased through his position as Chairman of the Chiefs of Staff Committee, but this still restricted him to being their spokesman. He had no power to override their views – a situation that, to a certain extent, Bramall was to inherit twenty years later. Before then, however, he was to appreciate the degree of independence still available to him as Chief of the General Staff (Head of the Army) during the Falklands War, and, following his retirement from military service, an even closer integration of the centre of the Ministry of Defence was introduced before the wars in the Balkans and against Saddam Hussein.

The New Year's Honours List of 1965 announced the appointment of Lieutenant-Colonel E.N.W. Bramall MC to be an Officer of the Most Excellent Order of the British Empire (OBE) for the manner in which he had dealt with the difficult and diverse problems connected with the reorganisation. This was followed by a personal letter from Mountbatten saying how delighted he was, adding that Bramall now had an unrivalled knowledge of Whitehall and that he would expect him to reach high rank in the Army. By then Bramall was turning his attention to a rather different challenge – active service in command of an infantry battalion in South-East Asia.

7

Operational Command

Success in command of a battalion, or a regiment if in the armoured corps, artillery or engineers, is the determining factor for the rest of an officer's career. If he turns in an outstanding performance, he can usually depend on at least the command of a brigade, but if no opportunity arises for him to shine – or he doesn't when the opportunity is there – he will be stuck. As it matters little what he has achieved beforehand, everyone hopes he will command on active service, where his true worth may be reliably judged. Dwin Bramall was therefore fortunate to be given command just as his battalion was being sent to the Far East to face an operational situation.

His appointment in January 1965 to command 2nd Green Jackets (KRRC) occurred during the Indonesian 'Confrontation' with the recently formed Federation of Malaysia. Governments and international observers alike had been taken by surprise by this 'war' as, although he was recognised as a chauvinist, few had anticipated that President Sukarno of Indonesia would risk widespread condemnation by attacking his predominantly Muslim neighbour. An uprising by a handful of dissidents in Brunei, which also lies on the North Borneo coastline, had long been thought to be on the cards, but that was an entirely separate matter and had been dealt with, with British help, before the Confrontation began.

Sukarno was the hero of his countrymen's assertion of independence from the Dutch at the end of the Second World War, but he remained power-hungry. He had briefly put forward the concept of a federation incorporating Malaya, the Philippines and

Indonesia to be titled 'Maphilindo', which would – he doubtless supposed – have brought the British protectorates of North Borneo and Sarawak under his control. Both lay on the northern coast of the vast and mainly Indonesian island of Borneo (Kalimantan). As early as 1961, talk of enlargement of the Federation of Malaya to become 'Malaysia', embracing Singapore and the two Borneo protectorates – plus possibly Brunei – ended Sukarno's dream of 'Maphilindo'. But when British forces were requested to put down the indigenous uprising against the Sultan of Brunei the following year, some evidence suggested that the uprising might have been inspired from Jakarta. Then in January 1963, even before the Federation had come into being, Sukarno announced a policy of 'confrontation with Malaysia, at present accomplices of neo-imperialistic forces pursuing a policy hostile towards Indonesia'.

Two days after the new Federation of Malaysia had been inaugurated on 16 September 1963, a mob set fire to the British Embassy in Jakarta. Earlier, in August, British Gurkha troops and Indonesian 'volunteers' had clashed in the jungle-covered mountainous region of the Sarawak border. At the request of the Malaysian government, Britain agreed to reinforce the infantry brigade sent to Brunei, where it was still hunting the last of the insurgents, so as to increase security in what had become East Malaysia.

There was some concern in London about the logistical implications of this initiative. Until then, contingency preparations in the Far East had focused almost exclusively on the supposed threat from Communist China through Thailand to peninsular Malaysia and Singapore. Instructions were therefore issued by the Ministry of Defence to Far East Command headquarters in Singapore to the effect that reserves of ammunition and supplies stockpiled against the Communist China contingency were not to be used in East Malaysia. Inevitably, staff officers on the spot had to ignore the instruction.

Fifteen months before Bramall and 2nd Green Jackets arrived on Penang, the island that was to be their base while in the Far East, Indonesia had begun cross-border raids into East Malaysia, and this had led to substantial reinforcement of the North Borneo territories of Sarawak and Sabah by British and Commonwealth forces. Three brigades of British, Gurkha and Commonwealth troops were deployed from Kuching, in the administrative First Division of Sarawak in the west, along the Indonesian frontier region as far as Sabah, as British North Borneo had become, in the north-east of the island of Kalimantan. British, Australian and New Zealand ships and aircraft carried provisions from Singapore, and Royal Navy and RAF helicopters lifted troops into and out of the jungle and flew in supplies. Army helicopters were used for liaison flying and reconnaissance. Overall command was exercised by the experienced and resolute Major-General Walter Walker situated on the island of Labuan, just off the Brunei coast.

Unlike a number of battalion commanders training their soldiers for operations in East Malaysia, Bramall had not fought in Burma during the Second World War, nor had he served in Malaya during the twelve-year-long Communist insurrection. He therefore knew nothing about operations in jungle conditions. Consequently, he had to start from scratch but was not too proud to ask for advice, in particular from Lieutenant-Colonel D.F. 'Nicky' Neill commanding 2nd Battalion 2nd Goorkhas and probably the British Army's most experienced jungle fighter at the time. 'Tell me all you know,' he invited Neill. That was indeed a tall order, but Bramall and his battalion received great benefit from what he heard.

Although it may have seemed illogical, as it did to many Malaysian troops taking part in these operations, that two nations largely of the same ethnic group, language and religion should engage in armed conflict, the Malaysian political leaders and senior military officers knew only too well about Indonesian President Sukarno's territorial ambitions, recognising that the Indonesian incursions into Malaysian territory had to be met by force.

In the early months of the campaign, the British-led security forces concentrated on containing and repelling Indonesian incursions. But it soon became clear that the enemy would retain the initiative as long as it could choose its points of entry and withdraw to base camps on the Indonesian side of the border, usually littering its exit track with anti-personnel mines.

Consequently, authority was discreetly obtained from the British and Malaysian governments for cross-border attacks on enemy base camps and ambushing of border approach routes, under the code name 'Claret'.

The 2nd Green Jackets' first operational tour of duty in Borneo was with West Brigade (99 Gurkha Infantry Brigade) in the administrative 'First Division' of Sarawak. The brigade was commanded by Brigadier W.W. Cheyne, a determined and dynamic officer who was struck down a few years later by motor neurone disease shortly before taking over command of a division in the British Army of the Rhine. West Brigade faced the Indonesian 5th Brigade supported by what was assessed as the heaviest concentration of artillery and mortars along the 1,000-mile length of the Sarawak border. There was plenty of local intelligence in the area, although much of it was of doubtful quality. Family connections transcended the political frontier, and custom-free cross-border trade using tracks between the border visits had existed for generations. The battalion sector covered some 20 miles of meandering frontier, much of it ill defined, with a depth of 40 miles back to the coast at the narrowest point. The jungle-clad Bungoh range of hills, which rose to 4,000–5,000-feet-high knife-edge ridges, intruded into the sector to a depth of 8 miles, with the Sarawak river flowing from it and on north-westwards to Kuching, the Sarawak state capital. The jungle was intersected by streams liable to flooding by shoulder-high torrents after a rainstorm.

A thought recurrent in the minds of all commanders in the West Brigade area was the relatively short distance Kuching lay from the frontier. From the Green Jackets' right forward company position the distance to Kuching was only 25 miles. While that might be thought enough ground in which to fight a decisive delaying battle against any Indonesian advance, there was a more insidious threat. During the early stages of the campaign, Chinese Communist elements had sought to take advantage of the uncertain security situation concurrent with the Brunei rebellion to make trouble in West Sarawak. The region had a reputation for banditry dating back to the days of the Brooke 'rajahs' in the employ of the Sultan of

Brunei, who ruled the territory in the mid-nineteenth century. Although the Communist insurrection in peninsular Malaysia had been finally suppressed by 1960, some Chinese Communist cells remained in East Malaysia. Therefore the ground between Bramall's battalion headquarters, close to Kuching airport, and his forward companies was secure only where his troops occupied it.

In the three months between arriving in Penang and deploying to Borneo, Bramall subjected his battalion to a vigorous training regime. A selection of officers and NCOs had been sent in advance to the Jungle Warfare School in south Johore so that they could instruct the rifle companies in the requisite skills of finding their way and operating in the tropical rainforest. The reconnaissance platoon trained to work with Iban trackers from Borneo, who were completely at home in the jungle and could interpret the least mark or disturbed leaf into accurate information of who had passed that way. Finally, the entire battalion went to Johore for three weeks' jungle training under Bramall's personal supervision.

Training was and would remain the persistent bee in Bramall's bonnet. This was in no sense unusual in the Green Jackets' psyche, as individual and specialist training had been their watchword ever since General Sir John Moore had introduced riflemen skirmishers operating in advance and on the flanks of the main infantry formations, and not infrequently as their rearguard, in the Peninsular War. But, dispersed to small garrison stations between wars, the British Army easily degenerates into a colonial gendarmerie preoccupied with local internal security duties, allowing the battlefield lessons of the past to be forgotten. If not exactly a battlefield, Borneo – with its jungle and wide, fast-flowing rivers – offered plenty of physical hazards even before the enemy joined in.

In the sector Bramall inherited from 1st Scots Guards, the frontier area was controlled from two fortified base camps, each occupied by a rifle company. This situation led to conflicting demands for human resources. The camps had to be fortified with sand-bagged posts, barbed wire and all the paraphernalia of static defence to avoid being over-run if attacked by the Indonesians in a strength up to a battalion group supported by heavy mortars. Manning and maintenance of these defences, in face of daily torrential rain, insects and rats, called for men who would otherwise be patrolling the jungle or ambushing possible enemy approach routes. Bramall insisted that at least 50 per cent of the forward companies' manpower was out in the jungle at any time. Patrols lasted for up to five days, occasionally as many as ten, and included regular but unscheduled visits to local villages close to the frontier to gain intelligence.

It was perhaps not surprising that military commanders and staff remote from the Borneo conflict tended to view it as an extension of the Malayan Emergency, concluded three years earlier. In fact, except for the terrain in which it was conducted – and that in Borneo was considerably harsher and more physically demanding than in most of peninsular Malaya – it was quite different, particularly in its objectives. In Malaya the aim was to persuade the majority of the Communist terrorists of the hopelessness of their cause, bring about their surrender and hunt down the hard core who continued their campaign of terror from jungle sanctuaries. In Borneo, the campaign was essentially defensive and so largely reactive in nature, but its focus on the frontier introduced a key element absent in the earlier campaign, except for the Thai frontier in the extreme north. The Kalimantan border imposed itself on the thinking of commanders at all levels, rather like the front line in a conventional campaign. Aside from the question over the reliability of the Chinese workers in rear areas, there was only one way to look.

From the earliest stages, it was apparent that the Indonesian soldiers, in particular the Javanese, were brave, resolute and would fight hard, often without officer leadership. Bramall had gleaned all this through study of the background and conduct of the campaign before his arrival in the Far East, but his instinct was to analyse what was happening and draw his own conclusions. Over the years since he had been a motor platoon commander in Normandy, he had evolved his own concept of leadership. He had a draft of a pamphlet explaining this in mind when he took over command of his battalion, but avoided going into print until after his first stint in Borneo.

There was difficulty over tactical innovation, however. Although the campaign did not fit the mould of what became known as 'framework operations', with units hunting the enemy within a chessboard of areas of responsibility, changes to the situation of forward company base camps – and even of the few individual platoon positions – were difficult to achieve. Aside from the fact that someone must have decided there was merit in establishing where they were in the first place, much sweat and material had gone into building and fortifying them against Indonesian attack. The greatest single limitation on redeployment from one jungle base camp to a new site was the tightly controlled availability of helicopter flying hours. Men could be moved easily enough, but lifting forward significant tonnage of corrugated iron, pickets and barbed wire was acutely extravagant in flying hours unless the threat could be shown to have changed.

The central sector of the West Brigade area (see Map 4) had a workmanlike layout, with two company base camps well forward on either side of the Bungoh Range and a third company in reserve to the rear. The battalion structure, designed for war in Europe, comprised only three rifle companies, but each had its own section of 81mm mortars and an anti-tank section. The latter were clearly not going to be required in their primary role, but, as generally more mature men than the average riflemen, the gun crews proved a useful boost to the strength of the rifle platoons. Theoretically, on mobilisation a fourth rifle company would be added from the Territorial Army, but, of course, this was not available in Borneo. Bramall was, however, able to use the headquarters of this 'shadow' company to oversee the reconnaissance and assault pioneer platoons, the former having become the tracker platoon with an increment of Iban trackers and Labrador dogs. Two Sioux light helicopters were also available for reconnaissance, although, as little could be seen through the jungle canopy, their principal value was for liaison sorties or to act as an airborne battalion command post.

Two features of the inherited layout gave Bramall concern. First was the need to maintain three detached platoons very close to the border. Aside from their isolated vulnerability, he considered that

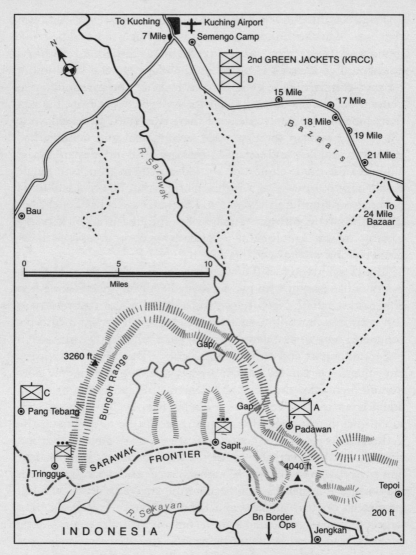

Map 4. *Central Sector of West Brigade area, 1965.*

their persistent demand for defensive manpower infringed the principle of concentration and economy of effort. Patrol activity was inevitably restricted in scale by men being tied down to defending five locations, instead of just two company base camps. He particularly disliked the platoon base at Sapit, right on the frontier and detached from 'A' Company in the east of the Bungoh Range. It was an old fortified camp originally set up to watch over a village subjected to Marxist propaganda. While the Commander of West Brigade could see the force of Bramall's argument, the political view that the village needed a military presence to prevent defection prevailed.

His second concern was the 4,000-foot peak overlooking 'A' Company's base camp and visible from a ridge occupied by a company of 2nd Battalion The Parachute Regiment from the east, across the inter-battalion boundary. He succeeded in having the battalion boundary shifted to the east, and 'D' Company took over the Parachute battalion position at Tepoi, around which there had been considerable enemy activity, in late May. The penalty paid was that only one platoon, detached from 'D' Company, remained as battalion reserve, but the forward area was more secure.

Relationships between officers and men of the Green Jackets had long been less formal than in most infantry regiments. This stemmed partly from the naturally uninhibited nature of the riflemen, many of whom came from the East End of London, and partly from the liberal approach of the officers.

Bramall's genuinely friendly attitude to everyone and a good memory for names and faces gave his NCOs and soldiers the certain impression that he knew who they were and what they were supposed to be doing. This did not lead to any unwanted informality, just straightforward answers to his questions. Company sergeant-majors saw it was purposeless to warn the rifleman not to raise complaints to the commanding officer, as he would discover any problems by his natural curiosity.

On taking over command, he had reflected on how to advise his officers and NCOs on how to deal with the inevitable easing of formal relations with the men that is inseparable from the stress of active operations and danger. He baulked at the use of forenames, as had occasionally arisen during the war, as that could only be applied downwards if proper discipline were to be kept. Instead he introduced the system of everyone having a handle to his name. Thus, rather than a private soldier being addressed by his surname alone, he became 'Rifleman' Jones on all but the most pressing occasion.

The first crisis to arise during the 1965 operational tour in Borneo put the heat on him rather more than on anyone else. Shortly before midnight of 27 June the police station at Milestone 18 on the road running south-east from Kuching was attacked and, simultaneously, an attempt made to blow up the bridge over the river at Milestone 24, where a civilian was murdered. While the order to deal with these events – arriving at 2325 hours – caused Bramall some frustration, it allowed him until daylight to make his plan, issue orders and deploy the additional units put under his command. Success or failure subsequently hinged on his insight, military skill and leadership. A switch in operating style was also required.

Assuming the perpetrators were Indonesians, who would head for the border, Bramall decided to establish cut-off points on tracks to the south. He gave orders for battalion tactical headquarters to move to Padawan and 'C' Company, commanded by Major Peter Welsh, to join him there by helicopter soon after first light, leaving only a base protection party at Pang Tebang. From Padawan, he would be in a position to react to any information on the enemy expected to be moving towards him. Shortly after 0230 hours, news came through that the police had recaptured their station at Milestone 18, having suffered some casualties, and the enemy, estimated to be around a hundred strong, were thought to be heading westwards, but had left no tracks. Despite the apparent change in the direction of the enemy's withdrawal, Bramall continued with his planned deployment and instructed a company of 1st/6th Gurkha Rifles, placed under his command, to assist the police in searching and clearing the area of Milestone 18 and extend the curfew southwards.

The next day brought two negative developments. A corporal of 'D' Company on patrol in the border region was injured by an Indonesian anti-personnel mine, leading to the loss of his leg, and a curfew breaker shot by 'C' Company after failing to respond to the statutory three challenges turned out to be a mental patient. Late on 29 June, HQ West Brigade intelligence sources identified the enemy as Chinese Communists attempting to spark off an insurrection in a manner that characterised the onset of the Malayan Emergency in 1948. This news changed Bramall's plan.

Aware that the terrorists would try to set up bases among Chinese workers living away from the settled areas, he sought and received West Brigade's authority to concentrate the outlying Chinese in kampongs along the main road. Under the rather unfortunately code-named Operation 'Hammer', he gave instructions for the five bazaars between Milestones 15 and 24 to be cordoned off, while villagers in the outlying kampongs were concentrated within the cordons secure from terrorist pressure. Although essentially humanitarian in intention, this operation had to be carried out in a good-humoured and persuasive manner if those being moved were not to be alienated. The operation began at first light on 6 July, and by nightfall some 2,500 Chinese had been gathered in from outlying settlements and escorts provided for them to tend their cultivations and livestock without threat of terrorist intimidation. As was often the case with such incidents, no conclusive evidence of the fate of the terrorists came to light, but the speed and comprehensive nature of the operation seem to have been sufficient to prevent any further hostile activity in the area.

The operation to deal with incipient Communist insurrection in the rear area marked a change of emphasis in 2nd Green Jackets' activities on the border. Now confident that his forward companies had acquired as good a feel for the terrain on the Indonesian side as they could get without actually going there, Bramall decided to carry the campaign to the enemy. Although cross-border patrols to locate enemy base camps beyond the frontier and to ambush routes from them had been agreed by London and Kuala Lumpur, such operations were not advertised because of political sensitivity. Bramall's operational plans reflected a structured sequence, which, if successful, would leave West Brigade's central sector in better shape than he had found it. He also wanted to get rid of the Sapit commitment.

Urgency was given to these operations by identification of an Indonesian regular army unit immediately across the border. Unless put back onto the defensive, this unit could undermine the confidence and so allegiance of the Malaysian population living along the Malaysian side of the border through its presence alone. As he intended to start on the east of the Bungoh Range only 3 miles from Sapit, Bramall decided the time was ripe for him to convince the Resident (Governor) of Sarawak's 1st Division, the Kuching District Officer and the local people that Sapit need no longer be manned. Much hinged on undermining the morale of the Indonesian troops opposite the village, so putting them on the defensive.

The proximity of the Indonesian camp to a local village precluded a direct attack, if unacceptably high civilian and military casualties were to be avoided. Consequently, he decided to isolate the camp by ambushing its supply routes and harass the occupants with intermittent fire until they withdrew. This had to be a two-company operation, so Bramall set up a forward command post on a border ridge line that overlooked the whole area and provided an excellent base for radio communications. While 'C' Company, under Major Peter Welsh, swam a river to lay ambushes on the main supply route to the camp from the east, 'A' Company, under Major Gerald Carter, kept the valley under observation from the north, ambushed the line of the river in case of its use by enemy craft and provided protection for the battalion mortars that had been brought forward. In the opening moves, a platoon of 'A' Company commanded by Lieutenant Michael Dunning ambushed a military supply boat on the river, killing five Indonesian soldiers without loss. When this produced mortar fire from the enemy camp, the battalion mortars were brought into action, silencing the defensive fire and causing panic within the camp. A number of Indonesian soldiers ran down the track and into the ambushes laid by Major Welsh's 'C' Company. The camp was abandoned shortly afterwards.

Bramall next turned his attention to an Indonesian camp at Mankau to the south of 'C' Company's area. This was similarly dealt with and more casualties inflicted without loss. It is worth drawing the distinction again between the ambush techniques used in

Borneo and those used against Communist terrorists in Malaya. In Malaya, the terrorists would flee when fired upon and gather at a pre-arranged rendezvous. The Indonesians were more resolute adversaries. They would retaliate with fire, both direct and indirect. This meant that each British ambush party had to have a back-up force ready to give support with mortars and artillery and on which it could fall back if significantly outnumbered. The operation against the Mankau camp was conducted using all these features, including artillery fire on an ambush position after it had been sprung and then abandoned.

Stringent operating procedures governed the conduct of cross-border patrols, and commanding officers were not permitted to accompany them. This was a sensible precaution against giving the Indonesians a propaganda coup should a senior officer fall into their hands, as well as encouraging COs to get on with their own job rather than that of their subordinates. That said, every commander wishes to show that he is up to doing all he asks his soldiers to do. Having got the brigade commander's permission, Bramall accompanied a patrol of the New Zealand SAS across the border to join up with one of his own patrols and then, having seen them at work, marched out with them over a period of three days.

A final operation against the Indonesian unit across the border was carried out by 'D' Company, skilfully commanded by Major Robert Pascoe (later the Adjutant General). An Indonesian relief unit moving towards Mankau was ambushed and six enemy killed after putting up a stiff fight; the rest withdrew in confusion. This inflicted a serious blow to enemy confidence and morale, and the number of border incursions in the West Brigade central sector fell dramatically. Bramall was mentioned in despatches for his period in charge of the sector, and two of his officers, Major Peter Welsh, rated by Bramall as an outstanding company commander, and Lieutenant Mike Robertson, were awarded the Military Cross.

The 2nd Green Jackets returned to Penang in September 1965 feeling they had acquitted themselves well in Borneo. During the immediately previous two months they had fought six successful carefully planned and executed actions; forty-three of the enemy had been accounted for and possibly also another forty. On the debit side, the battalion had lost one man killed in action and two wounded. Above all, under Bramall's perceptive and considerate leadership his officers, NCOs and riflemen had acquired a self-confidence on jungle operations that, without being cocksure, left them feeling self-assured about the next tour due to begin in January 1966.

Two events marked the next four and a half months before Bramall was due to return to operations, this time in Sabah on the north-eastern tip of East Malaysia. The more public of the two was the change of his regiment's title from 2nd Green Jackets (King's Royal Rifle Corps) to 2nd Battalion The Royal Green Jackets. This may seem a minor modification, but the change brought into being a new regiment – the Royal Green Jackets – and ended the separate existence of the three former regiments: the Oxfordshire and Buckinghamshire Light Infantry (43rd and 52nd), the King's Royal Rifle Corps and the Rifle Brigade. All were well known in the Army for their fine fighting records, for excellence in shooting and field craft, and the intellectual awareness of their officers. The change was part of an infantry-wide policy of bringing single battalion regiments into close affiliation, so as to facilitate the transfer of individuals, officers and soldiers between them.

The 60th Rifles had been the centre of Dwin Bramall's life for the previous twenty-three years and the thought of being their last commanding officer weighed with him. The change took effect at midnight on 31 December 1965, following ceremonial Sounding of Retreat at the battalion's base of Minden Barracks, Penang. His address to the battalion and audience included the following words:

In this life, if you are sensible and particularly if you are young, you look forward and not back, and indeed it is the tradition of riflemen that they are progressive and move with the times. But we would not be human if we did not feel very considerable sadness at the passing of a regiment with such a proud and wonderful history; and one in which so many of us have had such splendid times and such great comradeship, some, for close on a quarter of a century. The name of the King's Royal Rifle Corps, the 60th Rifles, will always have a very special place in our hearts and that is exactly as it should be.

The parade marched off to the 60th Rifles march – Lützow's 'Wild Hunt' – which was to remain as the 2nd Battalion's own quick march.

During the period between operational tours of duty in Borneo, Bramall wrote, or in fact refined and perfected, a pamphlet entitled 'Leadership the Green Jacket Way'. It expresses much more than the tenets of command and encouragement that had become clear during the preparatory training and execution of the first period of active service in Borneo. It set out much of Bramall's philosophy of military life, which he carried through in his day-to-day dealings with riflemen, NCOs and subordinate officers. Although he completed and refined the draft between the two Borneo tours, he chose not to publish it until the final month of the second tour.

The pamphlet was taken into use by his battalion and is still extant 40 years later. The complete text appears in Chapter 8, but Dwin Bramall's words on discipline on active service have a particular relevance in this chapter.

Discipline on active service means having the capacity to carry out an essential, irksome or arduous task without supervision; keeping going and staying awake when fatigue is overpowering; obeying unpleasant but necessary orders; and above all continuing to fight when the instinct of self preservation is advocating something totally different.

The 2nd Battalion Royal Green Jackets, as they had become, faced a radically different situation and deployment on their second tour in Borneo in early 1966. There are opposing views on the merits of returning units to operational areas with which they are familiar. The principal argument for return is that the ground, roads, tracks, in this instance helicopter LZs, and local officials and police will be familiar, leaving only knowledge of the enemy's positions and habits to be updated. The argument for change is psychological: the troops will be more alert because of the newness of their situation, more curious and enterprising than if returning to somewhere well known. Ideally, choice could be applied to both unit and the locality, but the decision will usually be determined by expediency: a change in deployment priorities, the fixed period between a unit's tours of duty, when its period in theatre begins or ends or the changeover of a commanding officer.

Although none of these factors appeared to apply in this instance, instead of returning to the West Brigade area, Bramall's battalion went to Tawau in the East Brigade area of south-east Sabah, again taking over from 1st Scots Guards. It was a politically sensitive sector, as the Indonesian border runs through Sebatik Island across Wallace Bay from Tawau and, in December 1963, two platoons of a Royal Malay Regiment battalion had been surprised at prayer by 120 of the enemy and suffered eight men killed and nineteen wounded. The East Brigade area had consequently become something of a symbol of Malaysian resistance to Indonesian confrontation, where the slightest reverse would be viewed with alarm in Kuala Lumpur.

The eastern seaboard of East Malaysia is low-lying with an intricate and irregular pattern of estuaries and inland waterways separated by mangrove swamp and sand spits. It offered opportunities for Indonesian incursion and speedy getaway, but, possibly because they faced – at least for the main part – their ethnic brothers rather than the 'imperialists', the enemy held back and were rarely encountered. East Brigade comprised two Malaysian battalions and one British or Gurkha battalion. Some degree of tact was required of the British or Gurkha commanding officers, as they were likely to be more operationally experienced than their Malay counterparts and even the brigade commander. Their troops were also of very different stock from the Malays, who, at that early stage of national independence, were rather better at military ceremonial than jungle fighting.

The 2nd Royal Green Jackets' front covered some 70 miles of messy deployment, coping with which could become almost a full-time activity. Battalion tactical headquarters, with 'D' Company in reserve, were at Kalabakan, at the north-western end of Wallace Bay, where the attack on the Malaysian battalion had occurred in 1963. One of the two forward positions was at Serudong Ulu (jungle) on a ridge overlooking the frontier, in a situation familiar from the West Brigade sector, but the other at Serudong Laut (sea) lay on a river bank where it was possible to construct defence works only by building them up, giving the camp a wild-west fortlike appearance (see Map 5).

These two positions and responsibility for operations around them were undertaken by 'A' Company (Major Robin Montgomery) and 'C' Company (Major Peter Welsh) respectively. B Company (Major Geoffrey Hopton), comprising the assault pioneers and reconnaissance platoon, came under command of the Tawau Assault Group, a mixed force of British, Commonwealth and Malaysian soldiers and sailors, operating a variety of small craft responsible for patrolling the inland waterways and swamps.

The battalion's assault pioneers had been trained in watermanship in Penang and ran their own patrol programme in boats fitted with outboard motors. In many ways the operational tasks and deployment in the East Brigade area offered even more scope for initiative by junior officers and NCOs than the West Brigade area had done. The enemy threat proved to be so low that the risk of complacency, which could lead to carelessness on operations or accidents, began to give Bramall concern. Before the halfway point of the tour, two riflemen were drowned in the fast-flowing Kalabakan river, and, despite a changeover between 'A' Company at Serudong Ulu and 'D' Company, commanded by Major John Mason, in reserve, he recognised that he had to raise the tempo.

Despite an intensive patrol programme up to the border where it could be reached, there was an almost total lack of intelligence on the more remote regions. Bramall set about correcting that omission, and 'C' Company had a brief clash and exchange of fire in the Serudong Laut sector in May. One Indonesian was killed and another wounded, but this low level of activity was an unwelcome contrast with the challenges of the West Brigade area

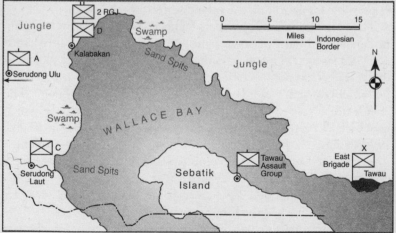

Map 5. Tawau Sector of East Brigade area, 1966.

and, with a third operational tour expected during his battalion's two-year period in the Far East, Bramall could not allow his men to go off the boil.

He looked at a variety of options for the final weeks in Tawau, rejecting the intensification of patrol activity simply to provoke Indonesian reaction. Not only would such a course be contrary to his nature, he was conscious that his battalion was in Tawau in an essentially defensive role, with the safety of the Malay, Chinese, Philippino and locally domiciled Indonesian population a priority. Training was of course always in his mind and all arms training in particular, so he decided to use the local conditions for this while being wary of giving his riflemen an impression they were no longer on operations – and kept away from their families – simply for training.

Having call on the 105mm pack howitzers of 40 Light Regiment RA to support his border and waterborne patrols, he made every opportunity to position the guns by helicopter and rehearse the infantry fire control drills down to junior NCO level as part of their military education. This technique, well known but all too seldom applied in anger, had been used with instant effect after the initial exchange of small-arms fire in the brief clash with the enemy in the 'C' Company sector in May. When no further opportunities for this activity presented themselves, he introduced live firing exercises using artillery and the battalion's own 81-mm mortars, still in the context of practising weapon drills relevant to the task in hand.

Some stimulating variety was nevertheless essential, and the availability of Royal Navy destroyers, for fire support if required, prompted some practice beach landings with troops up to platoon strength as they could be spared. Straightforward recreational activity, as a change from jungle or river patrol, was found by the establishment of a rest camp on a small coral island off the coast. There the riflemen could swim, water-ski and drink cold beer to their hearts' content. More challengingly, each of the three rifle companies organised expeditions to climb the 13,455-foot Mount Kinabalu, the highest peak between the Himalayas and New Guinea, which rises 40 miles from Kota Kinabalu (formerly

Jesselton), the capital of Sabah, where each party spent a few days after completion of their climb.

The battalion returned to Penang in mid-June anticipating another four to five months' break before returning to Borneo for a third operational tour. But three developments made a third tour unnecessary. In March that year the 1st/10th Gurkha Rifles had scored a spectacular success in the Bau sector of West Brigade by killing thirty-seven Indonesian soldiers in an ambush without any loss to themselves. More significant still, President Sukarno had totally undermined his authority in Jakarta by seeking alliance with the Chinese-dominated local Communist Party. He quickly became President in name only, with authority slipping into the hands of the Army Commander, General Suharto, who put out peace feelers to Kuala Lumpur. An agreement was signed in Jakarta on 11 August 1966 that brought the confrontation with Malaysia to an end.

8

Leadership the Green Jacket Way

In between two four-month periods of operational duty in Borneo, Lieutenant-Colonel Bramall turned his attention to writing a short booklet on leadership for the benefit of the young officers in his battalion. He had had this idea in mind for some time but completion of a successful period on operations, in which many of his principles had been tested, led him to put pen to paper. The booklet was aimed at those in command of platoons of around thirty men, but the tenets expressed have relevance higher up the chain of command; and the main principles could apply equally well to leadership in commerce and industry. The text that follows was still in use as a guide in battalions of the Royal Green Jackets forty years later, modified only by use of updated military terms and expressions. Although associated with a particular regimental ethos at the time of writing, the concepts the original booklet expressed are now more usually seen in the British Army as a whole than they were half a century ago.

Foreword
When a young officer first joins a Battalion he is often confused about how he is expected to handle his platoon. He has presumably basic leadership qualities, otherwise he would not have been commissioned in the first place and he will certainly have been taught something about command; but he does not yet understand the basic philosophy of the regiment he is joining nor will he know of the particular whims and idiosyncrasies of the battalion to which he is posted. He may be nervous at being

thought too zealous by his brother officers and diffident about throwing his weight around with a comparatively experienced platoon and an even more experienced platoon sergeant. He will also almost certainly be uncertain of the type of discipline and degree of strictness required in his platoon, and he will be acutely aware that his platoon will be watching carefully the action he takes and the decisions he makes in the first few weeks.

Altogether the new officer will be naturally and understandably unsure of himself and may well be hoping for some positive guidance which will help him to act in the approved way and allow him to take the right decisions. He may get this from his company commander or the adjutant or even CO, but a suitable opportunity does not always present itself and before it does, he may find himself 'putting his foot in it' and getting a number of 'rockets', all of which will increase his confusion and uncertainty. It is so easy for people to assume that he will soon pick it up as he goes along, as so many have had to do before him, but this is not always a very helpful attitude.

It is therefore for the benefit of these young officers who may be seeking guidance that I have prepared this short booklet. The ideas advanced are not revolutionary but represent what I have always believed to be the genuine Green Jacket philosophy and approach to matters of leadership, discipline, man management and training. Ever since their formation, the Regiments which now make up the Royal Green Jackets have been ahead of their time. It is not surprising, therefore, that their way of doing things remains completely up to date and in tune with modern conditions and requirements. I hope this booklet will help the young officer face the challenges of his new command with greater confidence and understanding.

Dwin Bramall   Borneo, April 1966.

THE AIM – HIGH MORALE

When you take command of a platoon or later of a company or even a battalion, you should always have one constant aim: that is to ensure that the men for whom you are responsible have what is generally described as a 'high morale'. If you achieve this you will be doing your job; for if there is high morale it means that not only are all ranks individually and collectively contented, but that they have also acquired that spirit of service and self-discipline which is so necessary if they are to carry out their duty properly and stand up to discomfort and danger. A body of men with high morale is both happy and efficient and in every way capable of carrying out these demanding military commitments. Nothing less will suffice and no officer should rest or be content until he is quite satisfied that he has achieved this aim. The challenge is exciting, but will demand hard work and dedication and a thoroughly professional approach to the job. On the other hand the fruits of success will be infinitely rewarding.

There is nothing particularly complicated about high morale. Its main ingredients are:

a. Confidence. b. Discipline. c. Self-respect.

CONFIDENCE

The confidence required is bred from an appreciation by all ranks of the all round efficiency of the unit or sub unit and of its leaders. It can only be brought about by a properly planned and supervised training programme which is demanding, progressive and interesting and, ultimately, by success in active operations. It also requires the leader to exercise his leadership in a positive and dynamic way.

Training

The first thing you must do as a leader is to see that the training of your men is right, so that they all become and remain proficient in their military skills. These will include, amongst other things, shooting, weapon training, fitness and agility (including marching and swimming), first aid and health training, map reading and navigation, signals, tactical training, and certain special skills applicable to a particular theatre of operations such as the jungle or the desert.

Soldiers must not only be taught their trade but must also come to have complete confidence in their own and their comrades' skill. This will not happen by accident, but will be achieved if the training is carefully and imaginatively conceived, clearly explained, is interesting and progressive, and leads up to a real challenge which offers, when met, a proper sense of achievement. Officers who believe their soldiers will be grateful for soft and easy training do not understand human nature and will never succeed in producing high morale. The expert trainer of troops is the one who, despite the protestations of Jeremiahs, can select an objective which, although it appears unobtainable, is in fact just within the capabilities of his soldiers.

Then having won through, his men will feel that they have done the impossible and their sense of achievement and morale will be correspondingly great. The difficulty in peacetime is thinking up tasks of sufficient challenge without undue risk to life and limb; and normally this means falling back on tests of endurance in adverse weather conditions. Crossing of water obstacles and scaling cliffs are always good training, provided that an expert and the necessary equipment are available and elementary precautions are taken. There are also certain tricks of the trade with live firing guns which can make field firing appear dangerous to the participants when, in fact, there is no risk whatsoever. All these and other ways of encouraging self-reliance help to make training realistic and build up confidence. In an active service theatre, operations and training often overlap and there is no difficulty in producing the necessary 'needle' and risk and therefore the maximum sense of achievement.

A good trainer, like a good organiser, must think every training session or exercise right through to the end. In this way every development is anticipated, the timings are realistic and go according to plan and every training aid and piece of equipment required is readily available. The training will then be appreciated by the soldiers, who will have confidence in its value and realism. A good trainer will also take the trouble to brief his troops beforehand on what is expected of them, and to discuss the exercise at a post-mortem at the end, in order to bring out the lessons and ensure that the soldiers fully identify themselves with the training and appreciate the progress being made.

Training syllabi will usually be laid down by the commanding officer or the second-in-command and training programmes will normally be the province of the company commander, but a platoon commander will often find spare time on his hands when he will have a chance of showing initiative and of originating training which is both interesting and useful.

Shooting

In a Green Jacket Battalion, shooting naturally has a very high priority and this will always remain so. The advantage of competition shooting is that it enables a regiment to maintain a well distributed shooting elite who are enthusiastic about their shooting and ready to pass on their skill and enthusiasm to young soldiers. This helps to raise the standard of every type of shooting. When preparing for active service, however, it is not enough to classify once a year, shoot the non-central matches and send a well trained team to Bisley and Command rifle meetings. Under these circumstances, shooting must have a practical application to the sort of conditions likely to be met. Tactics are valueless if when the enemy is met at close quarters there is a failure to kill him, and the trained infantry soldier should be given a regular diet of handling his weapons from cramped battle positions, at realistic combat ranges and at night. With the help of the shooting gallery type of range, steps should be taken to make shooting interesting and stimulating for everyone.

Weapon Training

Weapon training, particularly the advanced handling of weapons (eg safety stages, firing from cover and rapid reloading etc) represents one of the basic infantry skills which must be continually practised. Weapon training must never be allowed to degenerate into something which merely fills the gaps in the programme. It must always be progressive and taught as part of a syllabus or series of tests, and lessons must be fully prepared by the instructor. An officer will usually supervise but must be prepared to take a lesson himself.

Fitness and Toughening Training
A fit soldier can meet most of the demands made on him, including competing with the climate. If he is unfit, he will probably collapse under conditions of extreme heat or cold as well as being a liability in battle. An officer must therefore aim, from the start, at a state of affairs in which every man, whatever his rank, feels that he has a personal obligation to keep himself fit; and as a result will take exercise on the playing field and in the gymnasium, swimming bath or squash court of his own accord. Exercise which strengthens the upper limbs (to help in carrying heavy weights), roping down from helicopters and crossing obstacles and builds up stamina should be particularly encouraged; unarmed combat and swimming are also important.

As the tone of physical fitness comes from the top, all officers and senior NCOs must set an example. A good opportunity to do this occurs if an officer will play games with his men. Sports and games not only increase fitness but also build up high morale in other ways, and soldiers have a right to expect plenty of time to play games in the Army, and a high standard of organisation. By fully identifying himself with these games as a player or referee, rather than only as a watcher, however consistent, an officer will help to foster enthusiasm and a good team spirit.

First Aid, Health and Hygiene, Map Reading and Signal Training
These are all subjects which to some extent should be mastered by all ranks, not only by NCOs and specialists. They build up confidence.

Current Affairs
Giving him some knowledge of the world around him is a useful method of building up a soldier's self respect and maturity.

Moreover the modern professional soldier needs to have a proper understanding of the people and problems of the areas of the world in which he may have to fight. But care must be taken to see that these subjects are not put over in an amateurish and slipshod way. Too often in the past current affairs periods left to platoon commanders have produced varied and erratic results, with barrack room lawyers often taking control. Either the subject must be meticulously prepared or outside lecturers, who are experts on these subjects, must be brought in to give the instruction.

Drill

This is another subject which must be approached with caution and a real understanding. Close order drill is no longer a major factor in building up battle discipline, as it was when first introduced. It is however very necessary in order to maintain a smart public appearance, as is expected of the British Army by the British Nation, and in preparation for some special parade at which a battalion wants to show itself off to an audience. In this context, riflemen have always demonstrated their ability to drill hard for a special performance when required. Drill is also a contributory factor in building up pride and self respect, particularly amongst junior NCOs. Drill should therefore not be ignored but form part of a definite programme working up to a definite objective. At times when there are more pressing operational matters, only sufficient drill should be done to keep up an acceptable standard of bearing and turnout and to ensure that the technique of close order drill is not lost completely; it can easily be recaptured when the need arises. Morning muster parades and a simple guard mounting drill are normally sufficient to achieve this.

When drill is done, in the same way as weapon training, it must never be allowed to become a stopgap in the programme, or something which the NCOs can take without preparation, or a period which the platoon commander considers he need not attend. Drill of that kind makes no contribution to the professional efficiency of the soldier or to his morale.

Tactics

Finally there is the question of tactical training, which is the officer's main responsibility. The successful teaching of tactics depends on enthusiasm and an ability to get realism into exercises. A good tactical trainer should possess or acquire the imagination to think up tactical situations which could well occur and confront his troops at some future date, and he should then reproduce these as realistically as possible in the training he has planned. Time spent in stage managing background incidents, eg producing character sketches of 'wanted terrorists', or dressing up characters who will contribute to the realism of a situation, will not be wasted, because the heightened atmosphere will make the soldier give that much more in his training, will highlight the lessons and enhance the sense of achievement. Instruction on tactics will vary from theatre to theatre, but the following general principles may be helpful:

a) Patrolling in section or half platoon strength should be given a very high priority.

b) Tactical exercises with troops (if the aim is to teach rather than to test) should, where possible, be preceded by a tactical exercise without troops (TEWT), involving officers and NCOs only, or a model exercise over the same or simulated pieces of ground. . . . This will ensure that officers and NCOs develop their full potential and fully understand what they are doing, and that, in consequence, the soldiers get the maximum value out of the training exercise.

c) All advance and attack training should be based on the principle of fire and movement or skirmishing, ie manoeuvring into a position from where our own weapons can be brought to bear on the enemy with maximum effectiveness.

d) All defence training should include the digging of fire trenches and, wherever possible, the provision of overhead cover. This is a science often neglected on training but reverted to quickly enough when the shells and mortar bombs are landing in earnest.

e) As large a proportion as possible (up to 25%) of tactical training should be conducted at night. Rather like jungle training, nothing will build up confidence (and morale) quicker than coming to terms with this rather unnatural but effective way of operating against the enemy.

Success in Active Operations

However well an officer trains his soldiers, there will be no substitute for success in the face of the enemy in building up a truly high morale. Naturally, if the training is well done, the better will be the chance of achieving this success. Because the results of an engagement on active service have such a significant effect on a soldier's morale, it is important that when troops are first committed to battle they are, as far as possible, given tasks which are fully consistent with their training and experience, and, where possible, are allowed to progress steadily from strength to strength and from small successes to larger ones. In this way, and in each operation, the soldiers and their leaders will have the sense of achievement derived from an earlier encounter to inspire them in their task and give them confidence. This will not always be possible and the urgency of the threat may justify risks being taken, but it is the ideal. Many a commander in the past has carefully engineered a comparatively easily won and minor victory early in his command, in order to produce the necessary sense of achievement and pride which can act as a springboard for the greater and more important challenges ahead.

This is sound practice and commanders at every level should look for ways for their men to win their spurs without undue cost. Once they have gained a sense of achievement in battle, high morale will be assured.

Leadership

Leadership must always be executed in a positive, personal and dynamic way. A leader must not only have a policy and be capable of leading but he must be seen to be doing so. It is no excuse for a young officer to plead that has not made much contact with his men, because they do not really wish to see him all that much, or because he is shy or bad at addressing men in public. If he takes this line he will never get his personality across and never be recognised as living up to his responsibilities. It is up to him to cure himself of any shyness and impeding inhibitions.

A leader requires certain basic qualities: courage, robustness, judgement to name three, but it is likely that every officer possesses these to some degree. But these qualities must be fully recognised by those that one leads, if the necessary confidence is to be there; and in the early days of command a certain amount of showmanship may be required to get these points across. Until fully accepted, an officer may have to work harder, expose himself (not his men) to more risks, take more trouble and show more versatility and endurance than are strictly necessary for carrying out the command function. This is in order to imprint your personality on your men. The important thing is that when men are ordered to do anything tough or risky, they must not have a moment's doubt that those who order it are capable of doing such a task themselves and have probably done it many times before. If still doubtful, they must be shown this.

If already well known for some achievement in another field, such as athletics, mountain climbing, skiing, shooting, boxing, to name but a few, this will be all to the good, as the prestige that results from these will help a leader get fully accepted.

Leading men in war needs a certain amount of luck, although luck normally comes to those that deserve it and particularly to those who have thought carefully and anticipated most eventualities. Certainly an officer need not have misgivings about recognising his luck, because to have the reputation amongst soldiers of being a lucky commander is one of the highest compliments possible. Once success has come in a unit, whether it be operational success or of another type, it never hurts for a commander to remind men of their past achievements together, and of the benefits obtained under his leadership. Men will only have faith in a leader who himself is confident and has faith in himself.

To sum up, leadership is exercised first and foremost by example, secondly by successful results, thirdly and still importantly by the spoken word in briefing men about the future and reminding them of past achievements. A leader must cultivate all these methods in order to exercise proper leadership and win men's confidence to the fullest extent.

DISCIPLINE

Once the training is developing on the right lines, attention should be turned with a critical eye to discipline and here the young officer may well run into a maze of uncertainty and conflicting standards.

What constitutes discipline? What are the standards worth keeping and what should be discarded in the interests of progress? Certainly the methods of instilling discipline have changed, as indeed they must; otherwise we would still be in the era of the lash and the gun wheel. But the need for discipline is as great as ever it was, and must never be neglected or lost sight of when commanding men. Soldiers will never go happily into a battle unless they know themselves to be a disciplined body of men, in which every member of the team is to be trusted. In fact without discipline they rapidly become a collection of frightened and unhappy individuals. In barracks, discipline is necessary if soldiers are to project a good public image and be respected by the local inhabitants.

Discipline on active service means having the capacity to carry out an essential, irksome or arduous task without supervision; keeping going and staying awake when fatigue is overpowering; obeying unpleasant but necessary orders; and above all continuing to fight when the instinct of self-preservation is advocating something totally different. Discipline in barracks implies an absence of crime and displaying a good soldier-like appearance to the outside world. A smart bearing, good manners and good saluting are an outward and visible sign that all is well, and if the discipline is right, these things should follow on without too much of a conscious effort being made. The problem is how to instil the necessary discipline in the most economical way and in a way that does not insult the intelligence of the normal soldier of today.

In the Green Jackets, the emphasis is rightly put on self-discipline rather than the imposed variety favoured by some others. By good leadership, example, explaining what is happening and generally treating soldiers with humanity and common sense, we seek to evoke a loyal response and produce the sense of responsibility needed. This is a policy to be proud of and it has proved to be extremely effective. The end product is more deep seated because it is based on the individual's own will power, and it usually creates a fine atmosphere of trust and mutual respect which manifests itself in a sensible adult approach to problems and a marked absence of crime. At the same time, the leader must be careful not to deny the weaker and more rebellious characters the stiffening discipline without which they cannot come up to scratch; and he must remember that the battlefield requires men who are mentally as well as physically tough, and that this cannot be achieved by excessive leniency.

The build-up and maintenance of discipline, like so many other things in life, demands a middle but consistent course to be found and followed. This course should be one that encourages self-discipline, whilst at the same time giving the individual man plenty of opportunity to prove he is worthy of this trust. It should also make provision for 'turning the screw' (by increasing punishments) if results are not being obtained, collectively or individually, or if a certain aspect of discipline is particularly important, needs stressing or is being neglected. Examples of this are a lapse in the alertness of sentries on active service, a prevalence of accidental discharges or a fall in standards of turnout in a place like Berlin. Officers and NCOs can then be ordered to tighten up on the particular point. The important thing is to keep the aim always in mind and not get obsessed by the means to the end. Drill, and ultra high standards of turnout, are not ends in themselves. A man with a shaven head will not necessarily be a more disciplined man than one with a normal haircut, nor a man with 'bulled' boots better than one with clean boots; although a generally dirty and untidy man will almost certainly have poor self-discipline and require checking. What is required is a reasonable standard of turnout with special pre-announced spurts if special results are required, or if these are indications that discipline is suffering. This also applies to drill, where there should be a reasonable constant emphasis with a special drive for special occasions.

Discipline, however, is far more easily 'caught' than 'taught'. Men will react to some degree to the threat of punishment, particularly pay stoppages; to a much greater extent to having it explained to them why certain orders and routines are necessary both in the field and in barracks; but most of all to seeing that those who administer discipline and give them orders are disciplined men themselves, with all that implies in terms of punctuality, turnout and obeying themselves the orders they enforce. The rest will then follow provided they are given the opportunity to display their self-discipline and are taken to task whenever they fall down on what they are supposed to do. What must be avoided at all costs is the bullying, blustering type of junior leader who covers up his own incompetence and lack of leadership by shouting and swearing. That is not discipline under any circumstances.

Although the ways of enforcing discipline may be varied from station to station, and in the light of the end product, there must be consistency for a particular period, and the men must know exactly where they stand. It is up to the officers at every level to make it clear from time to time the standard which they expect in the various fields of military conduct and routine such as instant obedience to orders, alertness of sentries, cleanliness and serviceability of weapons, personal and room hygiene, and behaviour, bearing and turnout in public. For infringement of these and other things which may be applicable at the time, it is wise for any commander to announce penalties which will be well known to all ranks and will help to clarify the issues on which no compromise is possible. If you are uncertain of the strictness to be imposed, you should seek guidance from the commander above you.

To sum up, as a leader you should explain what is necessary and announce your standards, set an example, give your men the opportunity to do what is required of them without bullying, and then 'hammer' them with a fair but stern punishment if they do not make the grade. The chance is that next time they will. To put it another way, you should decide where to draw your line and make it clear to everyone where that line is and what will happen to them if they cross it. There can then be no uncertainty or misunderstanding.

SELF-RESPECT

The final ingredient of high morale is what can be best described as self-respect – the individual soldier's conviction that he is a respected member of a respected and honourable profession with a worthwhile job to do. This self-respect or healthy personal esteem will of course be helped greatly by the other two ingredients which have been discussed – by the confidence each man feels and by the intelligent discipline which each man acknowledges and is proud to possess. It can also be acquired and improved in other ways; and every officer, whatever his rank, has some responsibility for seeing that the following conditions are met.

Information

First and foremost positive steps must be taken to see that all ranks are kept informed about battalion's policy, and the reasons for it, and about what is expected of them. This has already been mentioned in connection with the building up of confidence, the exercise of leadership and the instilling of discipline; but it is also a significant factor in the building up of self-respect. It invokes appreciation and co-operation on the man's part out of all proportion to the effort involved. This may well be done by the commanding officer or a company commander at frequent informal talks and question periods, but it is the duty of every officer, within the bounds of security, to pass on to his men what he knows, and to keep them 'in the picture' about what the future may bring.

Living Conditions

Secondly there is the question of high living standards in barracks. Men will not respect their occupation or themselves, unless their life and their training is varied, interesting and tough; but this toughness should not extend to conditions in barracks. Here they should be provided with a high standard of feeding, sleeping accommodation and amenities and recreation facilities generally; and the young officer should take, and be seen to take, an interest in these and should be prepared to tangle with authority in fighting for the best possible conditions for his men. There is also the question of really well run messes for warrant officers and sergeants and for corporals, with ever rising standards of taste and dignity. These help in building up the self-respect of the NCO and also help him maintain that slight but significant psychological separation from the other ranks, without which the implementation of even the most humane and intelligent discipline becomes difficult.

Public Relations

Next there is the need for good lively public relations. Everyone likes to know that their activities are appreciated, and soldiers are no exception. Both morale and recruiting benefit if articles and photographs of a unit's activities can be got into the national and local press. In the past, officers have often shown a hostile and suspicious attitude to journalists, but by doing so have defeated their own ends. It is a laudable aim of any young officer to show off his command in the best possible light and, again within the bounds of security, get them the type of publicity which will enhance their pride and influence others to follow the same calling. Within a unit there is also scope for some private publicity in the form of a newsletter or news-sheet. This enhances the family spirit and keeps men and their families informed in a light hearted unpompous way of what is going on in the rest of the unit.

Families

All the above conditions apply equally to married men and their families – an ever increasing company in the modern army. Married men should not, under any circumstances, get preferential treatment in their share of military duties, but no effort should be spared in seeing that they and their families live happy, comfortable and civilised lives. The families need to be kept in the picture about a unit's affairs just as much as the men (particularly as married men are notoriously bad about passing on information to their wives)!

The living conditions of families are also every bit as much the responsibility of a unit as those of the single man, and there must be in every unit a good welfare organisation to give really speedy practical help, if it is required, both with quartering and other human problems. The young officer can act as a link with this organisation, as can the wives of senior ranks, who can bring sympathy, understanding and a helping hand to families with welfare problems. All this contributes towards the married man's peace of mind, without which he cannot have confidence in himself as a soldier.

Punishments and the Redress of Grievances

Then there is the question of dignity of punishments and of redress of grievances. Leniency for proven prevalent and significant military offences will incur no respect from well trained and disciplined men, but punishments should be constructive and not debase the human spirit. Hit his pocket, restrict his privileges, and toughen him up on useful training, but never degrade him. It must not be forgotten that a man is innocent until he is proved guilty at his summary trial and he should be treated with this in mind. It should be appreciated also that, however fair the administration of justice may be in a unit, there are bound to be the odd injustices and misunderstandings which if allowed to persist may cause quite unnecessary discontentment. If the only method of drawing attention to them is by asking for an interview through the usual channels, i.e. the same machinery used to punish him, a man may feel he is not in a position to get a square deal. Besides, the matter may be confidential and he may be diffident about raising it through the usual channels (although he should always be encouraged to do so). As a result, a small irritant which could be disposed of early on may easily become a smouldering ulcer without anyone knowing much about it.

It is therefore the duty of every officer, from the Commanding Officer downwards, to be approachable so that a man can feel that he can have a private talk without a formal application for interview. It is very unlikely that this concession will be abused and quite unnecessary, if the officer handles the interview intelligently, for the wires to get crossed or disloyalty to be condoned. The officer should naturally not commit himself too much until he has investigated the problem with all concerned, but he should convince the man of his readiness to hear him and help him if he can. In this way the officer helps activate a very useful safety valve as well as, in the case of a commanding officer, keeping in close touch with many aspects of battalion life. The principle of direct access to officers has been accepted by the Green Jackets for many years and has always worked most effectively.

Addressing Soldiers

Finally there is the small but significant question of the way officers and senior NCOs address the ordinary soldiers. The surname alone is of course the conventional way; but these days this may be thought to have rather a patronising and peremptory ring about it. After all, a man expects to be given the prefix 'Mr' in civilian life, whatever his position. The use of a Christian name on the other hand, as well as being novel, would be interpreted as being familiar rather than friendly. This form of address could certainly not be reciprocated without familiarity and ill discipline creeping in and, unless used consistently and impartially, it would also lead to charges of favouritism.

The use of the rank followed by the surname (e.g. Rifleman

Jones) provides an ideal answer. The term 'Rifleman' is a proud and honourable one and by so addressing a soldier you give him a certain status, prestige and dignity which is often quickly reflected in his behaviour. Although this form of address seems strange at first to someone who is unused to it, it quickly catches on (after all, NCOs have always been addressed in this way). Soon the soldiers start addressing each other in this manner and then you get the very healthy use of rank titles downwards and sideways as well as upwards, with a very beneficial effect on the general self-respect of all ranks.

CONCLUSION

This then is the Green Jacket way – pride in fighting qualities and professional skill, intelligent and humane discipline, sympathy and understanding between all ranks and concern for the individual for his welfare and for that of his dependants. The young officer who applies the ideas in this booklet should have no difficulty in having a platoon which has a high morale and a healthy self-esteem that they are the best platoon, of the best battalion and of the best regiment in the British Army. A battalion committed to these principles could well be reported on in the words General Sir John Moore used when inspecting the 52nd (now the 1st Battalion Royal Green Jackets) in Sicily in 1806: 'I have the pleasure to observe that this regiment possesses an excellent spirit and that both officers and men take a pride in doing their duty. Their movement in the field is perfect; it is evident that not only the officers, but that each individual soldier knows perfectly what he has to do; the discipline is carried on without severity: the officers are attached to the men, the men to the officers.'

This must represent what all officers are seeking to achieve, for it is impossible to think of a higher compliment being paid to a regiment. Results like this should be a reward in themselves for all the hard work and dedication needed to achieve them; but for officers who are looking for further incentive or sense of purpose perhaps this final quotation (from the Seamanship

Manual of 1865), may have a message despite the dated and rather pedantic language, 'Remember, then, that your life's vocation deliberately chosen, is war – war, as I have said as the means of peace; but still war – and in singleness of purpose, for England's fame, prepare for the time when the welfare and honour of the service may come to be in your keeping; that by your skill and valour when that time arrives, and fortune comes your way, you may revive the spirit and perpetuate the glory of the days that tingle in our hearts and fill our memories.'

It must be the aim of every officer holding the Queen's Commission that they and their men are, in all senses and in every way, ready for that moment when it arrives.

9

'The Author and his Due'

Having completed a testing Grade 1 staff appointment before commanding his battalion on active service – and commanding well – Dwin Bramall had reasonable expectations of a brigade command in 1967. He was forty-four, the usual age for such an appointment at the time, but not even promotion to colonel in a 'brigade commander-in-waiting' type of job came his way. He therefore had cause to question where his future in the Army lay when sent back to Camberley as the GSO 1 (Author) and still a lieutenant-colonel ten years after he had first worn the badges of rank.

There is usually a career plot sketched out for individuals as promising as Bramall, but the Military Secretary is inclined to keep this close to his chest until the moment is ripe. No matter how brightly an officer's star may shine, there is always a chance he might run off the rails in one way or another. Although aware of this, Bramall felt he needed some crumb of comfort so made a discreet enquiry to General Sir Michael Carver, his former brigade commander and by then C-in-C Far East. Carver replied assuring him that his abilities were recognised but, meanwhile, he should get on with his authorship, a job which urgently needed attention.

It will be remembered from Chapter 5 that when he was responsible for tactical coordination at the Staff College in 1961,

This chapter title is a quotation from Francis Bacon, *The Advancement of Learning* (1605).

Bramall had begun to write the series of instructional pamphlets for use by the Army as a whole. This was the work to which he returned in 1967 and the first result was *Land Operations, Volume I – The Fundamentals, Part 1 – The Application of Force*. This was the theme to which he would return in an even wider context when a student at the Imperial Defence College; meanwhile, the structure and salient features of this first volume merit careful scrutiny. He began by setting out the different *types* of armed conflict for which the Army should be trained, equipped and ready to fight. Although accorded no priority of likelihood the inference was apparent; the types were: Cold War, with emphasis on the nuclear deterrent; revolutionary operations, which included insurgency and guerrilla warfare; Limited War, i.e. one of limited geographical scope in which selective use of tactical nuclear weapons was a remote but still feasible option; and General War, which would be dominated by at least the threat of a nuclear exchange. Then in sections of comparable status, he dealt with three topics of mounting concern: the Influence of Nuclear Weapons, the Significance of Chemical Weapons and Political Control, the last having the telling sub-section 'Public Opinion'. One might think all this pretty heady stuff, but these were the awkward topics to be addressed as the experiences and wisdom of the Second World War faded from memory.

Over the ensuing ten months, Bramall developed his series so that there was a pamphlet for each type of warfare listed in his introductory volume. Volume I, totalling some 10,000 words, dealt in three chapters with 'The Characteristics and Uses of Force', 'The Principles of War' – describing each of them in turn, including the tenth, 'First win the Air Battle' added by Field Marshal Lord Montgomery after the Second World War – and 'the Elements of Tactics'. Much has already been written about all these topics, but there are sections of his paragraphs on 'Political Control', the 'Prerequisites for Success' and 'Tactical Principles' which merit looking at in greater detail.

Concluding the Political Control section under the heading 'Public Opinion', he wrote,

It is important that military operations are displayed to the world in their most favourable light and that world reaction should be taken into account when using force. This should form part of the political guidance and support which a military commander may expect to receive, but he himself can contribute by being fully aware of the problem and taking positive steps to ensure that the actions and attitudes of the forces under his command are well presented to the public and the press. He will have to pay constant attention to this aspect, and this will include taking members of the press into his confidence when appropriate and with adequate safeguards.

Written before the intrusion of television cameras into the very heart of every military action, these were prescient words.

He began his section on the 'Pre-requisites for Success' with the premise that even the most brilliant and inspired military commander cannot hope for victory unless certain conditions are available in the way of organisation and equipment as well as superiority of some kind, be it manoeuvrability, technical advances, local knowledge and support or simply strength. Then, after touching on three of the principles of war already mentioned: a clear aim, high morale and sound administration, he went on to highlight the critical importance of accurate information and a satisfactory air situation.

As evidence of Bramall's industry while GSO 1 (Author) at Camberley in 1967, his 'Land Operations' series of pamphlets was published under the imprint of the Defence Council and remained the accepted doctrine for three decades. According to his instructions, he was required to send the draft for each volume to a wide range of authorities for comment but, knowing that most of the recipients would not be in a position, from either experience or intellect to contribute anything worthwhile, he sent the drafts only to General Carver – and received his 'go-ahead' virtually without comment in every case. Over the years the pamphlets were amended and revised in light of new experience or operational forecasts, but their principles stood and still stand the test of time.

During the summer of 1967, he heard that in November he was to be given command of the 5th Airportable Brigade based on Salisbury Plain. This was welcome news. The brigade was part of the UK-based Strategic Reserve with a variety of contingency tasks, including reinforcement of the NATO flanks and possibly of the Central Front, but also available for any emergency affecting British interests anywhere in the world. Its three battalions were individually on call for service in Northern Ireland or any of the rotational operational posts overseas, such as Belize and Cyprus. Therefore, although it lacked the more stable composition and clearly identified tasks of a brigade in the Army of the Rhine, the brigade commander had significant freedom of choice in deciding his training priorities. In addition, he was responsible for the training of the Allied Command Europe (ACE) Mobile Force battalion, in this case 1st Battalion Coldstream Guards, in preparation for its several contingency tasks.

Training fascinated Bramall and he knew that the divisional commander, Major-General Tony Deane-Drummond, who had served at Arnhem and later commanded 22nd Special Air Service Regiment, was unlikely to interfere in his plans as long as he developed an imaginative and vigorous training regime. So that became his overriding priority while he went round to see the units of his brigade to judge their capabilities and weaknesses and to let the officers and men of each see him. That his name was already widely known in the Army as someone of established reputation for intelligence and understanding helped a great deal, bringing everyone together in their support of what he wished to accomplish.

On 24 November 1967, the day after he assumed command, he wrote to all the commanding officers, including those commanding the smaller and administrative units. Before reminding them that the priority in 1968 would be training for Limited War – the theme set by the divisional commander – he stressed that he wished to be able to visit units without undue fuss and formality, with the aim of discussing current aspirations and problems with the commanding officer and getting to know the officers, NCOs and men. There was nothing new in these ideals, but resolution is required to carry them through at unit level. An otherwise enlightening visit can so easily be soured by a young officer's over-casual comment, or one from a soldier for whom a new and friendly face provides a seeming opportunity to air a grievance or deliberately 'drop in' a superior he doesn't like. Rather than bridle at such incidents, as if his own authority were threatened, Bramall would respond with a half-laugh and an incisive comment on how the point might best be dealt with. The technique did not always work but it put everyone on their mettle, including the would-be troublemakers.

His units lived in separate barracks but most of them within the area of the Tidworth Garrison, with its excellent shared sporting and recreational facilities. A distinct brigade identity existed but not with the sense of close cohesion that is demanded by war or even lower-tempo operations. Brigade study periods conducted in a reasonably convivial atmosphere are a sure way of improving cohesion and Bramall held three, each with a different operational theme, in each year of his command. He would decide the theme after reflection on what he saw about him, choose the location and then leave the detailed preparation very largely to his staff. That said, he did not shrink from putting up new ideas on content or presentation at any time, drawing heavily on the patient good humour of his subordinates. It was hard work, sometimes very hard work, but it was always appreciated. He also organised a Brigade Cricket Week for all units and sub-units in his brigade and played a prominent part, captaining the headquarters side and the brigade side against a visiting eleven, helping to foster a brigade spirit.

Bramall introduced his Directive Number 1 of 1968 as follows:

The Brigade's priority task for 1968 is to train for Limited War and I want you all to study the problems involved with *imagination, originality and a restless seeking after improvement*. In this way, I hope we can perfect existing techniques, introduce and evaluate new ones and make a really significant contribution not only to enhancing the comparatively limited resources of our Strategic Reserve, but also to guiding the future training and development of the Army as a whole. We are lucky to have such an interesting role to get our teeth into.

The words in the author's italics reflected Bramall's outlook not only on military training but on the conduct of his life in every sphere of activity he entered, of which there were already many and would be many more. Any stereotyped approach was an anathema to him, as was the affected and pompous way in which some officers still spoke and conducted themselves to project a studied, old-fashioned impression they considered 'smart' and of the elite. With Eton and the 60th Rifles behind him, Bramall was in an impregnable situation in this regard.

During the summing up of his autumn study period in 1968 he quoted a dictum of General Sir John Moore, founder of the Light Division to fight in the Peninsular War and hero of the battle of Corunna, which required his officers 'to display real professional knowledge and good temper and to exercise kind treatment of their men in order to enlist their zeal and encourage their intelligence and initiative'. Bramall appreciated and applied this dictum. His friendly disposition would usually push aside any pretensions, and plain speaking invariably caught his ear and lodged the point in his mind for future attention.

His first training directive was more detailed than his contemporaries would have produced and addressed awkward issues from which most might shy away. It spelt out what had to be done at each level of command over a wide range of activities, focusing on three points that indicated his particular interest and thoughts for the future: limitations on conventional offensive operations; the importance of professionalism; and the training of NCOs.

By 1967, most military planners had recognised that the use of nuclear weapons in 'limited war' was highly unlikely. The Korean War was the only experience from which to plan; use of nuclear weapons during that conflict had been firmly rejected by the President of the United States as politically unacceptable – even when the American-led UN Force was in dire straits. This left military planners and commanders seeking a new and credible scenario against which to train their units, credible in the minds of the men they wished to train and feasible in terms of resources.

In addressing this problem, Bramall drew on his experience of writing the 'Limited War' volume of the Land Battle series. His first training directive conceded 'because of extraneous political factors, our Limited War operations may have to be largely defensive in the early stages'. This was certainly so, and examples he gave were credible: blocking enemy thrusts, protecting entry points while strength is built up (airfields and ports), but even more interesting were his ideas for offensive action during the preliminary defensive phase – 'subtle and indirect tactical manoeuvres such as carefully planned raids and penetration into the enemy's rear areas by small bodies of troops'.

Here he caught the balance between what was credible and what might be achieved by providing units with a challenging scenario against which to train, even when only a handful of men were available to train. Distractions from training were and remain today a constant bugbear to units in the UK and only to a slightly lesser extent overseas. As commanding officers are bidden to have every man trained in outlook and capability to be ready for the unexpected, so they are directed to mount recruiting activities for the Army as a whole, provide administrative support for cadet training camps, prepare for the rigorous audit of the states of their weapons, equipment and vehicles, and administer themselves meticulously and economically.

In touching on 'professionalism' in his training directive, Bramall knew that what he had to say would appeal to some units under his command – the 1st Royal Green Jackets for example, but officers in other units would recoil from the word. At that time, there were still officers who revelled in being amateurs at their profession, blithely confident that through their courage and ability to muddle through everything would be 'all right on the night'. Whoever stole that phrase from the world of theatre for use in a military context did a service only to our enemies. Without defining exactly what he meant by professionalism, Bramall associated it with readiness to meet the 'unexpected and unusual circumstances'.

His recognition that the aspirations of NCOs were growing at a radical rate and that many intended to achieve commissioned rank, other than through the quartermaster route, put Bramall in the vanguard of manpower planners for the Army of the future. The officer intake since the end of the Second World War was significantly different from that immediately before it. Many postwar public schoolboys lacked the financial means to supplement meagre service salaries to a level to match the lifestyles of their forebears and so turned to business or the City.

While boys from Grammar and Secondary Modern Schools came forward, there was still a gap to be filled by young, ambitious, sports-oriented NCOs ready for the challenge. To encourage this development, Bramall directed that NCOs should be included in study periods so that they could have 'an opportunity to learn about and discuss a wide range of subjects dealing with not only the facts and techniques of their own particular job, but *also with topical and contentious problems of general interest*'.

As well as providing a platform for him to explain his tactical philosophy and ideas, his study days brought him further publicity – indeed reputation – as a forward military thinker but, of course, it was all theoretical. He therefore decided to mount a large-scale exercise involving all arms to test the more crucial aspects of the modern land battle which concerned him. It was a risk because, however well it is prepared and commanders and troops are briefed, an exercise can go disastrously wrong. The weather, in particular torrential rain, can obscure the view and quench the keenest spirit. As with the daily news, the bad has precedence over the good and other rising stars would not have been too upset to see Bramall suffer an embarrassment. 'Not so hot when he gets out on the ground,' one could imagine a few of them chuckle, had the exercise turned out a catastrophe.

Not through his choice, the exercise was named 'Iron Duke' but the bold concept, scale, choice of ground and meticulous preparation all bore his hallmark. It addressed the most challenging contingency role his brigade might have to face – halting or holding a Warsaw Pact armoured thrust either on the NATO northern flank in Schleswig-Holstein or Jutland, or even on the Central Front. To ensure the outcome of the exercise battle was credible, real unit strengths and weapon capabilities were used and all logistic units were moved forward to their operational locations. No exercise expedients were permitted. Stringent criteria are not unusual in planning a test exercise but they are difficult to maintain as other events collide with the planning process or the availability of troops and resources.

The exercise was one of the first to use a significant number of RAF helicopters to move troops around the battlefield in the manner of air-mobile operations carried out by the US Army. In consequence, reserves and anti-tank detachments could be repositioned quickly in the counter-penetration role, to exploit an enemy open flank and reinforce forward units who had seized bridges, ahead of the brigade position, by infiltration at night, much as had been achieved by the Argyll and Sutherland Highlanders during the 'Epsom' battle in Normandy. All the helicopter operations were co-ordinated at brigade headquarters by a Forward Air Commander.

As for battle, Bramall resolved that nothing but the unpredictable should be left to chance and, as far as possible, made provision to deal with that. The exercise was set for 3–9 August 1968 and one month earlier he held a study period in the Tidworth officers club to put across to commanders down to platoon and artillery/tank troop level what was required of them. He explained that the exercise was intended to determine detailed tactics for a non-mechanised infantry brigade operating under command of the 3rd Division in the Allied Forces Northern Europe operational area.

Ground available for large-scale troop deployment, including tracked vehicles, that offers the type of broken and wooded terrain feasible for an infantry formation to use in halting or destroying an armoured force is not easily found in southern England. In the event, part of the Salisbury Plain training area was used. The tactical philosophy which the exercise was designed to test emphasised taking up blocking positions, the channelling of enemy armour, long-vista positions for anti-tank guns and radar, reverse-slope positions for guns sited in depth, the whole to be conducted with an eye to deception, concealment and surprise. He received a surprise himself when the exercise controller, Brigadier John Badcock, introduced an 'enemy' tank thrust from a direction judged impossible, as it came from an area where tanks were not allowed on Salisbury Plain. (Badcock had prevailed on the chief range warden to allow an exception – and Bramall, who was also being exercised, managed a swift tactical riposte.)

He described surprise in his first Training Directive of 1968 as the 'most effective and powerful influence in war' and its elements as 'secrecy, concealment, originality, audacity and speed'. He encouraged all under his command to seek ways of mystifying and misleading an opponent.

Exercise 'Iron Duke' was an undoubted success and was well attended by observers. The Soviet Defence Attaché, who was a general, first asked Bramall where he was holding his nuclear weapons and then, when told that as a brigade commander he had none, he was asked how many enemy tanks he expected to face. Having scraped together all the tanks on which he could lay his hands in the United Kingdom, Bramall replied, 'Sixty.' 'Sixty!' snorted the Russian, 'I would be only interested in 6,000!'

Shortly after this exchange, Bramall was walking over to visit 1st Royal Green Jackets when two riflemen, with typical perkiness, asked if he could settle a bet between them. 'Well, I'll certainly try,' he replied. 'Is it true that there is a Russian officer here today?' one asked. 'Yes, quite true,' said Bramall, 'He is just over there and I will get him to come over and talk to you.' 'Well,' said the second rifleman, 'maybe you could settle another bet: Is Russia in NATO?' (It should be borne in mind that this was forty years ago. Today, it would be quite a pertinent question.) The brigade commander went off to find the Russian to ask him whether he would come over and talk to the two soldiers who had asked if Russia was in NATO. Needless to say, the Russian did not know what to make of the matter and may have thought his leg was being pulled, so he kept away from the two curious riflemen.

The exercise led the GOC 3rd Division to commission Bramall

and the brigadier commanding the Strategic Reserve armoured units to develop a concept to 'enable a non-mechanised division with limited anti-armour capability to operate effectively in Europe against a sophisticated and predominantly armoured enemy'. We will return to this project later but now it is time to turn to Bramall's outlook on discipline in his brigade.

Lieutenant-Colonel Henry Illing of the Royal Warwickshire Fusiliers had recently written an article published in the *British Army Review* entitled 'A Philosophy of Leadership and Discipline'. It was generally interpreted as a criticism of a 'modern idiom' of military discipline adopted by some units in response to the dawn of the non-deferential culture in the late 1960s. Colonel Illing was well known in the Army as a man who had won two MCs in the North-West European campaign and also an officer of uncompromising Christian principle. His article had created something of a stir, in particular his stress on the value of self-discipline and, where this was shown to be lacking, insistence that discipline must be imposed.

Bramall chose Illing's article as his theme when summing up the autumn study period of 1968, having first arranged for it to be widely circulated. His words reflected his deeply held views of discipline, or what the Army would term 'man-management', and also the sort of discipline to which the 60th Rifles aspired, as explained in his booklet 'Leadership the Green Jacket Way'. The key passage bears reproduction in full.

I think Colonel Illing's article focused attention on one of the more pressing and fascinating problems of our time and one which must be of deep and continuous concern to all who command men. Personally I think that he drew a false conclusion about 'units who, in an effort to conform with the modern idiom, have abandoned or relaxed more formal traditional disciplinary habits'. It is exactly this form of informal discipline with 'magnetic' or even good personal leadership which can, does and indeed must work in war. For in war, such is the turnover of men, there is little if any opportunity for 'formal disciplinary habits' and one must rely exclusively on the competence, example and leadership of the more senior ranks: in fact on respect and persuasion rather than on authority or fear.

It is in peacetime when the abandonment of all the more formal methods of discipline may have harmful side effects. When there are not the pressing problems and excitement of active service to absorb youthful exuberance and retain interest, excessive freedom of action and too little direction [and regimentation] is liable to lead to inconsistency and a feeling of uncertainty. This can be disturbing to immature young men and have a harmful effect on the morale of the non-commissioned officers who have such a vital part to play in the chain of command.

No commanding officer can ignore a unit's public image. A crowd of young military men, even if they are courageous and have their hearts in the right place, can create an objectionable impression amongst the citizens of the local cathedral or market town if their behaviour and dress are excessively contemporary. This is often quite unacceptable not only for the unit's reputation but also for its self-esteem.

The real issue raised in Colonel Illing's philosophy is where exactly does a commanding officer draw the line? In deciding this, I would take a rather more optimistic view of the young men who come into the Army than he appears to do. Provided positive, well thought out measures are taken to explain policy and the reasons for less obvious orders; providing training is always progressive, imaginative and interesting – instead of repetitive, pedestrian and boring – and, as Colonel Illing says, provided the example is there so that those who give the orders are seen to be disciplined men themselves, then I believe discipline can be a voluntary, cheerful and self-satisfying business.

Some may prefer to look back nostalgically and romantically on the 'good old days' when discipline was based on an inflexible and unquestioning acceptance of convention, routine and ritual. I have possibly overstated this point, but no-one will deny that there is a marked contrast in approach between the post-war and pre-war armies; and that today many of the old traditional methods must clearly be seen to be time wasting, irrational and irrelevant. It would be a retrograde step if the opponents of sensible change were to gain strength unintentionally from Colonel Illing's article.

He concluded with the quotation from General Sir John Moore on the encouragement of intelligence and initiative mentioned earlier and then remarked,

This he practised with conspicuous success with the Light Division over 150 years ago. It is therefore perhaps not surprising that far from wanting to put the clock back, some people may feel frustrated that we have not yet found the courage or acquired the knowledge and confidence to take another stride forward in this vital field of human relations.

There are some strong principles expressed here and the summary also provides an insight into a part of Dwin Bramall's personality which would emerge again when, as Chief of the General Staff or Chief of the Defence Staff, he was in a position to give advice to Ministers. It was seldom or ever his way to tell people *precisely* what he considered they should do, but rather to put forward an argument from which he hoped they would reach the same conclusion as he had done. This is the intellectual's way, but it does leave the door open to counter-interpretation, accidental or deliberate, or for the argument to be put aside as an opinion rather than a recommendation as to a specific course of action.

Command of the 3rd Division changed at the end of 1968 when Major-General Terence McMeekin took over. He knew all about Exercise 'Iron Duke' and the conclusions drawn from it, so it was not surprising that he decided to carry Bramall's theories on anti-armour tactics a step further. He gave instructions for Bramall and the BRAC (the brigadier commanding the armoured and armoured car regiments in the Strategic Reserve) to develop a concept of anti-armour operations against a predominantly armoured enemy in the NATO Central Region. In setting this task, McMeekin acknowledged that his division was non-mechanised and had only a limited anti-armour capability.

As a preliminary, the two brigadiers wrote a paper entitled 'The Killing of Armour'. This included an analysis of the threat posed by armoured formations of the Warsaw Pact, such as the 3rd Division would face in the NATO Central Region, and recommended what equipment, organisation and additional units the division would need to have a reasonable chance of success. This analysis and recommendations were examined at the Army Strategic Command study period in March 1969 and Bramall was subsequently directed to relate the conclusions to a brigade group battle on a suitable piece of ground and then report on the detailed tactics which should be employed.

This was a formidable challenge. He had been thinking about the development of anti-armour tactics ever since his period of responsibility for tactical coordination at Camberley in 1961 and now had an opportunity to put his ideas to the test. He was in his second year of brigade command, knew his subordinates well and had trained or perhaps more accurately, *influenced* his headquarters staff to think and react in the same way as he did. Moreover, he could be certain that the conduct and conclusions of the study would receive the attention of his divisional and army commander – and very probably a far wider audience.

General McMeekin's reference to a 'suitable piece of ground' suggested that the tactics to be developed should be tested by a divisional scale exercise, in effect an up-graded 'Iron Duke'. If that idea occurred to Bramall he was quick to discard it. Limitations of space and military resources in England would be bound to curtail the scope of a divisional-sized exercise to an extent that would be certain to cast doubt on its conclusions. Therefore he decided it should be a theoretical battle but over well-chosen ground.

His 'Formation Tactics' pamphlet acknowledged that a non-mechanised brigade would probably have to hold a defensive frontage of between 3 and 8 kilometres in the NATO Central Region. He took the worst case and chose a 16-kilometre-wide area bounded by the River Avon and the outskirts of Andover as the divisional area of responsibility with two brigades forward and one in reserve. Similar ground was available on the Larkhill artillery ranges or Salisbury Plain training area, but these were largely devoid of the copses, farms and hamlets critical to his concept of defence. The area he chose also had ready access for the commanders and staff officers engaged in the study.

At the outset of the study, 3rd Division was theoretically deployed with the 5th and 19th Infantry Brigades facing an anticipated enemy armoured advance from the south, up the A338 axis from Shipton Bellinger through Tidworth. The 24th Infantry Brigade was in reserve south of the Kennet and Avon Canal covering the 'vital ground' – that is the area which, if lost, would open the way for a breakthrough into the divisional area as a whole. Bramall ran the study through a series of discussion and planning sessions supplemented by ground and air reconnaissance he and his subordinate commanders and staff would carry out in preparation before battle was joined. Having determined the likely principal line of the enemy's advance, he focused on the 5th Infantry Brigade sector on the right (western) forward flank. In this way, he was able to meet General McMeekin's remit to relate the problem of destroying enemy armour to the brigade group battle and report on the detailed tactics to be employed.

To ensure a realistic appraisal, it was necessary to consider the allocation of troops, manoeuvre and timings for two distinct phases of the battle: first would be the 'covering force battle' to detect the enemy's main thrust within the divisional boundaries and to impose sufficient delay on his advance for the deployment of the infantry brigade groups in the main defensive zone, where the second and decisive phase of the battle would be fought out.

Bramall and the BRAC decided on the covering force's composition as: the divisional armoured reconnaissance regiment, less one squadron, an armoured regiment, less one of its (three) tank squadrons with a medium artillery regiment of 18 x 5.5-inch howitzers in direct support, plus support from the remainder of the divisional artillery and include the main part of an engineer field squadron, an infantry battalion equipped with wheeled troop carriers and six Scout helicopters.

The covering-force concept of operations was the imposition of delay on the enemy armoured formations while passing back such information as it could gather on the enemy's main thrusts; then, on being forced back to the line of the Salibury–Andover railway, swing back in two roughly equal groups to positions obliquely flanking the enemy's main axis. From there, it would protect divisional boundaries and inflict casualties on the enemy armour as it was canalised into the main tank-killing zone. Covering force operations had to provide sufficient time (24 to 36 hours) for deployment of the infantry and close support tanks in conformity with Bramall's concept of operations within the main tank-killing zone. The speed of the infantry deployment was to be assisted by helicopter-borne reconnaissance parties and order groups onto the ground as main bodies of troops, tanks and anti-tank weapons moved forward and, of crucial importance, the engineers laid minefields across the gaps between the tank and anti-tank positions situated in depth.

It will be apparent that the traditional 'two battalions up and one back' infantry brigade defensive deployment was abandoned. Instead, there were front to rear linear zones of responsibility allotted to battalions, but with tanks and anti-tank guided weapons positioned to cover the gaps and minefields, all in depth. The concept of operations at this decisive stage was to attack the enemy's armour at long range in the first instance, then at short range when his tanks had been channelled into the gaps between buildings and woods and towards the minefields in the gaps.

Controversially, the gun position areas allocated to the batteries of 5th Brigade's own close support artillery were dangerously far forward. Although Bramall's study report tactfully avoided giving the specific reasoning behind this, this deployment demonstrated these guns' short range (12,200 metres) and also allowed the study to take theoretical account of the pathetically insignificant part these guns were able to play in the battle against Soviet armour. (In fact, their replacement by the 105mm British Light Gun was already in train. This outstanding weapon system has a range far outstripping that of the medium guns which formed part of the 3rd Division's arsenal in 1969 and a more destructive shell.)

It would be ungenerous to other senior participants to give Bramall all the credit for the design, execution and report on the study, but his was unquestionably the driving force and guiding hand. His 25-page report submitted in December 1969 was inevitably theoretical in nature but its conclusions and recommendations were far-sighted and, with the exception of the cautious comments on the 105-mm light gun, uncompromising. He would also have been mindful of the success on the battlefield achieved by the German Army in Normandy in June 1944, when faced with greatly superior numbers of tanks and overwhelming fire support. Only the salient factors, conclusions and recommendations are summarised here.

Having selected the 5th Brigade mission as 'To halt the enemy before he could seize the (divisional) vital ground', i.e. before he could break out of the close country of the brigade defensive zone, he divided the battle into two elements:

Action of a Shield Force. This mobile, lightly armed group operating under brigade headquarters control comprised the reconnaissance platoons of the three infantry battalions, radar and guided weapon detachments and artillery forward observation officers (FOOs). Its fundamental task was to ensure co-ordination between the Covering Force and those preparing the main defensive zone and to ensure the latter were not surprised or attacked during their preparation phase.

Aggressive Defence. The aim of this main phase was to make it impossible for the enemy to get forward in sufficient strength to capture the vital ground, without first having to dismount and deploy his infantry to clear the anti-tank framework in the close country astride his main axis. Meanwhile, this framework sited in depth, using reverse slopes, natural obstacles and minefields would continue its work of dissipating the enemy's tank strength and preventing any decisive forward move.

The report made four key recommendations to improve the 3rd Division's anti-tank capability, all of which were organisational rather than tactical. The first was to increase the tank strength of the forward brigades from one squadron to two. This would allow for one squadron to be deployed in the anti-tank framework (as in the study) and a second used to form the striking force of the brigade reserve. The difficulty of implementation was the provision of a third armoured *regiment* for the 3rd Division.

The second recommendation was to put more emphasis, that is to say army *resources*, into arming suitable helicopters with anti-tank guided weapons. This was a 'hot' topic at the time and strongly contested by some elements in the Royal Armoured Corps, chiefly on grounds that helicopters could not survive at low altitudes over the modern battlefield. Despite the development of more manoeuvrable and well-protected helicopters since Bramall's report was written, the counter-argument has gathered strength in the form of evidence from battlefields such as Afghanistan and Iraq against enemies far less sophisticated than the Soviet Armed Forces, albeit often using weapons with which they had been equipped.

In a discursive paragraph on artillery, likely to have been written by the commander of the divisional artillery, there is a very worthwhile kernel of truth: 'If the long term policy is to give all the divisional artillery a heavier shell and virtually convert it to medium artillery, this would undoubtedly help our anti-tank capability.' The same paragraph goes on to suggest, 'it would be appropriate to deploy the guns where, in an emergency, they could bring direct fire (against tanks) to bear'.

The divisional artillery commander finally recommended that consideration should be given to the formation of a 'divisional anti-tank regiment'. This was not a new concept, as various units with only an anti-tank function had been used to good effect by the Germans and Russians in the Second World War and by the 8th Army in the Western Desert. Having had this option put forward,

Bramall seems to have felt obliged to knock it down on grounds of cost. Unless the unit were to be equipped with an existing tank, costs would have been high, but that was not a *tactical* consideration.

This study was Bramall's swan song before he gave up command of 5th Airportable Brigade to go to the Imperial Defence College. That it gave him a thorough grasp of the power of armour in the NATO Central Region there can be no doubt. A few years later, while visiting the small arms shooting competition at Bisley, someone scoffed at an RAC team which was not achieving high scores. Bramall turned on the speaker – also an infantry general – and said, 'Look, these are just popguns, the tank gun is the master of the battlefield today.'

Bramall's time commanding 5th Airportable Brigade had been happy and rewarding. The military side had been productive and worthwhile, it had included Exercise Iron Duke and the tactical studies flowing from it, smaller exercises in Schleswig-Holstein and Denmark and visits to the ACE Mobile Force battalion in Norway in mid-winter. He had represented the Chief of the General Staff at the annual study period of the Australian CGS in Canberra, as well as making visits to Northern Ireland whenever any of his battalions were on operations there. (Two of them were among the first to be deployed on the streets in Northern Ireland, when the troubles began in mid-August 1969, and were initially greeted as protectors by the Catholic population, who had been discriminated against.) He had also got ascending parachuting going in the brigade, a cheap way of introducing soldiers to the thrill and sense of achievement of *descending* by parachute.

From a family perspective, he and his wife Avril had lived in a charming farmhouse with a walled garden, provided by the Army, enabling them to play a part in the life of the local community and providing an ideal place for their two teenage children, Sara and Nicolas, to return to in school holidays. He had shot with the local shoot and played a lot of cricket on the Tidworth Garrison cricket ground, as well as club and regimental cricket, further afield. When 1969 came to an end with a year at the Imperial Defence College immediately before him, they had no home to go to. Thanks to Sir

James and Lady Scott they were able to rent a house on their estate near Alton, which proved an ideal place to commute to London to attend the IDC in Belgrave Square. As things turned out, the Bramalls were to stay in the house for a second year when he was given the task of helping with a study into the command structure of the United Kingdom Land Forces.

10

The Application of Force

Brigadier Dwin Bramall was a student at the Imperial Defence College (the Royal College of Defence Studies from the following year) in 1970. Alastair Buchan, son of the Scottish author and politician, had just been appointed the first civilian commandant of the establishment. Buchan's attitude towards the students, all men as militarily experienced as Bramall, was dismissive of their intellect and ability to express themselves.

Each student was required to write a thesis of his own choice during the year. This is a slightly abridged version of the thesis Bramall wrote, entitled 'The Application of Force'. In it, he concentrated his analysis on the immediate past and likely developments within the next ten years, but it has an acute, one might even say uncanny, relevance to the last three decades of the twentieth and even the start of the twenty-first century, which saw the Falklands War, the collapse of the Soviet Union and emergence of the single superpower situation, the recovery of Kuwait, spread of weapons of mass destruction, heightened international tension through fanatical Muslim opposition to Israel and the nations of the West, the rise of al-Qaeda and the invasion of Iraq. My explanatory and other comments are added as footnotes.

FORCE AND CONFLICT

Force has been defined in a variety of ways – as a revelation of strength and power, as coercion and compulsion, and simply as influence. It has often been considered as synonymous with military power or organised violence in some form. Undoubtedly force contains elements of all these things, but it is best equated with a form of strategy which comes into play whenever there is a clash of wills and interests. As such it covers all those measures which nations or communities can take either to compel others to do or accept something they would not do voluntarily, or to protect themselves or their property from the unacceptable interference of others. It also invariably confronts an opponent with a more disagreeable alternative in terms of loss, pain or grief than the compliance, acceptance or restraint which it seeks to impose.

In resolving a conflict of interests by the use of force it has not always been necessary to rely on directly applied violence; although violence is one important element of force. The threat of violence, on strength of evidence, has sometimes been quite sufficient, and even actual violence can be used highly selectively to illustrate and amplify a still greater threat to come. There are also a number of non-violent ways of exerting pressure and restraint which have been traditionally used by individuals and communities and are being increasingly used by nations and these should properly be considered to be part of force, because the pressure they can apply and the influence they can exert is often just as compelling. *Force must be considered a strategy for peace quite as much as it has always been for war.*

In past decades, violence has been a commonly accepted way of resolving international disputes once normal diplomacy has failed to produce a satisfactory answer. In attempting, therefore, to analyse the pattern and character of force in the future, the first problem to be resolved is whether this state of affairs has in some way radically altered. Is it possible, for instance, that within the present century the seeds of conflict itself will have so diminished that there will be no reasons left for using force at all; or could it be that the material, economic and moral costs of using violence will have become so great that no nation state will be able to use it, however much it might be tempted to do so, and that if force is to be applied at all, *it will have to be in a rather different form.*

A study of the current world scene and of recent experience gives little support to the first suggestion; recent years have seen the highest incidence of significant conflict of all types since the end of the Second World War. It is true that some of the more traditional seeds of conflict, notably the desire for territorial conquest for reasons of economic gain, scarce raw materials or missionary zeal, are no longer significant. It can also be argued that some of the instability and internal violence in the developing world can be directly attributed to the ideological and ethnic differences, and rivalries have continued and in some cases have become accentuated, and these have created potential flash points where the problems involved seem insoluble except by violence or an uneasy armed truce.

Perhaps most disturbing of all, a pattern of revolution is developing which transcends national boundaries and at times even ideological barriers. This manifests itself in local revolutionary movements which will gladly accept outside support from those who are interested in maintaining tension and struggle. But the common and underlying theme running through most of the revolutionary situations is undoubtedly 'anti-imperialism' which, in practical terms, simply means the disruption and turning upside down of the established world order and particularly of the status and position of the developed Western powers in that order. In the long term, such a movement probably poses as much a threat to a large and developed communist country such as the Soviet Union, as it does to the Western democracies. It may therefore be assumed that the world will remain a savage and unstable place and it seems certain that the ability to employ force will continue to circumscribe international relations for the foreseeable future.[1]

1. Since this section was written, the Soviet Union has fragmented with loss of its superpower status. In parallel, there has been an increase in the practice of revolutionary movements or nihilist cults seeking outside assistance and even 'fighters' to bring about such a degree of chaos in a state over which they wish to have control that the use of force, as an attempt at pacification, has become counter-productive and played into the insurgent's hands.

MAJOR CONSTRAINTS ON VIOLENCE

The circumstances under which it will be possible to apply force, however, and the form it will take, have been changing. Despite any impression given by statistics of conflict, the moral and economic costs of using organised violence have risen significantly since the end of the Second World War and there are now an increasing number of constraints on the use of military power for inter-state conflict.[2]

Some of these constraints are new, some stem from the unprecedented destructiveness of nuclear weapons and some are of even older origin. All are proving instrumental in channelling violence away from direct, prolonged and distinct military action at governmental level and into internal conflict in which the threat is altogether more subtle.

Still the most significant of these constraints is the possession of nuclear weapons by a growing number of powers. Because of the destructiveness and after effects of these weapons, no nation, however strong and dedicated, can afford to be subjected to them. Similarly, as the stigma attached to initiating nuclear war would be so great, the consequences of doing so, so unpredictable, and retaliation in kind from some direction so likely, the problems of using them seem insurmountable. This state of affairs makes it inconceivable that direct conflict between nuclear powers could break out by design, for no prize would be worth the risk of certain destruction of the homeland. It also imposes great restraint and caution on nuclear powers in all their dealings with one another, because, as long as nuclear weapons are held ready to be used, there is always a faint risk that a miscalculation of their own policies or of their opponents' determination might lead these countries into a spiral of nuclear escalation over which they had incomplete control. Indeed it is

---

2. Of the many conflicts since 1945, only the Korean War, Vietnam, the war between India and Pakistan in 1965, the Iran–Iraq War and the two wars against Saddam Hussein may genuinely by classified as inter-state conflicts.

on the prospect that, under certain circumstances, this could actually happen that the philosophy of the graduated deterrent is based.

Nuclear weapons may be virtually useless as agents of violence, but as a deterrent they still have a number of significant advantages over any conventional counterpart. They can provide a deterrent which not only super but all significant powers can afford; they impose as much self restraint as they do enforced restraint on an opponent; and to some degree their restraining influence can be extended into areas where it would not be possible to retain or introduce a formidable military presence.[3]

There will continue to be arguments on how credible a deterrent can be which palpably should never and, perhaps, could never be used. In the near future, however, the fear and uncertainty caused by a balance of nuclear weapons should continue to be the key factor in preserving the status quo in areas, such as Europe, where the vital interests of the super-powers are seen to be directly affected, and where fear of escalation carries most conviction. Indeed in Europe with the realities of mutual suicide conveniently forgotten, and with the nuclear threshold set at a plausible level, the avoidance by the super-powers of direct conflict with one another has taken priority over all other national interests.

The nuclear balance will also continue to produce prudence and caution in international relations throughout the world. Berlin in 1961, Cuba in 1963 and the conflicts in Korea, Indo-China and the Middle East are all examples of where the existence of nuclear weapons has exercised a degree of restraint

---

3. The most daunting development in this area is the acquisition or planned acquisition of nuclear weapons by powers with irrational foreign policies, of which North Korea is an example, or so factionalized internally, for example Iran, that there is a possibility of nuclear weapons being acquired by one faction to dominate another by threat of external use. In either case, the risk of accidental use is much greater than during the Cold War.

and limitation of conflict which probably would not have been present without them; and in future it is not difficult to envisage some degree of nuclear stabilisation dominating any confrontation between the Soviet Union and China. Although the possession of these weapons has in no way prevented organised violence, it has undoubtedly limited its scope and the geographical areas in which it can be used between nations at government level. It has also reduced the extent to which nuclear powers are prepared to intervene, in competition with one another, in areas outside their immediate spheres of influence.[4]

Enthusiasm for armed conflict between nations has also been steadily declining, with only minor variations, since the First World War. One of the main reasons for this is the cost of any conflict has escalated out of all proportion over the last 50 years, with each generation of weapons and equipment liable to cost double that of the previous generation. With the equipment costs of today running into many millions of pounds, the military stakes have to be very high indeed before any risks are taken. The nations of the world have also seen it established beyond doubt that the road to national wealth and economic power lies through education and investment and not through territorial conquest or military victory.[5]

We have witnessed the impact that the threatened withdrawal of United States financial support had on Britain's last attempt at large scale military operations at Suez in 1956. While Vietnam

4. The increased risk of nuclear weapons being used, either deliberately or accidentally, by what are now regarded as 'rogue' nuclear powers has so heightened the dangers that it has brought about co-operation between major powers likely to be affected in concerted efforts to avoid nuclear proliferation and to moderate the causes of conflict likely to lead to a nuclear exchange, e.g. the Indian–Pakistan dispute over Jammu–Kashmir.
5. Comparison of Capital Equipment Costs in the 1970s and immediately past generations of some British Army equipment:
    Armoured regiment £8.5m compared with £4.7m
    Armoured reconnaissance regiment £5.0m compared with £2.7m
    Medium artillery regiment £4.0m compared with £1.2m

presented the world with the pathetic spectacle of the richest nation on earth finding the level of expenditure, even in counter revolutionary operations, unacceptable in the light of higher national priorities. Moreover, while this has been happening, other nations, which have avoided war or been able to limit their military expenditure, have significantly increased their prosperity and standards of living, especially the Federal German Republic and Japan.

Today few nations can afford to spend more than 9 or 10 per cent of their Gross National Product on prolonged military expenditure and still draw on political and public support, and the great majority wish to spend less than half this amount.[6]

Expenditure at this lower figure may be adequate for self defence and internal security, but it would certainly not be sufficient for the prosecution of an inter-state conflict on any appreciable scale.

Moreover the more industrialised and wealthy the state, the higher its standard of living and the more it has to lose, the more pre-occupied it becomes with the pursuit of domestic issues and with progressive and costly social programmes, and the more reluctant it becomes to embark on a foreign policy which puts the capital investment involved at risk.

The second reason for the lack of enthusiasm for military adventures is the considerable moral repugnance for violence at government level. Not only are most governments inhibited from using substantial violence by the fear of the military and economic damage they will incur, *but the actual legitimacy of doing so*, even if they themselves consider the cause is just, is now subject to the most penetrating scrutiny both internationally and within their own countries. The moral and economic pressures which can be put on a country which flagrantly breaks international law and incurs international

6. In 1970, only the Soviet Union, Egypt, Israel and Iraq exceeded this percentage.

censure, although by no means binding, can be very embarrassing, inconvenient and irksome, and can never be ignored altogether. Far more serious for those who do defy this censure is the critical public opinion which can permeate within the offending country itself and amongst its allies, particularly if the scale of violence is thought to be in excess of what the situation strictly requires. No country can fly for ever in the face of these sort of pressures.[7]

Nowhere are these scruples of the popular conscience more marked than in the modern attitude towards territorial conquest. The right to deploy forces into neighbouring territory when truly vital interests of security are threatened can still be a compelling military requirement, as has been demonstrated by Israel and by the South Vietnamese in Cambodia and Laos; but nation states now have little interest in acquiring additional territorial possessions. The moral and economic costs of forcibly policing subject territory make it economically unprofitable and unrewarding, and there is also much less incentive and opportunity for conquest than there was in the 1930s when Mussolini was carving out an African empire and Germany and Japan were demanding room to expand. Large populations are now considered an asset for economic expansion, not a liability. Overt aggression has, therefore, to take into account not only physical frontiers, but also considerable psychological ones which few governments in their right mind would feel they had the nerve or capacity to cross.

Public opinion will be particularly significant in the future

---

7. The most obvious example of this is the American and British invasion of Iraq in 2003 which, in the absence of a more specific Security Council Resolution than 1441 and in the face of voiced opposition of three of the five veto-bearing permanent members of the Council, was of extremely doubtful validity in international law. Quite aside from the increased focus for acts of terror that the invasion provided, serious damage was done to the prestige and authority of the United Nations as an organisation to preserve world peace.

because it can now be developed around the catalyst of the mass communication media of television, enhanced by satellites, and transistor radios. These possess the capability of not only making all conflict and diplomacy public, however desirable it may be to keep them secret, but also of actually creating opinion, sympathy, anger and protest as well as reflecting these things. All the natural misgivings about war and its horrors can now be identified and diffused through this media, and those who report and commentate on violence throughout the world are not slow to exploit these capabilities.

The result of this is that emotion and protest are stimulated, particularly, but by no means exclusively, amongst the young and uncommitted, and the media then magnifies and re-diffuses this protest in such a way that the whole community soon feels implicated and involved and, very often, not a little guilty as well. When this occurs, democratic governments may feel obliged, because of the depth and persistence of the outcry, to take account of this public opinion, even when the normal processes of democratic government have been short-circuited. It can for instance be argued that it was largely because of public opinion that the President of the United States had to limit the depth and duration of the American sortie into Cambodia, irrespective of the military advice he received at the time.

For any nation which can get itself internationally recognised and accepted as the aggrieved party or 'underdog', international public opinion can be a powerful ally. If properly exploited, it can enable a small nation or minority faction to win a considerable psychological victory and restrict the options and the use of force by more powerful adversaries. It is not a new phenomenon for commanders and governments to suffer a psychological defeat in the mind when neither the strategic nor the tactical position really demanded it, but the unrelenting pressure of public opinion makes this failure of willpower even more likely to occur.

But if public opinion in most developed countries acts as a

restraining influence on organised violence at governmental level, it will not invariably do so.[8]

If a cause has the approval of local or international revolutionary movements, or indeed of a strong sectional interest, a section of public opinion may try to urge even greater violence on their governments, or at least get them to support others who are prepared to use it. The attitude of the 'New Left' to the activities of North Vietnam, to the using of organised violence against Rhodesia, to the Biafran rebellion and to rebel activity against Portugal and South Africa are all examples of this, as could be considered the approval of the use of violence in punitive operations between Israel and the Arab World by those who are emotionally involved in the Zionist or Arab causes. Moreover, because the mass media can transmit the challenge and record of emotion, protest and violence from one country to another, from one campus to another and from one revolutionary situation to another, public opinion may also encourage and stimulate internal violence at the lower end of the scale.

The constraint of public opinion can be reduced, as the Israelis illustrated in the Six Day War of 1967, by the speed with which violence can be initiated at government level and completed. Conversely, it may be increased by the remoteness of any violence from the homeland of the perpetrator.

IMPACT OF OTHER CONSTRAINTS IN AREAS OF MARGINAL CONCERN TO THE SUPER-POWERS

The constraints already mentioned do not have equal impact in every geographical area. In areas of the world which are in some

---

8. An example of the failure of public opinion to influence governmental policy was that in Britain against the invasion of Iraq in 2003, when thousands marched in London against the war, reflecting widespread views across the country as a whole. The more muted opposition in the United States may be attributed to the belief there that Saddam Hussein was in some way at least associated with the al-Qaeda attacks on the World Trade Center in 2001.

way linked to the East–West power rivalry but where the interests of the super-powers are less than vital, the situation is clearly less stable than in Central Europe. In certain respects, however, the relevance and influence of nuclear weapons has been extended. On the flanks of NATO, the multi-national Mobile Force has been formed to identify threats and to confront them on behalf of the Alliance as a whole, with all the nuclear constraint which this implies. In the Middle East, the Soviet support of Egypt, Syria and Iraq and the introduction of Soviet ships into the Eastern Mediterranean has virtually balanced the presence of the US 6th Fleet and the ultimate underpinning of Israel by the United States. While in the Far East, the United States involvement in South East Asia and the economic strength of Japan have to some extent been matched by the emergence of China as a nuclear power. All these developments tend to communicate to these areas some of the caution existing in central Europe, and to ensure a degree of compromise and limitation of local conflict should it occur.

In due course some limited proliferation of nuclear weapons to as yet non-nuclear powers, for the purpose of a local deterrent, may be inevitable. Whether this will be stabilising or destabilising will depend largely on the reciprocal balance of power which can be achieved and on the sense of responsibility amongst the local leaders at the time. For the moment, the best constraints on inter-state violence in these marginal areas will be very largely economic ones.

None of the constraints mentioned makes violence impossible, certainly not internal violence; nor are they utterly dependent on the nuclear influence to make themselves felt. But the constraints have collectively diminished the utility of inter-state war and they are that much more effective because of the continued existence of nuclear weapons. Together, they significantly limit the options of the great powers in inter-national relations, and they have reduced the extent to which chance, prestige, emotion and the corruption of power can govern the initiation and spread of conflict in the name of national interest.

Major Edmund Bramall.

Bridget 'Bryda' Bramall.

'Messenger Boy' – his first job – with
his brother Ashley.

Dwin with Mollie Neville in the early
1930s.

Juvenile batting competition judged by Mr D.R. Jardine, the current Test Captain of England, in Regent's Park, 13 June 1934. Dwin, the winner, is at the crease.

Varnishing Day, Royal Academy Summer Exhibition, 1940.

Member of the Eton XI, 1941.

Private in the Home Guard on his
seventeenth birthday, 1940.

Scoring the winning run in the Eton *v.* Harrow match, 1942.

Near Weert on the Belgian–Dutch border with Sergeant Rogerson of the 2nd/60th, September 1944.

Lieutenant Bramall receiving the MC ribbon from Field Marshal Sir Bernard Montgomery, February 1945.

Acting Major Bramall aged twenty-two, 1946.

Hiroshima, 1946.

Home from the war.

Wedding Day, 16 July 1949.

The newly weds.

Avril with Sara aged five and Nicolas aged four.

During the expedition to Kufra, 1957.

The Brandenburg Gate, as seen from the 2nd Green Jackets (KRRC) observation post on the roof of the Reichstag, 1961.

Commanding Officer, Borneo, 1965.

With the Soviet Military Attaché on Exercise 'Iron Duke', 1968.

At the Darmstadt Ski Meeting, 1972.

Arriving in Hong Kong met by Major-General 'Bunny' Burnett, November 1973.

Flagstaff House, Hong Kong, 1973.

With Gurkha officers, Hong Kong.

With HRH The Prince of Wales, Colonel-in-Chief of the 2nd King Edward VII's Own Goorkhas (The Sirmoor Rifles), and The Right Honourable John Nott MP, Secretary of State for Defence, at Church Crookham, February 1981.

The Chiefs of Staff during the Falklands War, Air Chief Marshal Sir Michael Beetham, Admiral Sir Henry Leach, Admiral of the Fleet Sir Terence Lewin and General Sir Edwin Bramall.

General Bramall with General Sir Frank Kitson, C-in-C United Kingdom Land Forces (left) and The Right Honourable John Nott MP, Secretary of State for Defence (right), seeing off troops bound for the Falkland Islands on the QE2, May 1982.

With his brother Sir Ashley Bramall when he was Chairman of the Greater London Council.

With The Right Honourable Michael Heseltine MP, Secretary of State for Defence, and General Jack Vessey, Chairman of the United States Joint Chiefs of Staff.

Lady Bramall during an official visit to Italy, 1982.

Sara and Nicolas at Sara's wedding, 27 June 1987.

Painting in retirement.

Lord Bramall as President of MCC, 1988–9, during the 'rebel' tours to South Africa, photographed in front of the Pavilion at Lords.

Above: In Belize with the SAS Regiment, of which Lord Bramall was Colonel Commandant.

Left: With grandchildren Charlotte and Alexander.

Receiving the Inter-Faith Gold Medallion from the International Council of Christians and Jews, 2001. *Left to right:* Baroness Boothroyd, Alexander Bramall (grandson), Sir Sigmund Sternberg, Patron International Council of Christians and Jews, Lord and Lady Bramall, Dr Rudy Vis MP and Nicolas Bramall (son).

As Lord Lieutenant with Her Majesty The Queen at the Parade of Veterans in the Mall to mark the fiftieth anniversary of VE-Day, 1995.

After installation as Knight of the Garter, walking in procession with the Duke of Wellington KG.

The Lord Lieutenant of Greater London in his office.

FUTURE PATTERN OF FORCE AND VIOLENCE

The major powers which have most to fear from escalation and the cost of conflict, and who often find their military superiority at a discount when confronting smaller nations, have become less and less inclined to get involved in any inter-state violence. They prefer the role of bystander or that of 'honest broker' to that of participant and, as a result, are carrying out critical reappraisals of their *own* hitherto vital interests. For these countries, inter-state war, in the distinct clear cut decisive pattern of earlier decades, will virtually cease to be an instrument of policy, and the avoidance of war will assume the same high priority as territorial integrity among their national interests.

The smaller and developing countries will also be subject to constraints, although perhaps to a lesser extent. There may still be some opportunities for limited inter-state violence between them, while the likelihood of internal violence will, if anything, increase. This state of affairs is partly because of the nature of the international problems themselves, partly because of the greater permissiveness in the international scene, and partly because it is in the field of internal violence that those who wish to get their own way, maintain struggle, and discredit the international order can do so without undue risk to themselves.

When force has to be used, the initiator will not only have to take account of the various constraints on violence but must also try to use them positively to his advantage. As far as possible, he will exert pressure or impose restraint by active diplomacy and other non-violent methods of force. Under certain circumstances, he may imply a threat of violence but will be careful not to place himself in a position where he automatically has to use it. If he feels he must resort to actual violence to achieve a particular aim, he is likely either to exploit opportunities for subversion, terrorism and even insurgency inside his opponent's country – the indirect approach; or he will concentrate on a more direct military 'confrontation' in which he initiates a series of punitive operations each with a precise and limited military or political aim; or he may attempt a combination of the direct and the indirect. If his punitive operations are to be of any scope and intensity, he is likely to try to complete his military action so quickly that he can, as the Israelis have done so effectively in the past, present the world with a *fait accompli* and, at the same time, so limit and localise the conflict as to transfer the main burden of constraints on to any outside power which may feel tempted to intervene. The victim, on the other hand, will naturally try to embroil others in the conflict from the outset, at least emotionally, so as to bring the maximum pressure of public opinion to his aid.

Should a major power require to intervene militarily in someone else's internal or external dispute, it should only be on the grounds that the alternative to refusing assistance would only create still greater risks in terms of the balance of power. Any military effort would then take place in conjunction with allies so as to broaden the base of military, financial and moral support, and would try to avoid too deep an involvement on the ground. Instead it would concentrate on building up the national organisation, military strength and morale of the country being assisted and on deterring any enlargement or escalation of the violence. It could do this with the help of military aid, such as arms sales, token and special forces, training teams and advisers, and by ostentatiously deploying, but trying to keep uncommitted, some superior element of military power which threatened a greater scale of violence than had hitherto been used.[9]

It will, however, be internal violence which is likely to prove the greatest threat to nation states in the future. This will arise from three basic causes. First, it may occur as a forceful protest against an internal or external political issue. Although this violence will be revolutionary in character, be in sympathy with

---

9. There can be no more cautionary example of creating greater risks, in this case in the international war against terror, of not gathering a broad base of military, financial and (above all) moral support and not avoiding too deep an involvement on the ground than in the 2003 US–British invasion of Iraq.

the pattern of world revolution and be decidedly tiresome for governments and security forces, it is unlikely to be pushed to the point of armed rebellion or insurrection.

Secondly, internal violence may be provoked by racial or religious rivalry and fear, or by deep social unrest brought about by labour disputes, maladministration or corruption. These, although local issues, are liable to have much deeper political undertones and support, and are capable of being exploited both for internal rebellion or civil war and to assist the hostile intentions of neighbouring states.

Finally, internal violence may be introduced as a principal element in the strategy of force, wherever there is an acute conflict of interests or the balance of power is in the process of adjustment. This revolutionary violence may still take some of its inspiration from ideological conflict; or, and even more likely, from ethnic conflict between black and white or Arab and Jew; or it may simply and blatantly be inspired by dissatisfaction with the existing world order, with the emerging states wanting to cause the downfall of those more inclined to be associated and aligned with that order. But whatever the guise, the internal violence in this third category is likely to be sponsored and directed from outside the threatened country.

STRATEGY OF FORCE

From this analysis of the pattern of international force and its constraints, it is possible to distinguish six ways in which a strategy of force can be applied which are infinitely more significant than the conventional and sustained use of military power. These can be described as pre-emptive diplomacy, psychological operations, threatened violence, revolutionary violence, punitive violence and peace-keeping. Each of these methods, with the exception of peace-keeping, has both an offensive and defensive aspect and each, depending on the aim of using force in the first place, may be either an alternative or complementary to one of the others. Indeed, it will usually not be possible to keep them in watertight compartments.

Pre-emptive diplomacy. With many constraints on the use of violence between states, there is both a greater tendency and a greater need for the nations of the world to safeguard their interests and achieve an acceptable balance of power in a particular area by means of diplomacy. As with other forms of force, the aim of this diplomacy may be to impose restraint on expansion; to exert pressure and influence on adversaries, rivals or non-aligned countries without incurring the risk of armed conflict; or it may be to maintain influence when others are trying to threaten it and substitute their own. Where possible this diplomacy should be pre-emptive so the onus of trying to change the *status quo* is placed firmly on an opponent.

Two of the main elements in this diplomacy will be economic aid and preferential trade, and military aid in the form of advice and supply of arms. The economic aid provides an opportunity to reduce poverty and economic disparity, which so often provides the conditions for internal and external instability. Moreover an acceptable local balance of power, which it is to be hoped will secure stability, will need some sort of economic equilibrium if it is to have a proper military and political balance. Although this aid will have definite links with the strategic and political interests of the donor, the humanitarian aspect may play an important part. The military aid can, if properly handled, produce an even greater and more direct incentive for recipient countries to follow policies compatible with those of the donor, and also to provide those donor countries with facilities and opportunities for strategic and economic expansion.

These two together, therefore, play a part in creating, consolidating and extending regional defence arrangements without the embarrassment or cost of an excessive military presence. They can also help to spread affluence, self-esteem and sophistication, with a corresponding local reluctance to lose this new wealth, to hitherto unstable areas. Using economic and military aid to create the right political climate for friendly and anti-communist governments to flourish has been a feature of United States policy since the Marshall Plan brought resuscitation to Europe after the Second World War. The application of force will always require sacrifice, but the sacrifices involved in reverting to the more traditional methods of having a large military presence and indulging in active military operations are likely to be far greater still.

By responsible behaviour in the trade of arms, the powers which have the virtual monopoly of manufacture have a real opportunity to use force in the interests of stability. If done scrupulously, the sale of arms can help developing nations achieve internal stability and a high morale; it can deter aggression, by giving small nations an adequate defensive capability; and it can achieve a solidifying balance of power in various regions. It is when armaments manifestly exceed these requirements, or when conflict has occurred and escalation is imminent, that the suppliers have an opportunity to contribute towards preventing violence spreading further. Differentiating between offensive and defensive weapons, or disassociating the actual supply or limitation of arms from political alignment and encouragement to one country or another, will never be easy; and agreement between the suppliers will still be influenced by a conflict of aims and interests.

Other forms of pre-emptive diplomacy are support and encouragement for ruling political parties, and the non-violent use of military forces for making a political point rather more strongly than it can be made by purely diplomatic means. If, for instance, a nation's military forces are retained in a particular area of traditional concern, or are moved into an area where they have not been previously, they may or may not pose a plausible threat of violence and be of some military value if put to the test. This will depend on their size, striking power, logistic support and ability to be reinforced. These forces can, however, without necessarily being used, give a measure of moral support to the host nation. They can show either a continuing or a novel interest and concern in local politics and trade, and can confirm or establish their nation as a factor to be taken into account; and they can start to balance the excessive influence of others, whether that influence is expressed in political, economic or military terms. They can, as deployment of Soviet naval forces in the Eastern Mediterranean has indicated, play a significant part in adjusting the balance of power *without* violence.

Psychological operations. One of the most important ways of applying pressure and restraint without resorting to violence, or as a supplement to that violence, will be through the medium of psychological operations which fall outside normal diplomacy. These cover the planned use of the whole range of the communications media to influence, to the initiator's advantage, the opinions, emotions, attitudes and behaviour of opponents, neutrals and allies. The ultimate aim of psychological operations is invariably to discredit an opponent's commitments and reduce his options, and thus force him into an attitude and line of action compatible with one's own. This can be done either by sowing doubt and dissension in the opponent's own ranks or by getting other influential countries to condemn him and thus put indirect pressure on him.

Propaganda designed to prepare the ground for violence and justify it subsequently has long been an instrument of conflict, and has been fully used by totalitarian regimes both for internal and external consumption. Nowadays, however, direct propaganda has an increasingly limited impact, because of the credibility gap which invariably develops, and as audiences both at home and abroad become more sophisticated and discerning. Direct propaganda can normally only be initiated by totalitarian countries with a controlled press and radio.

The emphasis in psychological operations today should be on getting the recipient nations, whether they be an actual opponent or other nations capable of influencing and discrediting that opponent, to implant and generate their own seeds of sympathy, anger and protest. In a free and democratic country it is comparatively easy to find the necessary sympathisers with any cause, particularly if that cause fits into a general pattern of 'anti-imperialism'. These sympathisers may be drawn from those who are politically involved, from those who are morally motivated and support the under-privileged and oppressed, or from those who prefer sensation to responsibility; or they may come from any of the religious or ethnic groups who may be identified with a particular struggle. Provided the cause they support has some substance, and provided the sympathisers can be properly organised to make full use of the mass media, they can play a significant part in any psychological operations directed at their country or at the world at large.

In circumstances which are less favourable for psychological operations, the initiator can introduce professionals in subversion using both traditional methods and modern methods of public relations. By these means, it is proving possible for small nations or dissident groups to restrict or stop altogether superior force being used against them. Successful psychological operations have been mounted by North Vietnam against the United States, by black Africa against South Africa, and by the Arab World against the British and French. An example was Biafra where a small breakaway province, with a plausible but none too sound a cause, was able, through the medium of a dynamic and well planned public relations campaign, to create such favourable public opinion throughout the world that it very nearly achieved its aim of international recognition.

The more totalitarian a regime, and the more a nation's territorial integrity is seen to be directly threatened, the greater will be its immunity to psychological operations. Psychological operations are therefore most likely to succeed when directed through countries where there is freedom of expression, and when conducted in opposition to policies which involve inter-state violence by a strong nation or group against a weak one.

How deeply damaging psychological operations will prove to nations who are particularly vulnerable to them, and who perhaps ignore their potential, is a matter of conjecture. It seems certain, however, that they will play a significant *role* in the strategy of force in the future and undoubtedly offer a rewarding field for clandestine diplomacy and subversion.

Threatened violence. No fully fledged state is as yet prepared to submit to a world body such as the United Nations, wholly and in advance, its security or indeed any other of its more vital interests. In any case UN intervention usually has to follow violence and not pre-empt it. As a basis of international order, therefore, all countries will continue to require military forces which can help deter any limited external aggression, or intimidation by threats of violence, or outside support for internal revolt.

A deterrent may take the form of a credible or at least plausible defensive capability (as in the case of Sweden), or it may be more appropriate and cheaper to base it on a nuclear counter threat. Precisely what constitutes a credible deterrent, and how much a potential aggressor is deterred by it, as opposed to being held back by 'other constraints', must remain a matter of speculation. A deterrent is clearly all the more credible if the vital interests of the deterring state and its capacity and will to defend them are seen to be clearly linked; but its effectiveness will also depend on the potential aggressor's intentions and resolve as well as his capabilities. The self confidence which a deterrent gives one's own side that it can exact an unacceptable toll from any potential aggressor is, in reality, just as important as the effect it has over an opponent.

For the time being, collective security based on an alliance of like interests, with some ultimate call on an effective strike capability, seems to offer the best method of deterring external threats; of maintaining confidence and stability where tensions between states still exist; and of encouraging self restraint by subordinating any local disputes to the needs of an alliance as a whole. This particularly applies to Europe, but it may be equally desirable for countries which lie outside Europe and in areas where tensions exist but where super-power interest is not deeply involved, to adopt some form of collective security. In these areas, the main threat will probably be an internal one, and the main requirement enlightened and unprejudiced government with progressive social policies and practical plans for regional economic development. In these conditions, the deterrent value of any outside powers who, for reasons of traditional ties, might be persuaded to be associated with the local security arrangements, would be limited, and the capacity of any outside power to intervene in internal violence would be considerably curtailed by political and moral considerations.

If, in spite of local solidarity, hostilities broke out which could actually be attributed to outside aggression or frontier violation, as occurred in Korea, East Malaysia and on India's northern border; or if a super-power or nuclear power such as China started to indulge in intimidation and blackmail, and the balance of power looked like becoming seriously disturbed, then another super-power, with such allies as it could muster, could still feel obliged to intervene. It would then have to do so largely in a supplementary or extended deterrent role by moving to the threatened area, but trying to keep uncommitted some superior element of military power, as for example a naval task force, or strategic bombers or long range missiles; all with a real or imagined nuclear capability.

With these, a super-power might safely be able to restrict the level of violence by the aggressor, to deter any widening or enlargement, to counter any blackmail or intimidation, and to prevent any of the sponsors from intervening. Indeed it might succeed in extending to that area a depth of constraint to that which exists where the super-powers normally confront each other directly. If attacked such forces would have to defend themselves with minimum use of force. This was the strategic philosophy which lay behind the stationing of part of the RAF Strategic Bomber force at Singapore during the Indonesian confrontation, and it was seen in its most classic form in Soviet support to Egypt in the area of the Suez Canal.

The most difficult task which would face deterrent forces in the Middle East, Asia or indeed Europe would be if an aggressor, for punitive reasons or for reasons of political blackmail, seized some limited objective which manifestly did not justify massive retaliation but which, both on grounds of principle and expediency required some counteraction. To re-establish the credibility of the deterrent which had previously been ignored would require intense diplomatic activity backed by psychological operations, and also the ostentatious deployment of fresh forces, preferably those appropriate to an enlargement of the conflict, to key areas close to the point of aggression.

Today, the strategy of force is not the deployment and organisation of military power to ensure tactical advantages at a critical point and something approaching victory on a battlefield, but more the complicated and devious art of producing a constraining influence and a deterrent, of threat and counter threat and counter bluff. In this strategy, military forces which are deployed and threatened are often quite as valuable as if they had actually had to be used; for as long as they are uncommitted they provide their governments with some degree of freedom of action in handling a crisis. That there must be some credibility gap and some disbelief that threatened violence will never be used, is inevitable, but with stakes so high and the consequences of guessing wrong so serious, this need not be significant. Provided the power and the capability are there, uncertainty may well do the rest.

Revolutionary violence. The next method of applying force is by means of internal or revolutionary violence. It includes civil disturbances and civil disobedience, as well as those acts of violence which militant revolutionaries employ, both inside and outside their country, to harass, weaken and ultimately overthrow a government of which they disapprove and to put an alternative one in its place.

Revolutionary violence is a particular phenomenon of the era, but because of its emphasis on taking over states from within by internal upheaval rather than by direct aggression, it can also be a formidable way of applying the strategy of force. It can often circumvent international conflict with its risks of escalation; it can blur the distinction between spontaneous civil disobedience by a majority with a mandate for change, and a calculated campaign by a hard line minority, often with outside support; and it can reduce the censure normally reserved for aggression and make it difficult for more powerful military forces to intervene because on no single occasion will the threat seem large enough to justify it.

The most economic use of violence in effecting revolutionary change is the *coup d'état*. This differs from insurgency or 'revolutionary war' in that it tends to draw support from a different section of the community. It is quick, tidy, involves no one else and usually produces firm and comparatively capable and incorruptible administration. *Coups d'état* have been carried out effectively in the last 20 years in over 20 different countries, amongst them Brazil, Greece, Indonesia, Cambodia, and South Vietnam, Pakistan, Egypt and Nigeria. *Coups d'état* have their limitations. They can *only* effectively be organised with the active assistance of the armed forces. They tend to be autocratic, and are bound to be an anathema to many intellectuals, liberals and all those who look on freedom as more important than any other aspect of government and society, and on political struggle as an end in itself. Yet in a developing world many of the better educated citizens serve in the armed forces, and political acumen and a desire for modernisation and technological advance are as likely to be found there as elsewhere. Moreover, where education and living standards are abysmally low, the first priority would seem to be firm and good government rather than plurality of choice and free debate and protest.

How long this state of affairs can persist is debatable. Power corrupts and military revolutionary regimes, like all excessively autocratic regimes with a tendency to perpetuate themselves, are liable to become increasingly vulnerable to alternative revolutionary movements with international support. For the next decade, however, the *coup d'état* is likely to remain the most easily controlled instrument for change in the developing world.

The more infectious threat to international order will come from armed rebellion or insurgency, often with outside support, conducted against an established government which is fully backed by its security forces; and here again the pattern of revolutionary violence may be changing with increasing implications for the world at large.

As Che Guevara has pointed out, the right conditions for revolution may now have to be created rather than being inherited ready made, as envisaged by Mao Tse-tung.[10] As a result, old methods may prove too cumbersome for the somewhat more sophisticated and perhaps less dedicated revolutionary of today, who may prefer more dramatic and quicker results. Moreover, with improving communications, it is becoming increasingly difficult to find remote and inaccessible areas which provide a physical obstacle to security forces and a refuge for guerrillas in any full scale insurrection.

In the future there is likely, therefore, to be a significant shift of emphasis away from the steady progression of Mao Tse-tung's revolutionary war towards four particular areas of threat and violence, some of which will be directed through an outside party selected for its ability to publicise and help the revolutionary cause.

The first of these is likely to be urban violence. This has the potential for making a faster and more dramatic impact on a nation's stability and confidence, and since it can actively involve large numbers of comparatively innocent people, requires less personal sacrifice and hardship from the hard core insurgents. It is also likely to provoke the authorities and security forces into an excessive reaction and thus can quickly rally liberal and moderate support to the revolutionary cause.[11]

The second will cover such activities as kidnapping, intimidation and assassination. These have always had a

10. Mao Tse-tung and Che Guevara, *Guerilla Warfare* (London, 1962).
11. There can be little doubt that the British Army allowed itself to be unduly provoked into excessive reaction against the original IRA in Belfast in 1968 and this, indirectly, led to the formation of the more aggressive Provisional IRA, when the originals backed down, and the subsequent large-scale alienation of the Catholic and Republican elements of society.

traditional place in insurgency, but now they will be directed not only against the usual key officials in the revolutionaries' own country, but also against carefully selected foreign diplomats and national personalities, who may be used as hostages to blackmail a larger country into bringing its influence to bear in the revolutionary interest.

The third type will concentrate on attacks on the property, economy and the overseas trade both of the threatened country and of other influential powers. Aircraft, ships, oil installations and commercial premises may all be vulnerable. These tactics can be used offensively to draw attention to the cause, but will be particularly useful in trying to prevent retaliation and reaction to other forms of violence.

The final area of activity will be psychological operations, designed both to obtain the willing support of the indigenous population and harness world opinion to a massive psychological offensive against the government concerned. Psychological operations have always been an important element in insurgency, but now there will be considerable emphasis on the subtle and often imperceptible subversion of those with influence on the mass communication media, inside the country and in the world at large.

These methods will be aimed at rallying the population to anti-government causes; to giving the widest publicity to popular dissent; and to subjecting the government to such intolerable harassment that it becomes impossible, either economically or politically, for it to continue resistance. They may be infinitely more difficult to counter than the more military threat posed by guerrilla warfare in rural areas. To deal with this type of violence, a nation must make it clear that it will not succumb to exploitation and blackmail. It may have to mobilise its civil and military resources, to abandon some hostages to their fate, to amend its laws and to redesign and re-deploy its security forces. But unless this new style of revolutionary violence can be curbed effectively, international anarchy, in which both economic and military strength will be powerless, could result.

Punitive violence. Most nation states will wish to retain the capability to carry out and resist punitive operations. These will be designed to hurt and humiliate an opponent, usually a neighbour, without too much of a risk of getting involved in an unacceptable scale of conflict. A good example of this was China's attack on India in 1962. Punitive operations can also act as a more emphatic deterrent against future acts of violence.

Punitive operations may be part of a broad confrontation designed to bring about the eventual collapse of neighbouring regimes – or alliances, as in the case of Indonesia's confrontation against Malaysia in 1963–1966; or they may be intended to force an opponent either to make specific concessions or to negotiate, as in the case of Israel's activities along the Suez Canal. If threatened violence fails, or looks like failing, punitive operations might be considered to be the best way to bring home to an aggressor that aggressive policies will not succeed. Alternatively, punitive operations could simply be retaliatory for some hurt received earlier, and be used to register disapproval and maintain tension in an area of traditional dispute. Lastly, these operations could be designed to achieve a limited military objective, which could subsequently, as a piece of international blackmail, be negotiated or exchanged.

Fundamentally, punitive operations pose an external threat. However, if the aim is the ultimate overthrow of a nation state, there will inevitably be links with subversion and terrorism inside the opponent's country. This happened in East Malaysia and is occurring on the west bank of the Jordan. In such circumstances, the driving force of the punitive operations may swing towards the irregular element, who will then be in a position to dictate both the pattern and the intensity of the violence used. This may happen voluntarily because of the greater constraints on governmental violence or as a result of pressure from a revolutionary movement.

Because of the risks of escalation, which neither side will be prepared to accept, it will be incumbent on both participants, whether they be perpetrating the violence or resisting it, to restrict the level of violence used. It will be in the aggressor's interests to limit his tasks and objectives in case he may start something, in international terms, for which he is not prepared and cannot sustain. On the other hand, over-reaction by the defender could force the aggressor to use greater violence than the defender could hope to contain. Indeed commanders on both sides will have the difficult task of achieving their military aims and rendering the other side's efforts ineffective, without using greater or more prolonged force than is necessary, and without closing the door to sensible negotiations towards an advantageous political settlement.

Each and every punitive operation must be designed to achieve a strictly limited aim and no more, and where possible should be conducted in a geographical area where escalation is not so likely, such as barren country or in jungle or at sea. Political factors will feature very highly in military planning and success and failure will depend on the wisdom and political sensitivity of commanders as well as on their professional skill.

Peace-keeping. Any strategy of force requires a safety valve, so that those who voluntarily or involuntarily get involved in violence can have an opportunity to escape from it without undue loss of dignity and without, perhaps, abandoning some of the advantages they have gained. A nation or faction in an unfavourable military position may well wish to prevent further loss or damage. A stronger one could want to consolidate what he had achieved, whilst reducing the economic, moral and military burden on himself. They might both, therefore, be prepared, at least temporarily, to accept the considerable moral constraint imposed by peace-keeping activities under UN auspices.

These activities cover mediation and investigation of disputes by UN officials, supervision of agreements and cease-fires by UN observers and the interpositioning of an emergency force between two hostile factions to prevent violence or further violence breaking out.

It is easy to be cynical about these operations. To launch a peace-keeping operation, there has to be a degree of consent and identity of interests which is rare in international relations. By their very nature, UN operations call for a multinational force which has been improvised at the last moment to meet specific needs, which is, therefore, unused to working together and which lacks any proper command or logistic infrastructure. Moreover, the tasks of observers and interposed forces become more difficult and dangerous in the increasingly prevalent internal and revolutionary violence. Despite these difficulties, UN operations in some form have taken place on a number of occasions in the last 20 years and have achieved significant success in preventing or calming down violence and helping to create a climate in which negotiations for a political settlement became possible.

Perhaps the most valuable contribution of all that these operations make is that they provide the machinery for encouraging nation states and ethnic communities who share the same long term goal to co-exist with dignity despite their prejudices and hostilities. This is something that the parties concerned might have neither the political courage nor the popular support to achieve, if the decision was theirs alone. In a world which is no less turbulent and competitive, but which is less inclined to destroy itself, this is a form of compulsion and restraint which cannot be ignored.

CONCLUSIONS

There will be many similarities between the international scene in the future and that of the previous decade. The seeds of conflict will not in themselves have diminished, and the influence and constraint of nuclear weapons (and others of potential mass destruction) will still make themselves felt. The world will probably remain in a more or less continuous state of low level tension. At the same time all the various constraints on violence should increasingly impose themselves on all established governments during the next 10 years. *The issues over which nations, particularly advanced nations, are prepared to go to war, apart from the protection of their own territorial integrity, are becoming less and less, and distinct decisive, inter-state wars will have virtually ceased to be instruments of sound government policy.*

Despite the limitations on the scale of violence, however, the struggle for economic power and political influence and the rivalries and prejudices stemming from race and religion will continue unabated, and force in some form will still be required whenever there is a genuine conflict of national interests. It will be required in the form of threatened violence, to safeguard territorial integrity and to achieve or preserve an acceptable balance of power, without which the constraints on inter-state violence will not be fully effective; and, if the conflict of interests is particularly deep, it may still, in the form of limited violence, be required to hurt and give more emphatic warning of worse to come. It will also be evident in the handling of revolutionary situations which are likely to prove the greatest threat to nation states in the future.

At the same time, as sustained violence cannot now be considered a sound instrument of policy, it will normally be in the interests of established governments to confine force to pre-emptive diplomacy, psychological and economic pressures or to military or economic assistance and other non-violent measures and to keep in the background, as an ambiguous but still persuasive threat, the controlled deployment of military forces.

Unfortunately, this caution and discretion will only apply at governmental level. To revolutionaries who feel unrepresented, or still harbour deep social, ethnic or ideological grievances, any *status quo* will be an anathema. They will see the near future as a period of intense change, and will find a number of ways of using internal violence which may not yet incur the same penalties and constraints as inter-state violence, but which will have an increasing impact on the world as a whole.

None of these changes of emphasis will make defence planning any easier or cheaper. There will be the organisational problems of reconciling the requirements of military forces which must be raised and equipped to deter and make a political point, but are unlikely ever to be used, with those which will almost certainly have to be used in the increasingly specialised role of dealing with revolutionary and, particularly, urban violence. And there will be the difficult strategic problem of assessing how much revolutionary violence and threats of violence around the world represent the inevitable and even desirable process of change, and how much they can be attributed to militant minorities dedicated to the disruption of the world order and the unbalancing of an acceptable balance of power.

This situation presents an intriguing prospect for all the nations of the world, and it is clear that the controlled and thoughtful application of force will be no less significant than it has been in the past, nor any less of a challenge for political and military leaders.

11

Divisional Commander

In his account of the Second World War campaign in Burma, *Defeat into Victory*, Field Marshal Lord Slim described command of a division as one of the best, because a division is the smallest formation that is a complete orchestra of war and the largest in which every man can know *you*. Dwin Bramall was certainly aware of these factors when he took command of the 1st Division in the British Army of the Rhine (BAOR) in January 1972. When an occasional comment was made about an infantryman commanding what was in fact an armoured division, but not then so titled, Bramall was able to point out, light-heartedly, that Rommel – no mean exponent of armoured warfare – was an infantryman. While he had experience of fighting in close support of armour in the North-West European campaign of 1944–5, he was aware that, unlike many of his contemporaries, he had not previously served in the British Army of the Rhine. He had been with 2nd/60th Rifles in Berlin in 1962, which was a distinctly different matter from command of a first-line division facing the armies of the Warsaw Pact on the north German plain, so he had to learn the contemporary 'cries'.

At this stage there was no hint of East–West détente. Less than four years earlier, Soviet tanks had rolled into Wenceslas Square to crush Alexander Dubček's 'Prague Spring' and fix Czechoslovakia firmly back into the arch of Warsaw Pact confrontation with NATO in Europe. Berlin was still divided by the hated wall and no one outside Russia had heard of Mikhail Gorbachev who, eighteen years later, would cause it to be torn down. Consequently, the task of the armed forces of the NATO nations was to deter any Soviet military adventure into their territory by making unmistakably clear that any incursion would result in an unacceptable level of casualties and damage to the aggressor.

Whatever the perceptions of politicians and the civil population at large, Bramall held no illusions that, with the forces available, NATO would not be able to hold out for long without resort to at least battlefield nuclear weapons. It was his personal estimate that, if British ground and supporting air forces were used with skill and resolution, the enemy might be held up for five days. He knew that by then the NATO armies would have run out of munitions, space and, in all probability, of men, so his tactical philosophy and training directives were based on this assumption. He also recognised that, with German participation in defence plans for the NATO Central Region increasing very significantly, it would no longer be acceptable to think of all the territory east of the Rhine as a bargaining counter for time, while Western politicians found the nerve to use nuclear weapons.

Before Bramall arrived in the picturesque Niedersachsen town of Verden, where the 1st Division headquarters was situated south of the confluence of the rivers Aller and Weser, word had been sent round of what would be expected of the staff. Colonel Tom Jackson, the chief administrative and logistics officer, was a Royal Green Jacket who knew Bramall well. He let it be known that every department chief should have his brief for the new commander meticulously prepared, as he would want to go through each of them in detail. In the first few weeks the new commander gave priority to visiting units to assess them, their commanders, and to let them see him. His reputation went ahead of him, but his warm-hearted friendliness marked him out as a 'different' kind of general. That said, anyone who fumbled or gave a sloppy answer got a cool stare or crisp rebuke.

New as he was to Germany, Bramall was alert to any changes necessary for the pursuit of his tactical philosophy of how to delay a predominantly armoured enemy. The 1st Division was already organised to fight on a mixed armour/infantry structure at brigade and unit level and the artillery, engineers and supporting services were well integrated with the formations with which they would fight. At an early stage, he impressed on his two brigade commanders, Ian Baker commanding 7th Armoured Brigade and Robin Carnegie commanding 11th Armoured Brigade, that they should not maintain rigid groupings of infantry and armour – except for the basic training of combined arms tactics – as he believed that operations on the north German plain would demand flexibility and adroit manoeuvre. Both brigadiers responded by being innovative in their tactical thinking.

Behind this advice lay a more fundamental thought. The early years of the Second World War were littered with examples of how ill-trained British and Commonwealth troops had given up the fight because the tactical plan had not worked, their officers had been killed or they had become separated from their parent formations and supporting arms. A sense of 'What can we do now?' prevailed over any initiative to reorganise with what weapons they had and on the best ground available to hit the enemy hard to damage and delay him. (The defeat of the Australian, British and New Zealand defenders of Crete by a far smaller but more highly trained and motivated force of German parachute troops in just twelve days in the summer of 1941 is a case in point.) Bramall foresaw that in a battle against the Russians, British formations and units would inevitably be split up and have to fight on their own or with units not necessarily familiar to them.

He was shrewd enough not to try to put all these ideas across at one time or to give an impression, when speaking to soldiers *en masse*, that he was a new broom about to sweep away all they had learned or been trained to do. He knew that soldiers, and most officers too, remembered jokes generals told and any gaffes in their introductory speeches better than points of serious military philosophy. The latter were learned only through practical experience on exercises that tested them and their equipment to their limits. There would be plenty of opportunities for these later on; meanwhile he kept a watchful eye for promising military talent – and the weak links.

Until Dwin Bramall's arrival in Germany, relations between British senior officers and their West German counterparts in the *Bundeswehr* had been cordial but almost exclusively social. An exception was at high-level NATO study periods where matters of agreement were given emphasis, rather than differences in tactics. He was determined to break this mould by gaining the confidence and friendship of the German formation commanders who would be co-operating with the 1st Division and, if possible, get inside the minds of those who had first-hand experience of fighting the Russians on the Eastern Front during the Second World War.

He had learned some German at school but had insisted, before taking up his appointment, that the Ministry of Defence should arrange for him to attend an intensive language course at the Berlitz School of Languages. This was enough to give him confidence to use his German in speeches to German civilian and military audiences and on visits to officials. Before long, he became known as 'the General who spoke German', not because he spoke it all that well, but because few of his predecessors had troubled to speak it at all. He also took as his ADC Captain Jan-Dirk von Merveldt, the stepson of Captain Stuart Symington, a friend in the 60th Rifles who had been his company second-in-command when he was running the pre-OCTU company at Winchester in 1955–6. Although a British subject and an officer of the Royal Green Jackets, von Merveldt was from a Westphalian family dating from the twelfth century. Bilingual in English and German, with many contacts among the landed families in the region, he became an important means of contact with the German generals and their staffs whose experience Bramall wished to tap and ideas he wanted to hear.

Bramall's reasoning was: 'If we are to fight side by side with them, they must know what our intentions are and we theirs.' So a discourse began which was to burgeon into a fruitful two-way traffic as well as reveal some startling shortcomings in liaison between allies. For example, the forward operational deployment of the 1st Panzer Grenadier Division reached almost to the frontier wire at Wolfsburg, whilst the 7th Armoured Brigade on the Panzer

Grenadiers' right planned to engage the enemy 20 kilometres further back. Neither formation was thinking in terms of a First World War-style 'front line', yet the disparity of tactical concept needed sorting out. A more immediate problem concerned the bridges over the Mittelland Canal, which the 1st Division planned to destroy in the very early stages of an emergency deployment, while the Germans intended to use them for their re-supply.

The Chief of Staff of the 1st Division, Colonel Roger Plowden, was an experienced BAOR soldier and advised caution when his general said they must get round the map table with Major-General Horst Hildebrandt and his staff to resolve differences of emergency deployment and operational plans. Until then, it had not been the custom to discuss such matters with the Germans, except in the broadest outline at Army Group level. When the two generals met at the map table in the War Room at Verden, they discovered that the variations in their deployments were largely obscured by the thick line of the inter-Army Corps boundary on the trace showing the emergency deployment plan on a small-scale map.

Bramall established a close working and social relationship with General Hildebrandt, formerly ADC to General Hasso von Manteuffel, who commanded the 5th Panzer Army in the Ardennes offensive of December 1944 and, earlier, had been a successful exponent of mobile defence against the Russians in Romania. Such tactics were exactly those which Bramall sought to develop for use on the North German Plain against the Soviet Army. He also got to know the commanders of the 3rd Panzer Grenadier Division, Horst Ohrloff, based west of Hamburg at Buxtehüde, and Major-General Schubert of the Hannover Territorial Command.

It irritated Bramall to see that the British Army and the NATO Alliance as a whole were failing to make use of the vast fund of German experience against the Russians. Recognising Ohrloff as a man hardened by experience on the Eastern Front, Bramall sought his opinion on the perpetual debate in the 1st (British) Corps as to what was the ideal range at which to open fire on Soviet tanks. This was not just a matter of the effectiveness of various tank guns, guided weapons and artillery against enemy armour, but the tactical considerations of time available for other enemy tanks, not engaged in the immediate action, to react with fire and the consequent opportunity for British weapon systems to take cover. After taking these factors into account, Bramall ventured 1,500 metres as the ideal range. Ohrloff widened his eyes and replied, 'I would not open fire over 500 metres,' then added, 'But I agree for that you would need a very steady nerve.'

One of the examples of the closer contact on the military side was the holding of 'ein taktisches Picknick' attended by officers of both Armies, out on the ground where they not only enjoyed an excellent picnic but also discussed tactics on the exact ground over which they might have to fight.

An elegant lifestyle was available to Dwin and Avril Bramall at the Villa Strube, allocated to them as their private residence, complete with staff to relieve them of time-consuming chores and support their heavy programme of entertaining and accommodating official visitors from senior headquarters and England. They were generous, gracious, and above all imaginative hosts. He took immense care in his selection of couples from his divisional staff to complement other guests and ensure stimulating conversation through matching and contrasted interests. As well as the seating plan for lunch or dinner, there would be less apparent arrangements before and afterwards to avoid anyone becoming 'stuck' or of a topic being exhausted. On one occasion after dinner, their daughter Sara resisted being moved any further, exclaiming, 'I'm in the middle of the most fascinating conversation I've had for months, I'm going to stay here.' Her smiling father quietly conceded that he had lost that one.

One or two odd situations arose through his ADC Jan-Dirk von Merveldt being a member of a well-known German aristocratic family, something Bramall could not resist exploiting when opportunity arose. Returning by helicopter from a conference at Headquarters BAOR or 1st (British) Corps, he might spy a likely looking *Schloss* down below and, if von Merveldt knew the family, insist they land and invite themselves for 'Kaffee und Kuchen'. One gloomy October afternoon when he did not arrive to visit a 7th

Armoured Brigade exercise, Brigadier Ian Baker became very anxious. When at last the helicopter descended out of the mist around 7 p.m., it was discovered that not only had the Divisional Commander stayed late with his impromptu hosts, but the pilot had had trouble finding his way in the dark and radio contact with base was working only intermittently.

It was an intensely busy life and Bramall was fortunate that he had perfected the art of sensible delegation while commanding the 5th Brigade at Tidworth. It is all too easy to criticise commanders for lacking the self-confidence to delegate, but the judgement hangs on deciding just what may safely be left to whom and, having done that, on making certain one's instructions are clearly understood. One visit with a reputation for going wrong was that of the current course at the Royal College of Defence Studies (RCDS), as it comprises blasé young brigadiers or equivalent enjoying their final fling before starting the most testing phase of their careers and not hesitating to criticise if they felt like it. Bramall delegated responsibility for the RCDS visit in 1972 entirely to the Commander 7th Armoured Brigade, arriving only half an hour before his eighty-five guests to watch a demonstration of the armoured/infantry mobile battle on Lüneburg Heath.

There is no doubt that Bramall generated something of a breathless pace of activity in the early months of his command. This may have stemmed from his impatience at being out of the swim because of what he perceived as an over-long period at the RCDS as a student. Then, during the following year, when he had served as the Deputy Chairman of the Stainforth Committee before taking the RCDS tour round North America in the autumn, he had felt he was just kicking his heels.

Notwithstanding the pace he set the 1st Division in Germany, he still found time for painting, playing cricket whenever he had the chance and taking part in activities which allowed him to get in among the men under his command and their families. It was no bad thing for morale when the 1st Division cricket team, of course captained by the Divisional Commander, comfortably defeated both the 2nd and 4th Divisional sides. He encouraged extra-mural activities, as much as his own and others' military duties allowed, and did not hesitate to use his authority in both spheres. During the Kiel Sailing Week, he was in the 1st Division boat when the skipper went round the wrong side of an island in the Baltic, thus losing sight of the other competitors. The General's instant reaction was to order, 'Sails down; engine on' – to the delight of the rest of the crew, not least because the weather had turned foul.

He enjoyed complete freedom of thought and almost the same degree of action in the military field. His immediate superior, Commander 1st (British) Corps, was none other than his old friend Lieutenant-General Sir Roland Gibbs, with whom he had rejoined the 2nd/60th Rifles after they had been wounded in France on the same day in 1944. The epitome of calm self-confidence, Gibbs would never have thought of interfering with how Bramall was running the 1st Division or training it for war. Had guidance been requested, he would doubtless have provided some, although perhaps he would have been surprised to be asked.

Bramall's thoughts were seldom far from the battle he might have to fight should any political misjudgement occur in East–West relations. Aside from the ground on which he would have to face a Russian armoured advance, he had to consider fighting with the troops he had in hand and those on which he *might* rely if some warning of Soviet intentions came to be known and, equally problematical, whether the NATO political leadership would respond in a manner allowing for mobilisation and significant reinforcement of forces on the Continent.

The word 'mobilise', frequently misused by journalists when they mean the *movement* of troops already in service, is nevertheless highly emotive and enough to frighten most run-of-the-mill politicians out of their wits. When the Kaiser asked the head of the German General Staff whether he could order mobilisation of only *half* the German reserves in 1914, thinking this would send a negotiating message to London, Moscow and Paris, he was told that it was all or nothing, as *all* the reserves had to be moved by eleven thousand trains in meticulously planned schedules to their battle positions. Thus an attempt to avert an unnecessary and catastrophic war was frustrated. Bramall and other senior officers who pondered on such issues were worried lest the 1914 experience would influence the current political leadership *not* to order mobilisation, when to do so would send an unequivocal message to the Kremlin that the West intended to fight and so, in contrast to the situation in 1914, be a move to *prevent* war.

Around 48 hours' signal and satellite intelligence warning of a Warsaw Pact surprise attack was generally regarded as a sound basis for planning. That said, the movement of a Soviet tank division by rail in radio silence from the Murmansk Military District to the Czech border in 1968 gave NATO intelligence staffs something new to think about. Even with 48 hours' warning, British divisions in Germany in the 1970s could be lacking complete units, for example on emergency tours in Northern Ireland, as well as the men and, in many cases, the fourth company or other sub-units required to bring units they had up to war establishment. On the credit side, it was believed that, with so very little time in hand, the West German government would be more likely to agree to the demolition of key bridges than if time were available to weigh the likelihood of a Soviet invasion.

Whether or not additional units and reservists would have arrived in Germany, the battle for which Dwin Bramall had to train his division was essentially one of mobile defence. The rolling terrain of his sector was interspersed with woods and villages, giving good opportunity for him to develop further the tactics for eroding the enemy's armoured strength – tank killing in effect – that he had demonstrated on Salisbury Plain with the 5th Brigade in 1968. A study of armoured battles in the Second World War and in the Arab–Israeli Yom Kippur War of 1973 confirmed this, convincing him that the most effective use of armour was not to charge at the opposition, unless it had been severely weakened, but to position one's own armour on ground where the enemy would be forced to attack. To complement the manoeuvrable firepower of the 144 troop tanks of the four armoured regiments in his division, he had infantry anti-tank weapons and guided missiles to attack enemy tanks in the flank from the rearward part of the villages and woods.

One very significant weapon not available to him, but which would be to his successors, was the multi-launch rocket system capable of raining down dense concentrations of high-explosive or armour-penetrating warheads onto the vulnerable decks of the enemy tanks from above.

He planned to use one of his two armoured brigades, the 7th – still the 'Desert Rats' – in aggressive delaying action against expected Warsaw Pact formations with a three-to-one ratio of superiority of armour and infantry. The 11th Armoured Brigade would conduct the mobile defence using the back edges of the villages and woods, as well as other 'hides', for cover until ready to engage the congested phalanxes of enemy armour. He left the composition and deployment of battle groups to his brigade commanders, but the composition of individual units did not offer wide scope.

The aggressive delay brigade was grouped into four battle groups, two to be 'armour-heavy', comprising the two armoured regiments equipped with the far-from-reliable 'Chieftain' tanks, each less a squadron, but with an armoured infantry company – mobile in fighting vehicles AV 432 – under command. The 'infantry-heavy' battle groups were each based on an infantry battalion, less the company detached to one of the armour-heavy battle groups, but with an armoured squadron under command. This balanced structure was suited to the opening stages of the anticipated battle, but allowed virtually no capacity to maintain that balance after battle casualties were sustained.

The mobile defence brigade would usually be similarly grouped, although the 'villages and woods' tactics Bramall intended provided opportunities for effective smaller-scale action with far less dependence on control at battle-group level than in the aggressive delay battle. The two phases were interdependent, with the forward delaying brigade assisted by minefields and demolitions to channel the enemy advance into the 'killing areas' of the mobile defence battle groups of the more rearward brigade. These tactics of mobile defence in depth had been developed by the Commander of 11th Armoured Brigade, Brigadier Robin Carnegie, and his Chief of

Staff, Major Peter Inge (later Chief of the Defence Staff, a Field Marshal and Life Peer), and – in due course – helped to shape the new approach to the defence plan for the Northern Army Group sector under Field Marshal Sir Nigel Bagnall, when he was Commander-in-Chief Rhine Army from 1983 to 1985.

Such expressions as 'killing areas' and 'mobile defence' were set out in a booklet of 'Military Terms' Bramall compiled and published so that those under his command could know exactly what each term meant. Some years after he had relinquished command of the 1st Division and left Germany, a member of his staff familiar with his 'Military Terms' rushed into his office exclaiming, 'General, "killing areas" are out!' 'Do you mean,' Bramall asked, 'that someone has thought up a new name for the same thing or really thought of something new?' 'Oh, I don't know about that,' admitted the crestfallen subordinate. 'All I know is that killing areas are out.' (Of course they were nothing of the kind, but someone was trying to be smart.)

When Bramall began his two-year period of divisional command, German farmers and land-owners still took a relaxed view of damage to barns and fences caused by British troops during exercises, as well as to the churning up of crops by armoured vehicles, knowing they would receive generous financial compensation. As the policy of deterrence brought its reward and the threat of war receded, greater care had to be taken to avoid claims for compensation. This factor, together with British defence economies demanding reductions in the use of expensive vehicle spare parts and limitation on the mileage of every tank each year, gradually reduced the degree of realism under which training for war could be conducted.

One persistent difficulty with which Bramall and the other divisional commanders had to contend was the inherent lethargy in units, especially armoured regiments serving in Germany for as long as eight years and exercising over ground they knew like the backs of their hands. Orders for an attack might be boiled down to 'Just like we did this one last year, but with Toby on the left flank, instead of Charles.' To overcome these negative elements, he laid stress on squadron/company and troop/platoon training being as realistic as local circumstances allowed and exacting on the thinking and expertise of junior officers and NCOs. This in part, although not totally, avoided the risk of higher-level training being repetitive, consequently tedious and, worst of all, making false conclusions of what might be achieved in battle.

One aspect he insisted should be applied with strict accuracy was that of timing, even in command-post exercises – or NATO 'telephone battles' – with no troops on the ground. If a bridge would take x hours to build, then x hours were built into the exercise sequence, likewise the time it would take for an armoured battle group to cross the bridge once it was in place. His own battle experience had taught him that everything takes longer, sometimes five or six times longer, to accomplish than the expert thinks it will – and failure to appreciate this results in lives and battles being lost.

On taking over control of a functioning entity, whether a government department, commercial concern or a military formation, few individuals are able to resist the temptation to reorganise it. This instinct is often a defensive mechanism to do away with an aspect the new man does not fully understand or, unconsciously perhaps, to move a person to whom he has taken a dislike. Bramall certainly made changes to the internal working of Headquarters 1st Division, but that was simply to adapt it to suit his own working methods, for the convenience of everyone. He did allow, indeed positively encouraged, a year-long experiment which was costly in time and resources, into the re-organisation of an armoured brigade onto a four-unit or 'square' basis, instead of the current three-unit or triangular structure.

The idea was put forward by the Commander of 7th Armoured Brigade, Brigadier Ian Baker, late of the Royal Tank Regiment. The 'square' had no connection with the defensive battlefield square of the eighteenth and early nineteenth centuries, but related to the number of armoured squadrons and armoured infantry companies a battle group commander might have under command when fighting a battle.

Except in the case of the three-legged milking stool, the balance of a four-square organisation speaks for itself. Before the First World War, infantry battalions had four companies, each of four platoons of four sections. Brigades had four battalions until the beginning of 1918 when, ostensibly to increase the proportion of artillery to infantry, they were reduced to three. But the underlying reason was the forecast 33 per cent shortage of manpower to meet the draft intake for that year. In the campaigns of manoeuvre in the Second World War, in North Africa and North-West Europe, British armoured regiments had three tank squadrons, as it was considered that around 45 tanks were the most that the regimental commander could deploy and 'fight'. Infantry battalions still had four companies, but of three platoons each of three sections.

Postwar financial constraints led to the introduction of battalions of three rifle companies with, on paper, fourth companies made up from reservists on mobilisation, as were crews to man the tanks that armoured regiments held in preservation. Ian Baker was not the only realist to argue for a four-square armoured and infantry organisation in peace, knowing that the prompt arrival of reservists would be problematical, but it was he who proposed an extensive and testing field trial. To an extent, Bramall stuck his neck out in approving and backing him. It is one thing to be an idealistic unit or even brigade commander but, in divisional commanders, the hierarchy is on the lookout for pragmatic men with no stars in their eyes regarding the political hold on the military purse strings. But in this case, Bramall was no doubt influenced in believing that Baker was on to a good thing in his recollections of the Normandy battles when the British armour had become separated from the infantry with devastating results. This had led to each armoured regiment being grouped with an infantry battalion for the final eight months of the war in North-West Europe, an arrangement with most effective results.

In selecting the armoured regiment to conduct the trial, Baker cannot have failed to take into account the personality of the commanding officer of the Queen's Dragoon Guards. Fresh from being the Military Assistant to the Chief of the General Staff, Lieutenant-Colonel Maurice Johnston was not only a rising star but a man who could be relied upon to conduct an objective trial and write a cogent report. Lieutenant-Colonel Raymond Ashforth commanding the infantry battalion, 1st Green Howards, was rather less exacting, at least within the context of the trial. For example, his report that adding a Rarden gun or machine-gun turret to an armoured personnel carrier (APC) would not reduce the number of men the vehicle could carry was found to be mistaken.

Baker and Johnston lost no time in arranging the trial, which was to be conducted over a period of six months during the summer of 1973. The fact that demands of Northern Ireland for units on emergency tours precluded the trial being carried out on a brigade basis, which might have seemed ideal, actually resulted in a useful by-product; the other armoured regiment and infantry battalion in the brigade remained on the triangular organisation which allowed for a useful comparison of performance during exercises.

As one would expect, the report on the trial ran to many pages of facts and closely argued recommendations. Commander 7th Armoured Brigade's covering report to those of the two key unit commanders contained, in paragraph 54, the essential conclusion which merits repeating in full:

54. The implementation of the four square armoured regiment and mechanised battalion would enhance greatly the capabilities of brigades, and hence divisions, in the 1st (British) Corps. It would enable battle groups to be grouped so that four sub-units would be the norm, and not less than three sub-units at times when squadrons and companies have to be extracted as divisional reserves or for special tasks. It would provide more troops to cover our considerable areas of responsibility, a better fighting ratio and added ability to produce depth. In particular, the extra teeth in the shape of 48 battle tanks as against 36, and 36 rifle sections, as against 27, spell out the increased effectiveness that would be ours in both the armoured regiment and the infantry battalion.

The following paragraph acknowledged that there would be costs in terms of manpower and equipment which would have to be compensated for by reductions elsewhere in the Defence Budget, but pointed out that most if not all of these might very probably be achieved by cutting out unnecessary command manpower and vehicles.

It is interesting to reflect on how Bramall dealt with the outcome of the trial, which he must have known would prove favourable to the four-square organisation, and been aware of the financial and manpower requirements involved if all or part of the trial recommendation were to be implemented.

At that stage, only his service under Mountbatten in 1963/4 could be used to label him a 'Whitehall warrior' – and that was not enough to make such an epithet stick. There can be no doubt that he was convinced of the value of the trial and supported the thrust of Brigadier Baker's consequent recommendations. He forwarded the report to the Commander 1st (British) Corps endorsing Baker's advocacy of the four-square organisation and recommendation that it should be adopted. He also approved the suggestion that a study should be launched by the Ministry of Defence into how the compensating reductions of men and material might be found.

His memorandum forwarding the trial report was dated 18 October 1973, less than a month before the end of his time in command of the 1st Division, by when he knew he was to be promoted to go to Hong Kong. It might therefore be conjectured that he fired off the report knowing well that he would not be left to pick up the pieces as a director in the Ministry of Defence.

Indications as to his character and way of dealing with controversial issues suggest a different scenario. Coming so close to the end of his tenure as Divisional Commander, it would have been quite acceptable and some might argue *usual* for him to hand over the report to his successor for a second opinion. Instead, by sending it up the chain of command before handing over, he clearly intended that note should be taken of the report and action taken to implement its recommendations. In effect, he was not allowing his successor an opportunity to influence the future of the trial.

Although he had not been told by the Chief of the Defence Staff that the appointment to Hong Kong was a stepping stone to becoming head of the Army, and from there to become CDS, the implication was plain to see. (Certainly everyone else in the Army with half an eye to such matters could make that assumption.) He therefore knew that he would be required to address hard policy questions in Whitehall around the time the report had been thoroughly staffed as, even if he had not yet arrived there, he would be on hand either as C-in-C in Germany or in the United Kingdom for consultation.

So what happened? Some steps along the line of recommendations of the report had been achieved by the time 7th Armoured Brigade was required to go to war against Saddam Hussein's occupation of Kuwait in 1991. The two armoured regiments under Brigadier Patrick Cordingley's command each had four squadrons, as recommended by Ian Baker, of four troops of three tanks, achieving the recommended total of 48 troop tanks. The two infantry battalions had, however, been reduced to only one – and with the old three companies of three platoons organisation. It could be argued, however, that the infantry firepower and under-armour manoeuvrability had been increased by replacement of the thinly armoured AVs 432 with 'Warrior' armoured fighting vehicles, each mounting a 30-mm Rarden cannon and a 7.62-mm chain gun. But when planning his breakthrough of the Iraqi forward defence, Cordingley had felt himself short of infantry, in particular for holding open the minefield gaps.

The Strategic Review of 1996 restructured the Army for expeditionary operations. The 'squaring' or 'principle of four' was adopted with square brigades comprising 16 sub-units (8 armoured and 8 armoured infantry). Although this was achievable throughout the Royal Armoured Corps, it was clear that the infantry would not be able to recruit to a level to maintain companies of four platoons each. Consequently, 7th Armoured Brigade went to war in Iraq in 2003 on a 'square' organisation, except that the eight armoured infantry companies had only *three* platoons each of four 'Warrior' vehicles.

Writing after the return of 7th Armoured Brigade from Iraq, Brigadier Graham Binns, who had commanded the Desert Rats in the taking of Basra and subsequently, gave his opinion that 'A four unit brigade based on four sub-unit battle groups is right. Subsequent brigades deploying to Iraq for peace support operations had a minimum of four manoeuvre units.' It could therefore be said that the work of the 1st Division in the early 1970s contributed significantly to the adoption of this formation and that Bramall's time in command had resulted in the development of tactical thinking in the context of the armoured battle.

12

Hong Kong

Early in 1973 the Governor of Hong Kong, Sir Murray MacLehose, had written to the Chief of the General Staff regarding the successor to the Commander of British Forces (CBF) in the Colony the following November. 'Send me a General I can make a friend,' he wrote. This was not just a personal request, although the CBF at the time had a reputation as a highly efficient cold fish, but because the Governor knew that the Hong Kong Defence Costs Agreement with Her Majesty's Government was due for renewal by March 1976 and negotiations were likely to be difficult and protracted. Matters would be much easier to handle if he and the CBF enjoyed a friendly relationship.

The position of Commander of British Forces was unusual. Not only did he command the units of all three Armed Services, he was a member of the Colony's Executive Council and second only to the Governor in local protocol. This gave him direct access to political opinion reflected in the largely nominated Council and to the often widely disparate views of the expatriate and local business tycoons represented in the 'Parliament' or Legislative Council.

At the time of Dwin Bramall's arrival in Hong Kong in November 1973, the Colony was still, to a degree, traumatised by the widespread urban unrest and the attack by Chinese irregulars on the border village of Sha Tau Kok six years earlier. Both events had been precipitated by Mao Tse-tung's Cultural Revolution, resulting in the Chinese population of Hong Kong smashing up the 'Place Where Men Eat Fat Pork' with considerable vigour – this despite many thousands of them having fled either from the famine in

Kwangtung Province in 1962 or simply from the Communist regime. Many of the 22,000-strong police force and soldiers of 48th Gurkha Brigade stationed in the New Territories had been involved in containing this violence, consequently their officers expressed serious doubts about possible reductions in the garrison. So when the new CBF began to explain the need for economies in the United Kingdom defence budget, old Hong Kong hands – civilian as well as military – shook their heads and pointed to the commercial miracle the Colony had become and the entrée to the vast Chinese market it offered. The end of the lease from Beijing was still a generation away.

While his Service staffs examined how to reduce the garrison without serious prejudice to internal security and struggled to construct arguments designed to persuade the Hong Kong government to pay more for less, Sir Edwin – he had been appointed KCB in the 1974 New Year Honours List – set about planting the seeds of change. In this, for the first time in his career, he was very much on his own. He knew that Whitehall was seeking defence economies overall, but he had received no guidance from the Chiefs of Staff as to what reductions were expected in Hong Kong. This was partly because they were unable to agree on the matter themselves and partly because the individual Service Chiefs did not wish to defend too strongly any element of their Service in Hong Kong, knowing retention would be at the expense of the total budget. Bramall harboured a personal reservation. Having seen the essential need for close cooperation between the Services and their various arms in war, he had begun a crusade against the fatal habit of all but abandoning this principle in peace.

The Army was particularly vulnerable in this regard. Except in the Army of the Rhine, infantry battalions were used as an imperial gendarmerie in remote places still red on the map where training with armour, artillery and close-support aircraft was impossible. Because of a perceived threat to the Colony from Communist China in 1948, Hong Kong had been spared this predicament. Indeed, at the time of the Korean War of 1950–3, the garrison had been increased to a strength of almost one and a half divisions which, incidentally, was why the CBF was a lieutenant-general. Subsequently its strength had been cut but the border incursions of 1967 emphasised the need for an all-arms force in the New Territories. In 1967, the guns of the resident field artillery regiment had been driven ostentatiously northwards to positions in the New Territories at first light, when the peasant farmers were moving into their rice fields, then returned to base after dark ready to be moved north again, suggesting further reinforcement, next morning.

There was a strong view among the Hong Kong population that the very existence of the military garrison ensured that law and order would be maintained. Everyone with experience of rioting knew that if the violence reached a level where the police could not cope, the military would be called in. New towns in the New Territories, as well as the areas of dense population in Central, on the Island, and in Kowloon made it ever more likely that the Army would be required to act in support of the civil power, should serious trouble arise. There was also a useful psychological weapon available in the form of a government announcement that the garrison was to be reinforced, which tended to cool emotions.

Now that substantial savings had to be made in the Army as a whole and Mao's influence had waned in his last years, so Hong Kong's relationship with Beijing had improved. In the context of impending defence cuts, it was not surprising that the Governor should ask the CBF, 'Do I need all these tanks and artillery?' (Strictly speaking the 'tanks' were armoured reconnaissance vehicles, but they had tracks and gun-turrets and so were 'tanks' to the layman.) Moreover, owing to a recent accident, the artillery had earned a bad press in the Colony. Their use of live ammunition was confined to firing from a gun position in the New Territories onto one side of an uninhabited island. During a practice shoot, a salvo had overshot the island and burst over a party of young people canoeing in the bay beyond, killing one and injuring others. Bramall wished to retain some armour and artillery so that the garrison could maintain professional standards, but he would not be helped by attitudes either in Whitehall or Government House.

This was not the first occasion on which his wish to hear all sides of a question proved troublesome. His instinct to keep his own counsel until he had weighed up the various arguments was perfectly sound, but it could leave him open to criticism by those who had convinced themselves that they had convinced *him* of their case. He was careful not to commit himself in conversation, but would cock his head on one side and mutter ruminatively, 'I can see what you mean,' leaving his listeners with optimistic expectations.

His grasp of the local political and security complications was readily apparent. Speaking at a joint Army and Police study period shortly after taking over as CBF, he said,

> The Hong Kong Government will never be provocative to China; equally it must never be pushed around. If China's influence here is to be kept within manageable proportions, the Services must play their part, both along the border – deterring any attempt to erode our authority or dealing with incursions or illegal immigrants on a large scale – and giving moral and actual support to the police in their task of maintaining internal security and law and order.

Here he was putting down a marker in support of a balanced military force in the Colony but he concluded with a warning for the future: 'Never forget that China is the Mother Country of the Chinese people who live here and one day Hong Kong's status may have to change in accordance with China's wishes. The government has to walk a tightrope reconciling these contradictions.'

The Hong Kong administrative and commercial hierarchies were quick to appreciate they had a general rather different from his predecessors. He smiled, listened, answered questions in an interesting way, and if he did not wish to answer a question comprehensively, he would explain why and, as already mentioned, give the questioner a feeling that his concern had taken root. In all of this, unlike the much-respected but immensely tall Governor, he was helped by not towering over the Chinese dignitaries but conversed with them at eye level. From the outset, he took pains to get out and about to meet his Chinese colleagues and to win their confidence. Others might have waited in the office for them to come to him, but that was not his way, nor would such a tactic have worked had he tried it.

Demands for him as a speaker at official gatherings with which the Hong Kong calendar was packed came in thick and fast. This was not just because he was a new face to be seen and a personality to be judged, but because he was good at it, meticulously researching his audience as well as the subject and including jokes which at least most of those present had not heard. His voice gave a slightly breathless hint of possibly having arrived at the last minute or lost his notes, suggesting that some indiscreet revelation might result. He was never late, updated his notes as new thoughts struck him and kept everyone on the edge of their chairs. If he did risk an apparent indiscretion, it would be a deliberate straw in the wind. He would sometimes begin with a disarming, 'I don't know whether', allowing for a low-key withdrawal if the suggestion proved flawed. It became commonplace for Members of the Legislative Council to lobby him vehemently in the way the Chinese do without realising how worked up they appear. If the individual's passion was not matched by proper knowledge of the subject, Bramall would avoid the obvious short-cut solution to such a situation, but invite the person to lunch, politely test the theory advocated and explain the downside. His view was frequently sought on subjects quite outside the military sphere.

A year after taking up his appointment, he set out his military and political philosophy in a far more expansive manner than he had deemed appropriate on arrival. Again it was the annual study period for the Armed Services, with representatives of Hong Kong government and the Police present. The topics for presentation and discussion were the European attitude and contribution to the nuclear deterrent and the Arab–Israeli Yom Kippur War of 1973. A prominent, pro-European Member of Parliament gave a talk on the European Economic Community, as it then was, and this was followed by a presentation on the battles fought on the Golan Heights, in the Sinai Desert and in the air over both battle areas during the Yom Kippur War.

Summing up, he acknowledged that the nuclear deterrent had

kept the peace for thirty years but pointed to the pressures for a fresh approach, particularly the very high cost of defence. Bringing this point round to Hong Kong, but with reference to the Soviet Union rather than to Communist China, he said, 'There is a temptation to say that since the Russians do not want war we need not take defence seriously any longer.' He then reminded his audience of the Chinese philosopher Mo Tzu of 400 BC, who preached universal love but founded a society of fighting freemasons on the basis that those ambitious for power are deterred not by the turned cheek but by a credible system for defence.

His remarks on European integration made almost two decades before the collapse of the Soviet Union deserve analysis against the very different situation today.

If we are to get any reconciliation between defence contributions, resources and social priorities, we cannot function alone and there must be the closest possible integration with Europe, politically, economically and militarily and we must abandon the more selfish forms of nationalism. We must be prepared to forgo some sovereignty to achieve a broader base, more resources, more strength and more security at an economical cost and perhaps those of us who are so convinced should be prepared to say so from time to time.

It is easy to argue that these views were seen against United Kingdom accession to the EEC at the beginning of the previous year and were largely the aspirations – indeed the expectations – of those elements of the British population who bothered to think about the matter at all. Yet, even when examined in the light of subsequent developments, they still represent what the British people believe they should receive, in terms of increased prosperity, in consequence of joining the European Union. Bramall's views expressed in 1974, and especially his suggestion that people should stand up and be counted on the issue of EEC membership, indicate that not only was he a politically aware general but also prepared to be identified as one.

He concluded with three main points in the context of the pressing review of the Defence Costs Agreements, and its likely impact on Hong Kong, which would follow the conclusion of the previous one in April 1976. He expressed them as guiding factors or limitations for those in the Hong Kong government and the Armed Services working on the problem:

- At least for the foreseeable future, it was realistic to discard any idea of China taking over Hong Kong by force of arms.
- The British government was limited in what it could spend on defence outside the NATO region, on which there could be no compromise.
- In Hong Kong, the argument centred not so much on the level of forces to provide security, but rather on who would pay the bill.

Shorn of sophistry, these words indicated the degree to which he now felt he could begin to call the tune in contrast to his position as a new arrival 12 months earlier. To many businessmen in the Colony, whose influence in or on the Legislative Council was considerable, the first two assertions were not open to challenge, leaving only the third for somewhat grudging acceptance. The new realities were coming home to roost.

Suddenly, a new topic of conversation swept aside the likely implications of the Defence Review, except of course in the minds of Sir Edwin's immediate Service staffs. Rumour became rife that the Queen might call into the Colony on her way to a state visit to Japan in the spring of 1975. Despite being a commercial miracle, the characteristics of Hong Kong are those of a village – a Chinese village. Everyone who was anyone assumed that he or she would enjoy a leading role in events, and positions were quickly consolidated to avoid disappointment. The hitherto little-known figure of the government's adviser on protocol, a retired officer of the Foot Guards, sprang into prominence as soon as Her Majesty's visit was confirmed. If he had been short of invitations to extravagant lunches on board even more extravagant launches cruising the colony waters, his situation was soon reversed. Luckily, he proved tediously incorruptible so, bearing in mind that the Armed Services would be certain to stage a programme of their own, flagrant lobbying soon turned in their direction.

As detailed planning got under way, the cordial relationship between Hong Kong government staff and that of Commander British Forces began to show signs of strain. Sensibly, it was government policy to administer the local population as lightly as possible to achieve by consensus what was necessary to maintain the Colony's bounding prosperity. Consequently, the government structure was slight and soon proved inadequate to cope with the myriad of detailed arrangements in connection with the royal visit. The Services and the Army in particular were the ideal source of organisation and manpower but, instead of saying so openly and asking for the badly needed assistance, the government officials tried stealth. For example, the Services were invited to provide all the marshals and seating attendants for an evening carnival procession along Nathan Road in Kowloon – but were requested not to wear uniform. It all became rather petty.

The inference drawn by the Service staffs was that, because of the shadow cast by the Defence Review, with its attendant threat of Hong Kong being obliged to pay more for less, there was a wish by Hong Kong government officials to avoid giving the Services an opportunity to say 'There you are, you can't even manage a royal visit without us.' Relationships deteriorated to the extent that Bramall felt it necessary to call his friend the Colonial Secretary, in effect the Colony's prime minister, to ask that his officials might be more straightforward in their dealings with his staff. The plea was graciously accepted, but not much changed.

Then an unexpected turn of events brought the two elements into a new atmosphere of cooperation. At 8 a.m. on 3 May, the day before the Queen was due to arrive by air at 6 p.m. on the Sunday, the Army's Chief of Staff was asked to walk across to the Government Secretariat building to receive some news from the Secretary for Security. At 7.53 a.m. on 30 April the United States flag had been hauled down over their embassy in Saigon after the city had been under siege for a month, and South Vietnam civilians who feared for their lives or wealth had been leaving the country by any means they could find. The Dutch container ship *Clara Maersk* had sighted a sinking vessel in the South China Sea and taken all the estimated 2,800 men, women, complete families, unaccompanied children, all refugees from Vietnam, on board. These were the first Vietnamese boat people, and five of them urgently required medical attention. All but the seriously ill were crowded onto the stern or in the spaces between the stacked containers and the ship's rails, from where they had watched their own ship sink.

The Secretary for Security was a former naval officer and maintained the professional composure for which the Senior Service is rightly renowned, but he concluded with a message from the Master of the *Clara Maersk* to the effect that he was making for Hong Kong and expected to dock next day, Sunday, at 6 p.m. The old Kai Tak airport strip, built by the Japanese during the war with stones from the walls of the Walled City in Kowloon, juts directly into the harbour, so there was a good chance of Her Majesty having a clear view of her fellow guests during their simultaneous arrival.

On hearing this news, General Bramall advised his Chief of Staff to ask the Royal Hong Kong Police for all the men they could spare to help with the refugees' reception. 'I already have,' came the reply. 'They can spare eight, all the other 21,992 are involved with the royal visit.' There may have been a touch of exasperation in the Deputy Commissioner's reaction but, in the event, everything went smoothly. Two RAF helicopters winched down doctors and medical staff onto the *Clara Maersk* in exchange for a refugee with appendicitis. A couple of training camps near Kowloon were activated and tents for a third erected on the New Territories polo ground. Someone had the smart idea of using empty containers on the quayside to form corridors to segregate the refugees as they walked to buses to take them to the camps. Numbers had been underestimated. Some 3,400 disembarked, varying from families with nothing but the clothes they wore to gangsters carrying briefcases stuffed with US dollars and well-dressed young women who looked capable of dealing with any situation they might encounter.

All credit to the Hong Kong authorities with the Armed Services in close support, the royal visit and reception of the refugees proceeded in separate harmony. The Queen was informed, but decided against any personal intervention. As care and attention were lavished on the health and welfare of the refugees, Bramall ruefully remarked, 'We shouldn't make them feel too comfortable, you know. Otherwise we will be receiving a boatload every week.' Prophetic words: many thousands of refugees found their way to Hong Kong over the ensuing 20 years and it was not until May 1997 that the last group was forcibly returned to Vietnam.

Although seemingly callous, Bramall's comment was indicative of his way of looking at a situation not only in all its aspects but, through it, to the much longer-term implications. To some extent, the merit – or perhaps rather more the force – of advice he offered to governments over the years was tempered by the self-effacing half-smile which accompanied it or, if his views were in writing, by the humour inserted between the lines of what he guessed would be not wholly welcome counsel. It is difficult to judge whether this whimsical habit was deliberate or instinctive. Experience had certainly taught him that advice from servicemen with a reputation for laconic irascibility, or for taking a hard line whatever the issue, could be all too easily set aside by politicians as 'typical'. Conversely, his reflective and measured manner could result in his point being missed – particularly if it was an awkward one to accept.

The royal visit threw light on the generous side of his character. The four-day programme was packed with events involving the civilian population. Aside from a guard of honour for the Queen as she stepped ashore from the Governor's launch after crossing the harbour from the airport, the Services did not feature much. But the CBF was scheduled to give lunch to the royal couple on the penultimate day. Flagstaff House was not large, so the invitation had to be limited to the Service commanders and their wives. But he invited the forty-eight unit commanders and *their* wives to a pre-lunch reception in the garden, hoping that a few might be presented. Hardly had his guests assembled than a torrential cloudburst drove them indoors where, perspiring freely, they packed cheek by jowl into the drawing room. 'Good Lord', remarked the Duke of Edinburgh with his customary candour as he entered the room, 'I thought this was to be a *small* party!' The Queen appeared unconcerned, and those within reasonable reach were presented.

The summer and autumn of 1975 brought a recurrence of the problem of large-scale border crossings by Chinese from Kwangtung Province. A steady trickle of illegal entries to the Colony had continued ever since the exodus during the 1962 famine in the north, but those coming now were economic migrants and in numbers that were to prove embarrassing on both sides of the border. Many were very young, and a favoured mode of entry was by floating on inflated truck or tractor inner tubes to one of the islands in Mirs Bay in the east or across the misleadingly named Deep Bay to the west. It was a risky business, with sharks in both bays inflicting a significant attrition rate. Until this new exodus began, the Hong Kong government had adopted a part-humanitarian and part-pragmatic policy: if an illegal immigrant reached the outskirts of Kowloon undetected, he or she was accepted, but if caught in the New Territories border area they were returned to China, unless very persuasive extenuating humanitarian circumstances could be proved.

Save for the border violations of 1967, which they had instigated, the Chinese authorities had gone along with this policy, rigorously policing their side of the land border with watchtowers and patrols. Early in 1974, a peasant farmer attempting an opportunity crossing by swimming the 30-yards-wide Sum Chum river marking the border was ruthlessly shot.

The sheer scale of the crossings in 1975 demanded new measures by both sides. A 20-foot-high chain link fence was erected along the twisting 18-mile stretch between Deep Bay in the west and Starling Inlet in the east. It was not difficult to cut a hole in the fence, so a vehicle track was made along the 'home' side and the five infantry battalions of the garrison took turns to monitor it day and night. Between twenty and fifty refugees were apprehended every 24 hours and the majority returned to the Chinese authorities through a staging camp near the Lo Wu railway station. Before any repatriations began, an assurance had been given by the Kwangtung authorities that those returned would not be ill-treated in any way, although possibly sent to 're-education centres' to be made more aware of the advantages of the communist way of life. This assurance was certainly honoured, as confirmed by refugees apprehended for a second or even a third time. When 1st Battalion Grenadier Guards caught an appealing young girl for the third time, the commanding officer signalled Land Forces headquarters that he could not be responsible for the discipline of his men if obliged to hand her back yet again. This was a threat no one could take seriously, so back she went. Generally concerned only that the surveillance system was working properly, Bramall seemed upset by this incident.

When the wind changed in early October and the Hong Kong Chinese began wrapping their protesting children into warm clothing in anticipation of the cool winter, thoughts returned to the Defence Costs Agreement. The CBF's negotiation team had whittled away the objections to the removal or reduction of units and facilities which they judged no longer essential, while the Security Department raised proposals for more extensive cuts to reduce costs. The arguments were not about security, but about money.

It was announced that the final force structure and the slicing of the cake of costs would be negotiated in Hong Kong between the Governor and his advisers and a delegation from the United Kingdom Ministry of Defence. The London team was led by the Minister of State for Defence, Mr William Rodgers, MP, later to become one of the 'gang of four' founders of the Social Democrat Party and, later still, Lord Rodgers of Quarry Bank. It was a fascinating discussion lasting several days with no one anticipating the *coup de théâtre* the Governor would produce on the last day.

Seated between the Governor's and the London teams with his own group of advisers, the Commander British Forces had an uneven spectrum of possibilities to put forward. His proposal to keep the RAF component virtually unchanged was not difficult to defend. The flight of eight medium-lift helicopters based on Kai Tak airport east of Kowloon was popular in the Colony. The aircraft were often used for air–sea rescue missions and any local emergency where their lift capability was useful. The Royal Navy presented a more difficult problem in the way of force reductions, and the Army was vulnerable to 'death by a thousand cuts' as the Chinese members of the Legislative Council were apt to remark whenever given the chance.

The naval complement comprised a frigate and five wooden-hulled mine-sweepers. Short of China attempting to blockade the port with mines there were none to sweep, but the craft were a part of the Royal Navy's worldwide order of battle and, although they had neither the speed nor firepower to take on the pirates plaguing the South China Sea, they were useful for patrolling between the offshore islands. It was clear to anyone not wearing a dark blue uniform that the frigate was little more than an expensive and not very useful luxury, but the local Captain RN 'in charge' was under orders from the Naval Department in London to keep it if he could.

Discussion of what would survive of the Navy's complement was an early feature of the negotiations. The Hong Kong Secretary of Security had served with distinction in the Royal Navy and had been lobbied by the Captain in Charge. Hence he argued with charm but little conviction for retention of the frigate as if the vessel were the Colony's ultimate insurance against disaster. Seeing his own case for dispensing with the frigate being effectively if not intentionally argued from the Hong Kong side, Bramall was content to maintain silence, wearing an expression of rapt attention.

It was around this time that the negotiating skills of Bill Rodgers began to emerge. Given his patrician nature, the Governor, Sir Murray MacLehose, had doubtless expected to hold sway in the discussion, but he was put firmly into his place by Rodgers when he chimed in with a tentative word of support for the frigate. 'We are not here simply to maintain the *status quo*,' said Rodgers suavely and with the reasonableness of an Oxford don pointing a wayward graduate in the right direction. The Governor's 'flinch' was perceptible only from his frozen expression.

Nothing was decided at this early stage of discussion, but the frigate was put into square brackets and, to the unconcealed horror of the Captain in Charge, two of his five mine-sweepers were similarly encompassed. His argument that he needed four at some stage of rest and refit to keep one at sea sounded a bit lame. 'One on and four at the wash seems excessive,' remarked Rodgers impassively. 'Let's move on.'

Once it was accepted that the Army's logistic elements supporting all three Services should be trimmed to meet the needs of the final structure, there was not much left to discuss. Slightly contentious items such as the Veterinary Corps mule troop, swooped on by the Hong Kong government side because the stables also housed polo ponies, were included in the list of savings. This left only the field force of five infantry battalions, armoured reconnaissance squadron and the field artillery regiment. The Commander of British Forces tackled the discussion of their future from a philosophical standpoint.

He began by pointing out that Hong Kong was being asked to pay for only 75 per cent of the cost of the garrison. Consequently, the 25 per cent London was paying might reasonably be regarded as the element for the benefit of the Services. Rodgers raised an eyebrow of curiosity while the Governor looked doubtful. Bramall's argument was for the Army to keep the 'all-arms' element to maintain the professional standards of units of 48 Gurkha Brigade which seldom served elsewhere. Here he had a dual motive. Whilst he wished to square his own conscience by putting forward a point in which he had passionately believed for more than twenty years – opportunities for professional training – more prosaically, he wanted to demonstrate to the Naval and Air Force commanders that the Army was also under pressure to make cuts close to the bone.

Negotiations paused while the detailed implications of the proposed economies were examined, and resumed on the final afternoon to consider the results. Only the formal closure of the talks, and expected agreement on Hong Kong paying a great deal more for considerably less, was left for the morning before the Whitehall party was due to leave on the afternoon flight for

London. With the spice of drama the citizens of Hong Kong would relish, the local government side launched its proposals for acceptance in the *South China Morning Post*. If anything would smack of victory in the eyes of the commercially conscious Chinese, it would be the acquisition of *land*! The more senior Chinese members of the Executive Council had long had their eyes fixed on the considerable areas of service-owned land in Central and in Kowloon, the generous sports fields of RAF Kai Tak in particular.

Whoever thought up the land deal, initially breathtaking in its scope, had the issue thoroughly worked out, as it was accompanied by a solution to every objection. In return for Hong Kong paying 75 per cent of the defence costs, Victoria Barracks on the Island, containing Flagstaff House and the Army's Headquarters, plus various outlying installations and the acres of aircraft parking space and sports fields of RAF Kai Tak were all to be 'returned' to the Government. In compensation, a new house would be built for the CBF on the Peak, the Army's Headquarters would move into a new purpose-built skyscraper in HMS *Tamar* – the naval base on the waterfront – and, while RAF transport planes would continue to land and have facilities at Kai Tak civil airport, the helicopter flight would be co-located with the Army flight in the New Territories. Hong Kong's pride would be satisfied and the property developers have a bonanza.

Bramall had been given overnight warning of the deal and permitted himself a rueful smile of admiration as he worked through the detail of the document over breakfast. His contacts with businessmen on the Legislative Council and elsewhere had alerted him to the land hunger, but he had expected to assuage this by his offer of an extensive Service property on the north-east of the Island, plus the other small installations which now sat strangely with the tower blocks alongside them.

Unfortunately, the property he had planned to relinquish anyway had bad connotations for the Chinese, as many had been murdered there by the Japanese after capture of the Colony at Christmas 1941. But that was of little account in the context of the land deal as a whole. The Hong Kong government case was unanswerable and accepted as an imaginative and workmanlike solution by the Ministry of Defence team, who left for home well content that afternoon, leaving Bramall and his staff to work out the programme for implementation.

If he felt deceived, Bramall kept it to himself. Moreover, by delaying putting the land deal on the table until the last possible moment, the Governor, who had indeed made a friend of the General, saved him from serious embarrassment. The 'losers' in the matter were the Royal Navy, who were obliged to relinquish their preserve at Tamar, and the RAF who had to give up a popular station for lodging rights with the Army in the New Territories, where facilities were still relatively few. The Army's land losses would not affect any field force units, only headquarters staff. If the CBF had been obliged to 'sell' this solution to the Service commanders, he might have found himself accused of showing bias in favour of his own.

Conclusion of the Defence Costs Agreement was the last major event in Bramall's two-and-a-half year term as Commander British Forces. Both he and his wife Avril had made many friends in the Colony and most would prove lasting. They were in intense demand for farewell dinners and receptions during their final weeks, not in any sense of duty but simply because they were a popular couple in the Colony.

The always straight-speaking *South China Morning Post* published the following leader on 21 March 1976:

When in May 1975, Sir Edwin addressed the Rotary Club of Hong Kong on the subject of defence costs, he began by saying, 'I speak to you as a public servant of Hong Kong, responsible to the Governor and his Executive Council for the efficient operation of the armed forces here.' And it is in this role as public servant that distinguishes this brief tenure of Sir Edwin and *marks out the course which the Commander British Forces might be seen to assume more frequently in future*. It deserves to be said that Sir Edwin's term in Hong Kong was happily free of civil strife or border tension, he played a leading role in a far more delicate and difficult matter – the reduction in the size of the Garrison with the sequential discussions on the apportionment of costs. There may be some feelings today that the agreed cuts did not go far enough or that Hong Kong has been made to bear more than a fair share of the costs. But we all recognise the real debt to the way in which Sir Edwin managed to maintain his stance as both a public servant of Hong Kong and Britain, yet he has preserved his quiet charm and courtesy to emerge with greater respect and admiration. Little wonder that his statesmanship has won him promotion to the rank of full General and the high prestige of being appointed C-in-C of the United Kingdom Land Forces.

It had been a swift transition from divisional commander to Commander-in-Chief, and he said good-bye to Hong Kong with the confidence that, even though he might not yet have fully mastered the intricate nature of politics, nor their unpredictable twists and turns, he had been made well aware of their challenge.

13

Men and Money

Given the choice on leaving Hong Kong, it is virtually certain that, on purely military grounds, Dwin Bramall would have chosen to be Commander-in-Chief British Army of the Rhine rather than of United Kingdom Land Forces (UKLF). The two commands were entirely different and the strategic responsibilities of Commander Northern Army Group, comprising four Allied Army Corps to be deployed in the event of war with the Warsaw Pact, presented just the scale of military thinking to which Bramall would choose to set his mind. In contrast, UKLF – although not lacking prestige – had no single role, no single identified enemy and a command structure which, while simplified as a result of the recommendations of the Stainforth Committee, of which he had been Deputy Chairman, still gave the Ministry of Defence right of direct access to district and divisional commanders and staffs on certain subjects or when someone in Whitehall wanted to cut corners.

On the other hand, he had been overseas for almost five years and an appointment at home would enable him and his wife to see more of their family and friends, which both of them counted as very important. Their daughter Sara, then aged twenty-five, had recently completed the combined course of nursing at the Hospital for Sick Children at Great Ormond Street, which qualified her as a State Registered Nurse and also as a State Registered Sick Children's Nurse. She was working as a staff nurse at Great Ormond Street at the time and later married the distinguished neurologist, Dr Edwin Bickerstaff. The Bramalls' son Nicolas, who had been to Eton and followed his father into the Cricket XI, was twenty-four and attending agricultural college in Northampton. After getting married, he set up his own gardening business, specialising in garden design and consultancy.

During the period in question, the two Commanders-in-Chief were almost invariably the only contenders to be the next Chief of the General Staff, but sometimes one or the other would know he was in his last post or, at least, that he would not be head of the Army. Bramall had a shrewd idea that the intention was for him to be the one selected and so could concentrate on what he perceived as the priority tasks to be addressed from HQ UKLF before he moved to Whitehall. He was supported by a deputy C-in-C, initially Lieutenant-General Sir Allan Taylor and then Lieutenant-General Sir Hugh Beach – both men of outstanding intellect – and two major-generals, one as Chief of Staff and the other in charge of administration, MGA. These, together with the Command Secretary who ran the Command's not over-generous budget, gave him a powerful resource, which he was quick to harness.

The previous Commander-in-Chief was General (later Field Marshal) Sir Roland Gibbs, his old friend of the 60th Rifles who had been wounded on the same day in Normandy. The two men were totally different in their outlook on the day-to-day management of the Command. Gibbs considered that he had highly competent, immediately subordinate staff, so he stood well back and let them get on with the job. He was always ready to step in should a crisis arise, and there is no record of his calm judgement being either at fault or late in implementation. Bramall wished, or perhaps it would be more correct to say 'felt compelled', to have a much closer association with events and direct policy in areas that he judged were being neglected or likely to present problems in the future. He therefore dispensed with the Chief of Staff's and MGA's routine fortnightly briefings to him and the Deputy C-in-C, and introduced the Senior Staff Management Committee.

This group, comprising the senior officers mentioned and the Command Secretary, worked under Bramall's chairmanship in a manner similar to the Executive Committee of the Army Board, of which the C-in-C was a member. Instead of waiting to hear about projects and problems from the Chief of Staff and MGA, Bramall adopted a proactive approach by having papers produced for the Management Committee to examine and decide on. Subjects ranged from such issues as the Army's use of redundant RAF airfields for training to housing problems of servicemen about to end their military engagements with no home to take their families to on relinquishing their married quarters. These papers provided the Ministry of Defence with an understanding of where the Army at home stood on key issues but, as often as not, prompted consideration of the matter in London.

In keeping with his previous practice from platoon commander to C-in-C, Bramall made an early opportunity to address the entire staff of HQ UKLF all together. Given the salutary example set by Montgomery on taking over command of the Eighth Army in the Western Desert in 1942, it continues to be surprising why so many senior or even middle-ranking British officers neglect this means of putting over their personalities and intentions. One has only to look at the publicity attracted by Colonel Tim Collins when speaking to his soldiers of the Royal Irish Regiment on the eve of battle before the invasion of Iraq in 2003. Certainly he used some telling phrases, but it was as much his action as his words that drew the favourable press attention. As mentioned earlier, Dwin Bramall's style of public speaking – wry, reflective, sometimes even self-deprecatory, but always showing a real grasp of the background and interest of his audience – won him attention and respect, convincing his listeners they were hearing something they should know from someone who did.

In his own perception, his role was more that of an 'inspector-general' of the formations and units under his command than that of a Commander-in-Chief. He delegated responsibility for organising and directing training to the Deputy C-in-C, yet his abiding interest in this critical facet of military life meant that he could never resist getting down on the ground – literally – to check the sighting of a light machine-gun or whether a position taken by troops on exercise really gave them a good field of view and fire, while still protecting them from the view and fire of the enemy.

One preoccupation which became almost legendary was to persuade junior commanders to avoid siting positions on forward slopes or on the tops of hills, where they could be seen and defeated more or less at will. The British Army is often spoken of as the most professional in the world, but the skills of siting defensive positions and weapons need to be learned afresh by each generation, as does the essential drill of the senior man taking over command, even if only a private soldier, when the officer or senior NCO is killed. These techniques together with that of the immediate counter-attack after local defeat were the battle-winning tactics of the German Army that were ignored by the British for far too long and at severe cost.

An important element with which the new C-in-C had scant familiarity was the 75,000-strong Territorial Army. Like most senior officers whose career had followed the fast track, he had never served as adjutant of a Territorial Army unit, much less commanded one – the fate of the worthy rather than the high-flying regular officer. He had noted, however, the performance and limitations of Territorial Army reinforcements to the Army of the Rhine while commanding the 1st Division, noting in particular the technical and logistic units' competence in their respective tasks, while infantry units needed much longer to get the hang of what was required of them.

Governments of the day treated the Territorial Army throughout the twentieth century not so much with ambivalence but in the light of expediency. When danger threatened, it was rapidly expanded – complete Territorial divisions were serving with the British Expeditionary Force in France by September 1915 – and the number of Territorial Army divisions was doubled, at least on paper, from thirteen to twenty-six when war with Germany became inevitable in April 1939. In the years of so-called peace that followed the Second World War, the TA was gradually whittled down by successive defence economies. Then the threat of Soviet *Spetznaz* Special Force units having a virtually free hand in sabotage and assassination in the UK at the outset of war, when all remaining TA units had been despatched to the Continent, brought about a reappraisal. Some modest expansion was authorised in 1970, only to be reversed a few years later, before the end of the Soviet threat, when money again became tight.

Bramall's arrival at Wilton coincided with revival of the 'One Army Concept' of ground force defence of the 1st (British) Corps front in Central Europe and of the United Kingdom home base. It was an attractive slogan, but one which both the regular and Territorial Army knew would not work as the TA was then generally constituted.

The 'One Army Concept' demanded that the entire composite force, or at least those destined to fight on the Continent, on the one hand, and those responsible for defence of the home base, on the other, would have the same equipment, so that units and logistic support were compatible, even if they would not all be trained to combat standards. The equipment ideal was simply unrealistic: the TA units received ex-regular army weapons, fighting vehicles and radios as they were replaced by more modern items. Much of the outdated stuff was still appropriate for the home defence role, but the disparity in weapon and equipment handling level could never be reconciled.

Bramall grasped the 'One Army Concept' for what it was, concentrating on the truly realistic aspects but getting rid of such fantasies as regular infantry battalions being told to rely on a fourth company of TA soldiers arriving in time to complete their emergency deployment to meet the Soviet threat. He knew from his time in command of the 1st Division that even if they had the weapons and equipment, part-time soldiers training only for a strictly limited number of days each year, owing to the limited funds available, could never match the regular army units' battle-readiness. To his credit, he never abandoned the 'One Army Concept' as an idea but tried, through the Deputy C-in-C responsible for training, to allocate effort and resources in such a manner that each unit had an achievable operational role, even though officially allowed time for training made achievement an aspiration in some cases. Later, as Chief of the General Staff, he introduced the title of Inspector-General of the Territorial Army as an additional and specific responsibility of the Deputy C-in-C

UKLF. This well-intentioned gesture, intended to boost the TA's self-esteem, led to some difficulties when the Inspector-General found himself at odds with the Whitehall-based Director of the TA and Cadets, who controlled the TA purse strings.

The relentless demand for training and then re-training units for tours of operational duty in Northern Ireland cut across the much wider spectrum of training for war. During Bramall's period at Wilton from May 1976 to March 1978, troop levels in the Province continued to average 15,000 and, although the interval between these emergency tours was increased from the previous low point of eight months towards a target of eighteen, the strain on individuals of an 'unproductive' and seemingly open-ended commitment was significant. Northern Ireland Training Teams had been set up in both the Rhine Army and in England. The very best instructors were selected for this work and nothing was left to chance to ensure that the training reflected latest intelligence assessments of terrorist tactics and responsive security force techniques, but it was a long hard slog.

Bramall's role in the Northern Ireland commitment was principally to ensure support to the units shortly due for service in the Province and to ensure that their period 'in baulk' from commitments away from their UK base was honoured. This was not always possible and the 'in baulk' system had to be abandoned completely during the Firemen's strike in the winter of 1977–8. Some twenty thousand UK-based servicemen, the majority from the Army, had to be trained in firefighting duties, using antiquated 'Green Goddess' military fire engines, and deployed to TA drill halls and other bases remote from their unit barracks. In many cases, too, they had to leave their wives and children, to whom they had only very recently returned from unaccompanied service in Northern Ireland.

All this was a severe test of service morale, not least because the firemen striking for radical increases in pay were already paid more than the average servicemen replacing them. As the strike became prolonged, the Chiefs of Staff put it to Ministers that it would be utterly inequitable to make an increased pay offer to the striking firemen without honouring the recommendation of the Armed Forces Pay Review Body with regard to increases in service pay. This was to prove to be of no avail until after the 1979 General Election.

Bramall was determined that this aid to the civil power should be handled as efficiently as circumstances permitted, the Army working closely and harmoniously with the Police and those Fire Service officers still at their posts. There was to be no confrontation with those on strike who, after all, were acting constitutionally and had a good case. Consequently, he came down heavily on a car-load of cavalry officers returning from a study period who had childishly bombarded a firemen's picket round a brazier with the remnants of their haversack rations. As C-in-C UKLF he toured the country talking to and getting to know the police and fire chiefs, as well as encouraging the servicemen doing their utmost to fight fires and save lives with their antiquated 'Green Goddess' fire engines. When the dispute was eventually settled, with a fair deal for the firemen, it could be said that good relations had been maintained throughout a severely testing period.

The appointment of C-in-C UKLF carried *ex-officio* membership and the chairmanship – in rotation – of the United Kingdom Commanders-in-Chief Committee, UKCICC, which was divided into two sub-committees: Home and Overseas. The Home sub-committee, comprising the Commanders-in-Chief of Naval Home Command, UKLF and RAF Support Command, was responsible for examining and making recommendations to the Ministry of Defence on joint service issues arising during an approach to general war, i.e. one between NATO and the Warsaw Pact, and placing the United Kingdom on a war footing. It could also be convened to deal with an emergency situation involving all three Services in the United Kingdom that were well short of preparations for war, for example the deployment of servicemen to deal with an outbreak of an epidemic of foot and mouth disease.

C-in-C UKLF was also a member of the Overseas Committee, comprising C-in-C Fleet, himself and C-in-C Strike Command. The remit of this group was to prepare contingency plans for operations overseas, which ranged from large-scale reinforcement of

British forces on the Continent in the event of the threat of general war to the evacuation of British nationals from countries where their lives might be at risk and troop reinforcement to places abroad where the United Kingdom had implied or actual treaty responsibilities for security. In both cases, the matters for examination were either referred to the Committee by the Ministry of Defence or put forward by one of the five commands represented. A small secretariat to prepare draft papers for discussion, manned by officers of all three Services, was established at Wilton, alongside Headquarters UKLF, with a one-star officer in charge.

The quarterly meetings provided ideal opportunities for the Cs-in-C to get to know each other, understand each other's capabilities and resources before, in the case of perhaps half of them, becoming head of their respective Service and moving to Whitehall, where they would again find themselves working together. This was an atmosphere in which Bramall revelled, not least because he was a member of both Committees and, as he increasingly enjoyed doing, having a finger in every pie. It also gave him opportunity to build on his experience, gained as Commander British Forces Hong Kong, of dealing with equally senior officers of the other two Services who, more often than not, saw defence priorities in a different light from each other. The Royal Navy and RAF, both acutely conscious of the huge cost of their ships and aircraft and of deploying them away from their home bases for protracted periods, would often be sceptical of taking on commitments to which the Army could contribute more easily with its ability to provide an economical task force tailored specifically to widely varied requirements.

Bramall's time as C-in-C in England also gave him the opportunity to renew his close association with the soldiers of the Gurkha Rifles and their supporting units. This remarkable breed of fighting men from the hills of Nepal had served the British Crown for more than 180 years. It had all begun with a war the British had waged against the Kingdom of Nepal in 1815, which ended in a draw. The adversaries had formed such mutual regard, however, that the Gurkhas were ready to form regiments to serve under the Bengal-based Government of British India, one adopting British uniform. During the Indian Mutiny of native troops, they remained steadfastly loyal and since then have served the Crown in campaigns in many parts of the world. In the First World War, they fought on the Western Front and at Gallipoli and in the Second in the Western Desert, East Africa, Italy and Burma. Since then they have served in Malaya, Borneo, Cyprus, the Falklands, the Arabian Gulf, in Bosnia, Kosovo and Iraq. On Britain's behalf they have suffered thousands of casualties, won many decorations for bravery, including thirteen awards of the Victoria Cross. Deservedly described as 'the bravest of the brave', they are highly disciplined yet gentle when not on operations, invariably cheerful and well adjusted. The Whitehall statue commemorating their service bears the inscription, 'Never has a Country had more Faithful Friends than These'.

Having first come into contact with Gurkha troops when serving with the occupying force in Japan in 1945–6, Bramall had found himself alongside 2nd Battalion 2nd Goorkha Rifles (The Sirmoor Rifles) when commanding his own battalion in Borneo during the Indonesian 'Confrontation'. The 2nd Goorkhas had been affiliated to his own original regiment, the King's Royal Rifle Corps (60th Rifles) since the Indian Mutiny, which facilitated a certain amount of interchange of officers between the two battalions. Later, when he became Commander of British Forces in Hong Kong, he had a whole Gurkha brigade of three battalions under command. He consequently learned enough of the language to enable him to speak with individual soldiers and make short speeches to groups of them, as when greeted for the first time by a Gurkha guard of honour he was able to compliment them in Gurkhali. On leaving Hong Kong, he was invited to become Colonel of the 2nd King Edward VII's Own Goorkha Rifles (The Sirmoor Rifles), a post he was to hold for ten years.

He visited both battalions of the 2nd Goorkhas on many occasions during this period, including a magnificent parade of both of them together in Hong Kong in honour of the Regiment's Colonel-in-Chief HRH The Prince of Wales. That day was rounded off by a Gurkha 'nautch' at which His Royal Highness was offered a portion of snake. He took it a trifle hesitantly with the comment, 'What I do for England.'

This was a period, in the closing years of the Wilson/Callaghan Socialist administration, when the armed forces were becoming seriously underfunded, owing to the weakness of the British economy, and undermanned owing to service pay having fallen drastically behind that of their comparators in civilian life. The Navy and RAF were losing pilots and technical specialists at an alarming rate, as those leaving had little or no difficulty in finding much better remuneration for their skills outside the Service. In the meantime the Army had armoured and artillery regiments and infantry battalions struggling to function at up to 10 per cent below establishment, while still dealing with frequent operational tours in Northern Ireland.

These were issues Bramall saw at first hand during his frequent visits to troops in his own command and deployed from there to Northern Ireland. As is the British soldier's way, the troops were grudgingly cheerful no matter how wretched the circumstances while on actual operations or taking part in realistic and worthwhile training, but many made their point by leaving as soon as they were back with their families, either at the first opportunity to break their Service engagement or by premature release from it (PRE). This was an arrangement introduced to encourage recruits to join and trained men to continue, both in the knowledge that they could opt out at a time of their own choosing. It was the idea of the much-criticised but intellectually alert Minister of Defence, Fred Mulley, who was to bring Bramall into even closer contact with these problems than while he was C-in-C UKLF, although that was not the principal reason for it.

By this point, late in 1977, Prime Minister James Callaghan had accepted the recommendation of the Chief of the General Staff, General Sir Roland Gibbs, that Bramall should succeed him as head of the Army when he had completed his period in the post in mid-1979. Like his predecessor, General Sir Peter Hunt, Gibbs had a fine record of command in war and in what passed for peace in the years following 1945 but not, by any stretch of the imagination, could he be called a 'Whitehall Warrior'. It was not that either man lacked vision or decisiveness, but rather that they had had no grounding at junior rank in how the Ministry of Defence worked, in particular the role of civil servants in their lines of responsibility to a Minister. Mulley allowed himself to be quoted as saying that, if the country had to go to war, Sir Roland Gibbs would be the man he would want to have beside him. Gibbs's term of office was coming to an end, however, and, although Bramall had been Mountbatten's right hand in the reorganisation of the Ministry of Defence in the 1960s, he had no experience of Whitehall at a higher level. Mulley therefore insisted that he be brought to Whitehall early to learn the intricacies of the current structure.

The post chosen was Vice-Chief of the Defence Staff (Personnel and Logistics), a four-star post rotating between the three Services. London offered a markedly different prospect from enjoying the next year and a half in the quiet comfort of Bulford Manor, the country house allocated to the C-in-C, indulging in painting, slipping up to Lords to watch cricket and seeing rather more of his son and daughter than the pressure of recent years had allowed – in all, taking a reflective pause before beginning the last two endurance laps of his career as CGS and then perhaps Chief of the Defence Staff. He allowed one or two wry comments about enjoying a relatively quiet time to slip out in chat to his close friends, but he cheerfully packed up and headed for London. As there was no house or apartment associated with his new post, he moved into a married quarter in Tidworth – such as would usually be allocated to a brigadier – and stayed in the Royal Army Medical Corps officers' mess at Millbank during the middle part of the week.

While the pressing problems of service manpower and the money to pay servicemen and women a proper wage for the job were the most immediate on his horizon, they represented only one part of his overall remit as VCDS (P&L). The other part was the international logistics planning associated with contingency plans for war in the NATO Central Region. To help with this work he had a two-star assistant CDS (P&L), first in the form of Major-General Peter Blunt and, towards the end of his time, Air Vice-

Marshal John Miller. There were also two senior civil servants, each responsible for watching over one of the two sides of Bramall's main brief, Alistair Jaffray for the personnel aspects and Julian Dromgoole for logistics matters. Although both men perceived their principal line of reporting to be through the 2nd Permanent Under-Secretary, Sir Arthur Hockaday, to the PUS, Sir Frank Cooper, both men gave Bramall their absolute support. So, despite the difficulties before him being formidable, Bramall had an able team to help him and all were equally enthusiastic to see success.

In the early days of his new appointment, the demands on the NATO logistics side were insufficiently pressing that he felt able to leave much of this work to his ACDS, Peter Blunt, while still requiring his help over the demanding questions of service pay, conditions and dwindling manpower. Quite aside from the country's unenviable economic situation at that time – the 1978–9 'Winter of Discontent' – much of the pay problem lay at the door of the Wilson/Callaghan governments, which had imposed freezes on service pay to restrain expenditure, ignoring the recommendations of the Armed Forces Pay Review Body, specifically established to ensure that pay rates of the Services maintained parity with comparable civilian jobs. This situation was compounded, not only by the frequency of tours of duty in Northern Ireland and separation of servicemen from their families, but also by the rapid deterioration in the quality of life in the Services, with sub-standard married quarters, lack of interesting service abroad and pervading sense of being at the absolute bottom of the heap for resources allocation.

In March 1978, the Callaghan government told the Chiefs of Staff that there was virtually no chance of the gap of 37 per cent between service pay and that of their equivalents in civilian life being made good in the foreseeable future. The CDS of the day, Marshal of the Royal Air Force Sir Neil Cameron – a no-nonsense airman who had risen to the top of his profession from the rank of Sergeant Pilot and, through appointments there, knew the intricacies of the Ministry of Defence intimately – had put the regaining of pay comparability at the very top of his agenda and had a private discussion on the matter with Prime Minister James Callaghan on 17 March but received no satisfaction. Meanwhile, it became known to Cameron and his fellow Chiefs of Staff that Treasury officials were drafting a Cabinet Paper designed to preserve the wider pay freeze and therefore the current gap between service and civilian pay levels. Faced with this *impasse*, the Chiefs of Staff recognised that their only resource was to appeal to the public over the heads of the Cabinet.

As VCDS (P&L), Bramall stood at the centre of this impending storm, which was given additional point by the information media, press, radio and television alike, who were clamouring for a Ministry of Defence briefing on why premature release from engagements (PRE) had reached such alarming proportions and asking what was going to be done about it. This was further exacerbated by the situation in Northern Ireland where, despite the New Year message from the Secretary of State, Roy Mason, 'the tide has turned against the terrorists', there was precious little evidence of the Provisional IRA beginning to recognise that a campaign of violence would never achieve their political objective of a united Ireland.

Cameron and his fellow Chiefs decided that the combination of the Labour government's obduracy over bringing service pay into line and the media's continued probing into the still-rising PRE figures provided an opportunity for a straightforward factual press briefing of the facts and figures, but one devoid of political comment. As the officer responsible for service pay and conditions, Bramall was the obvious candidate to give the briefing, and his persuasive manner of speaking to a potentially hostile or, at best, disbelieving audience was well known.

The first presentation was well received and led to a perceptive article in *The Times* entitled 'The Queen's Shilling', which was broadly supportive of the Services' position and drew the public's attention to aircraft with empty cockpits, because the pilots had left to seek better-paid jobs with the civil airlines, and the acute undermanning in the infantry, stretched as they were by Northern Ireland and the firemen's strike. The Service Chiefs may have felt that they had discharged their responsibilities at that point, leaving the general public to bring about change, either by increasing clamour on the radio and television or, more probably – given the inevitability of a General Election in the not so distant future – through the ballot box.

Bramall was not prepared to let matters rest, however. Writing long after the events of the summer of 1978, Alistair Jaffray, the Deputy Under-Secretary responsible for watching over the personnel side of MoD policy, expressed the view that Bramall felt so strongly over the service pay issue that he may have allowed a more impulsive side of his character to take over. In Jaffray's judgement at least, the press briefing had built up a head of steam, both in Parliament and in the country at large, which was enough to bring about the required pay increases, if not immediately then in due course, making the initiative that Bramall took both risky and unnecessary.

At the time in question and until early 2004, each Service had a one-star officer in the Ministry of Defence appointed to be its spokesman on public relations. These were invariably men young for their rank and well informed, who knew their individual Service from top to bottom and were able to speak with authority. (This system was changed in early 2004 when the Prime Minister's then spokesman Alastair Campbell sought to confine significant statements to the media to his own office and the Service spokesmen were downgraded to the rank of colonel or equivalent.) The Director of Public Relations (Army) in Bramall's time was Brigadier Derek Boorman, a protégé of his who had commanded a brigade in Hong Kong when he was CBF. Quick-witted and good on his feet, Boorman was ideal for the post and eventually rose to be Deputy Chief of the Defence Staff (Intelligence) and Deputy Chairman of the Joint Intelligence Committee.

Having been given to understand that Bramall was not wholly satisfied that his official briefing of the media would bring about the desired result of a substantial increase in service pay, if not the full parity with civilian rates recommended, Boorman undertook to examine how the impact might be enhanced. The outcome was an off-the-record briefing of an Associated Press journalist, by Bramall, on the very day that Callaghan was due to speak in the Commons on the armed forces pay situation. Whether this idea was Bramall's or Boorman's, it is impossible to believe that either of these experienced and intelligent men did not perceive he was taking some risks with the whole pay initiative, not to mention his own future. The briefing to the Associated Press provided 'raw' statistical data on service pay, rather than the more selected and polished figures provided in the official presentation to the press at large. The new figures were flashed out as a news item via the ticker-tape just as James Callaghan rose in the House to answer questions on the subject. The ticker-tape material was already in the hands of the Opposition as he began and he was immediately presented with questioners better informed than he was. At first, he attempted to find a way forward by 'welcoming' the new figures as 'useful', but his questioners had the advantage and it was not long before he – perhaps uncharacteristically – described the release of the figures as 'malicious'. Thoroughly alerted to what was in the wind, the Commons Press Gallery was full to capacity and the Prime Minister's discomfiture received wide coverage in the evening papers and the whole issue full treatment in both the broadsheet and tabloid press next morning.

Opinion varies as to whether 'Bramall's risk' was worthwhile. Callaghan's usual benign good humour deserted him on this occasion and he ordered an inquiry into how the leak had occurred and who was responsible. In sharp contrast to the conduct of more recent inquiries, the answer was delivered before the chairman was appointed or the terms of reference given, even in preliminary draft. The Chiefs of Staff accepted full responsibility for what had occurred and their only public penalty was a Mac cartoon in the *Daily Mail* portraying the four Chiefs carrying out 'Jankers' kitchen fatigues under the sternly watchful eyes of the Prime Minister and Fred Mulley. The wider perception was that Mulley's hand in Cabinet had been strengthened by the carefully timed leak, and the proof of the pudding was that a good pay award was granted, with the Prime Minister receiving some credit with the banner headline

'Jim Gives the Forces what they Deserve'. For the time being, however, the Treasury allowed no proportional increase in the defence budget, so the cash difference had to be found from economies elsewhere.

Bramall certainly had no second thoughts on the matter, as the aim had been achieved and the drain on service manpower had been slowed. He had regarded his action in privately briefing the Associated Press journalist as carefully judged and not in the least impulsive on his part. It could be argued that his initiative was in keeping with what a national trades union leader might have done in comparable circumstances, although he was resolutely opposed to suggestions, put forward by former trades union officials then in Callaghan's Cabinet, that the Services should form their own trades union to contest their pay and conditions. The Labour government had gone a long way towards matching civilian rates, which were finally restored as one of the first measures of Margaret Thatcher's government after the 1979 General Election, with an appropriate actual increase in the Defence Budget to match it but, by then, Bramall had moved on to become Chief of the General Staff.

A story later appeared about the Associated Press journalist who had let the cat out of the bag immediately after the Bramall interview. Apparently a leak had occurred in the roof of his house during the night. As he climbed into the attic, having scrambled out of bed and into his dressing gown, his wife called out, 'Be careful up there, remember he who lives by the leak dies by the leak!'

14

Head of the Army

When Dwin Bramall walked along the corridor on the sixth floor of the Ministry of Defence to his new office as Chief of the General Staff and consequently professional head of the Army, he had as his right-hand man a lieutenant-general as the Vice-Chief. This was a powerful post in the area of Army policy-making and it was accepted practice that the incumbent was a man of exceptional quality and experience. It was, of course, ideal if his experience and expertise complemented those of the CGS but, even more importantly, that the two men got on together. At one period in the 1950s, the Chief of the Imperial General Staff – as the post was then portentously titled – and the Vice-Chief were not even on speaking terms. When they met by accident one morning in the War Office corridor, the Chief allegedly muttered, 'Oh, hello, I thought you were on leave,' and quickly passed on.

When Bramall took over in July 1979, the Vice-Chief was Lieutenant-General Sir John Stanier. During the eighteen months he had been in post, he had devoted much of his considerable energy into setting right changes in army organisation imposed by the 1976 Defence Review, a Treasury-driven round of economies. This was almost complete when Bramall took office and a pause in this work ensued. To close observers in the Ministry of Defence, of which there was no shortage, it appeared as if Stanier may have been a touch in awe of his new boss, most probably because he knew the reputation better than the man. He had commanded the 1st Division immediately after Bramall, but the two had not served together. It proved a sound partnership, however, and Stanier was

231

promoted to become C-in-C UKLF early in 1981 in preparation to succeed Bramall as CGS a year later. It was only in dealing with others that the two men differed significantly in their approach. Whereas Bramall looked after the careers of those who served him well – in the eyes of some almost to a fault – Stanier operated a less personal policy and seemingly lost little by it.

The Vice-Chief had an important role in the working of the Executive Committee of the Army Board, that is the board sitting under the CGS's chairmanship rather than that of the Secretary of State, or of a more junior minister, as the Vice-Chief spoke for the General Staff at a table round which sat the Adjutant-General, Quartermaster-General and the Master-General of the Ordnance. Stanier was entirely at home here; he had developed a reputation as a competent extempore speaker on military matters, invariably researched his subject thoroughly and was never too proud to seek a subordinate's advice on anything with which he was not entirely familiar. As Stanier's period of office neared its close, however, there was surprise in some quarters when it was announced that he was to be succeeded, on promotion, by Major-General Harry Dalzell Payne, then commanding the 3rd Armoured Division in Germany.

Like Stanier, Dalzell Payne was an armoured corps officer – indeed they had both begun their service in the 7th Hussars – highly professional in his grasp of military affairs, supremely self-confident and with a seemingly inexhaustible mental and physical stamina which permitted him a lifestyle more appropriate to the Edwardian era than to the final quarter of the twentieth century. He might be winning or losing at the tables in Baden-Baden until the early hours, but would be at the door of his headquarters at 8 a.m. ready to receive a visiting ministerial committee and deliver a briefing of outstanding lucidity. Dalzell Payne was a star, but Bramall was taking a risk, not only by promoting him ahead of his contemporaries, but by relying on him to restrain his extra-mural activities while working in London.

As things turned out, this aspect was not subjected to the test. A horse-box containing many of Dalzell Payne's belongings from his house in Germany was found also to contain a large quantity of port when it was inspected by HM Customs at Dover. The port was destined for the Cavalry Club, and, although the NCO bringing in the goods had a signed blank cheque to pay any duty required, the Customs and Excise lodged a report and the press were quick to seize on the story. In the event the adverse publicity surrounding the case compelled Bramall, after receiving advice from the Adjutant-General, who had gone into the matter most carefully, to request Dalzell Payne's resignation or retirement from the Army. Dalzell Payne was deeply hurt, but resigned, at great professional loss to the Service.

The CGS took care to forestall any criticism of making risky appointments by selecting a totally contrasting figure as his new Vice-Chief in the form of Lieutenant-General 'Tim' Morony. An elderly looking and donnish old Etonian slightly crippled by poliomyelitis, Morony had completed two jobs as a major-general and was widely respected for his sound judgement and acerbic wit. He proved a shrewd and often wily foil to Bramall, who used him to launch a project where he felt it necessary to test wider opinion on a contentious matter before entering the lists himself, a ploy he may have learned from Mountbatten. In consequence, the ensuing two years were probably less turbulent in the Army Department than may have been the case had Dalzell Payne been there.

Coming from the post of Vice-Chief of the Defence Staff (Personnel and Logistics), it was inevitable that Bramall brought with him when he became CGS some of the personnel 'baggage' he had been struggling with over the previous year. His main interests, however, were essentially strategy, tactics and training, rather than the hardware demanded by the Army's weapon and equipment programmes. This is not to suggest that he lacked the warmth of what is often termed a 'soldiers' general', meaning one who could speak to them in a language they understood. He could do that to perfection, not least because of his own experiences as a recruit and of living in the field with his men during the North-West European campaign and in Borneo.

Weapons and equipment programmes were to play a large part in decision-making in the months ahead, but as 'Tim' Morony had served as the MoD Director responsible for advising which weapons and equipment the Army should acquire, all but the key decisions could safely be left to him. There was, however, a question of major political and strategic significance to be decided shortly: whether the country's nuclear deterrent should be renewed when the Polaris missile system came to the end of its operational life and, if so, with what. The Harold Wilson government of 1964–70 had placated its CND-supporting left wing by undertaking to phase out Polaris without replacement, but Mrs Thatcher's government had no such intention; in fact it became one of the four pillars of her government's defence policy.

The options for replacing Polaris were complicated by the requirement to replace the submarines from which the missiles were launched, by the need to maintain commonality of equipment with the United States, to ensure a reliable source of replacements and spares, and by the decision's impact on the defence budget as a whole. These were exactly the type of complex and philosophical issues with which Bramall thoroughly enjoyed engaging his mind but, before they could be addressed, a distraction arose which demanded his attention while indicating a possible breakthrough in a seemingly intractable current political problem.

In September 1979, two months after Bramall had become Chief of the General Staff, an agreement was reached during a conference in Lancaster House between delegations from the black majority political parties in Rhodesia, the white minority, led by Mr Ian Smith, and Her Majesty's Government led by Lord Carrington – who chaired the meeting – whereby Britain would temporarily resume responsibility for governing Rhodesia while elections were held to replace what was regarded as the puppet government of Bishop Abel Muzorewa and assumption of power by the black majority. It was an agreement reached after various previous initiatives, some involving the United Nations and the United States, had failed to resolve the issues arising from Ian Smith's unilateral declaration of independence in 1965. The most immediate problem to be dealt with before any practical steps could be taken for the elections was to persuade the two main groups of guerrilla fighters of ZANU, led by Ndabiningi Sithole, with Robert Mugabe as his Secretary-General, and ZAPU, led by Joshua Nkomo, to cease all terrorist activity, emerge from the forest and participate in the elections.

A British governor, Sir Christopher (later Lord) Soames was appointed and it was clear that an independent and therefore British force would be required to monitor the process, but any large-scale influx of troops would inevitably create an impression of coercion, with disastrous consequences for the agreement. Following a first reconnaissance of the situation on the ground by the Vice-Chief, Sir John Stanier, Bramall hit on the idea of using the command elements of some thirty units serving in the United Kingdom to carry out the task of monitoring, while the majority of the soldiers remained behind. It was an unconventional solution but it worked because it brought close control and cohesion on the ground. To command the monitoring force, Bramall chose the self-confident Major-General John Acland, whom he considered could be depended upon to stand up to the Governor where necessary.

The guerrillas remained suspicious of British motives. A breakthrough was achieved, however, when an eight-man team under a second lieutenant, waiting in a ruined schoolhouse in the Mrewa district, suddenly found the forest around them alive with armed men. 'What do you think we should do?' the subaltern asked the wiry little company sergeant-major sitting beside him. 'Put your rifle down on the table, sir,' he advised. 'Then walk forward, hold up your arms and shout "Welcome, welcome."' The subaltern did as suggested and the guerrillas came out of the forest in their hundreds. The operation as a whole was regarded as a military and political *tour de force*, so it is distressing to witness Mugabe's subsequent betrayal of trust.

While what proved to be only an interim settlement of the Rhodesian issue augured well for the new British government and defence team, the abrupt invasion of Afghanistan by the Soviet Union, in December 1979, threw the Western Alliance nations into confusion as to how to react. While Moscow protested that the Soviet Army was carrying out a purely defensive move to protect the USSR's southern rim of Muslim states from the contagion of Muslim fundamentalism rampant in Iran, a similar 'defensive' argument had been deployed at the time of the Soviet invasion of Czechoslovakia in 1968 to put down the 'Prague Spring'. Although the Soviet move was not a direct threat to British interests, it provided a sharp reminder that the Soviet threat to world peace had not gone away and it was high time for the question of renewing the national nuclear deterrent to be addressed.

Bramall immersed himself in the nuclear issue, displaying his understanding of the position of the new Chief of the Defence Staff, Admiral Sir Terence Lewin, and his two fellow Chiefs of the Naval and Air Staffs, Admiral Sir Henry Leach and Air Chief Marshal Sir Michael Beetham. It was clear that refurbishing Polaris and replacing the associated submarines would be simply throwing away money on an outdated system. A second option, with which Bramall was personally in favour, was the submarine-launched Cruise missile system that he felt would provide the greatest operational flexibility. In the context of a sub-strategic situation, where it was apparent the United Kingdom might have to threaten or actually use nuclear weapons, it offered a much wider choice both in scale of attack and types of target, most crucially in the *lower* spectrum of each. Cruise missiles also had the option – since demonstrated in the wars against Iraq in 1992 and 2003 – of carrying conventional warheads.

The other options as perceived in mid-1980 carried problems over timing. The Trident I C4 missile system already deployed in the United States, with many years service yet foreseen, was to some degree overshadowed by the American Trident II D5. This was still in the development stage, however, and consequently not definite enough to be chosen by the British cabinet. Consideration continued, with a watchful eye being kept on the D5's progress. When President Reagan ordered the D5 programme to be advanced towards the end of 1980, the forecast for it coming into service coincided with the end of the operational life of Britain's Polaris. So Trident II D5 eventually became Britain's choice for continuation of the country's strategic deterrent.

The decision to adopt Trident II D5 was announced in March 1982, by when Brammall was in his final year at CGS. To his satisfaction, the submarine-launched Cruise missile was also added to the national armoury. Equipped with conventional warheads, this system could be widely deployed and used outside the NATO area, as in both Gulf wars.

While neither the question of the nuclear deterrent nor the acquisition of the conventional Cruise missile system were solved during the first year of Bramall's time as CGS, it was nevertheless a good year and he had reason for optimism. Then Thatcher monetarist disciplines to keep the national economy stable began to bite, the Treasury got down to the detail of long-term costing and the financial future for the armed forces began to look distinctly less rosy. In common with the governments of the other NATO powers, the Callaghan administration had given a commitment to NATO to raise defence spending by 3 per cent per year for the seven-year period beginning in 1980. Considered in real terms, this would only have been a possibility if the economy were growing at the same rate or better, which was not the case. But failure of a number of defence contractors to meet their delivery or payment-stage targets in the financial year 1979/80 had resulted in a rare cash *underspend* by the Ministry of Defence, providing the Treasury with an unrealistically low expenditure baseline from which to calculate the 3 per cent increases promised to NATO.

More immediate than the threat to the 3 per cent increases, deliveries by defence contractors began to speed up in 1980/1, as they were able to concentrate industrial effort on current contracts in the absence of new ones which, perforce, the MoD had felt obliged to cancel or postpone. By August 1980, those monitoring expenditure foresaw a very considerable overspend in the defence budget and urgent corrective measures were demanded. Blame for the expedient imposed was put on the shoulders of the Secretary of State for Defence, Francis Pym, but it really lay with the Permanent Under-Secretary, Sir Frank Cooper, who positively enjoyed wielding power in a ruthless manner. A moratorium on spending over a wide range of expenditure 'vote-heads' – the allocation of days' training undertaken by the Territorial Army, petrol, training involving travel over a certain distance, for example – was imposed, *without any choice being given to the two Command headquarters*: the British Army of the Rhine and the United Kingdom Land Forces.

As a former Commander-in-Chief, Bramall knew what would happen. But such was the power of the civil servants, through their closeness to Ministers, that he was powerless to avoid it. British soldiers, officers and men alike, know the rules governing their day-to-day activities only too well and it took only days, sometimes less than a couple of hours, to discover means of manoeuvring round the moratorium. It was surprising how activity banned under one vote-head could be paid for out of another and, as the Ministry of Defence was ridiculed, life went on much as usual.

A particular – and wholly unnecessary – fuss was made by a handful of constituency MPs and certain senior army officers over the curtailment of Territorial Army training days. There had been a consistent underspend in this area, even though a proportion of days not used in the early part of any financial year could be transferred to other men to use later. Therefore there was adequate scope for redistribution even under the terms of the moratorium. Regular army training on the larger training areas away from barrack locations did suffer, however, as there was little leeway to get round the restriction on use of petrol or on the reduction of 'track mileage' imposed on armoured regiments. An abrupt increase in the level of premature release from engagement (PRE), as servicemen became bored with life confined to barracks, was attributed to the moratorium. When consolidated figures were examined at the end of the financial year, it was discovered that the overall disruption of service life imposed by the moratorium had 'saved' more than twice the sum required to bring the budget in on target.

Bramall was quietly furious over what had occurred, not least by the lack of consultation with the Chiefs of Staff before the moratorium had been imposed. In his view, the outcome made the Chiefs look out of touch with their service people or simply uncaring. Around this time, the Secretary of State for Defence,

Francis Pym, was moved to become Leader of the Commons, reportedly because Margaret Thatcher was aware he would not quietly acquiesce to the Chancellor's insistence on defence budget levels certain to make major surgery inevitable somewhere in the defence programme. He was replaced by the little-known Minister of Trade and former merchant banker John Nott. His arrival in the Ministry of Defence was to set up far greater waves than those of alleged financial mismanagement he had been appointed to quell.

By an odd coincidence, Nott had served as a young officer with the 2nd Goorkha Rifles, of which, as we have seen, Bramall had become Colonel in 1976. While recognising that this was but a small basis on which to build mutual confidence and trust, he resolved to try to do so. Well aware of the link, Nott once replied to a memo Bramall had sent to him with the words, 'Well, if the Colonel of my Regiment tells me to do something. I had best do as I am told.' Had time and rather different circumstances allowed, the two men might have become quite close friends. In his 'Recollections of an errant politician', *Here Today Gone Tomorrow*, Nott acknowledges that Bramall was more of a 'cerebral man' than any of his fellow Chiefs of Staff, including Admiral Sir Terence Lewin, the then Chief of the Defence Staff. But they differed distinctly in both character and style. Nott was impatient, headstrong and very confident of his own intellectual powers – something he would occasionally acknowledge with the benefit of hindsight – and rather than stepping warily in order to avoid gratuitous offence, he did not hesitate to upset people, not improbably in order to judge their reaction or gain insight into a matter the other person may be trying to obscure, which is not a new technique. Bramall's carefully planned and persuasive approach was at odds with this, although he was perfectly capable of perceiving the line the Minister was adopting and why.

He realised that it was incumbent on each Chief of Staff to be completely frank and straightforward when discussing his own Service's commitments and resources bilaterally with the Secretary of State. He recognised that the Royal Air Force have a relatively easy hand to play in any contest for resources arising from a conflict between a predominantly continental and a maritime strategy, merely claiming that aircraft could fly in support of operations over land or sea as required. From the point of view of the Army, although reasonably confident that the demands of NATO would call for retention of the 55,000 to 60,000 men in Germany to defend the 65 kilometres of the Central Front allocated to 1st (British) Corps, he insisted – against the advice of the General Staff, who feared he might be offering a hostage to fortune – that John Nott be given an alternative option. This was to reduce the Army of the Rhine to a force of around 25,000 men, such as is there today, which would be in keeping with Britain's historical role *vis-à-vis* the Continent.

With a less specific role and its surface fleet vulnerable to Warsaw Pact attack in the north Norwegian Sea, the Royal Navy had the hardest task to convince the Secretary of State that no further reduction in capability could be made. The Navy's case was not helped by the Chief of Naval Staff making clear that the size and shape of a balanced fleet was a matter for the Navy to decide, not the Secretary of State, which was no way to treat a determined politician. It soon became clear that with Nott's exclusive focus on the country's NATO responsibilities – and with possible action to defend the Falkland Islands not even a glimmer in anyone's eye – the Navy was to be the target for cuts in the review to bring defence expenditure and the government's cash provision into line.

Before these differences could be crystallised into any form of priority, an across-the-board cut in defence spending over the next seven years was imposed through Nott persuading the Cabinet to change the 3 per cent increase per annum in defence spending, as had been promised to NATO by the previous administration, to a 21 per cent increase over seven years. This was done with an eye to reality, as he knew the Treasury would not be able to sustain a 3 per cent per year increase, but not only was the future cash available reduced by the compound interest factor, but scope was provided for year-on-year variations in cash provision which could play havoc with procurement programmes. Nott made these harsh adjustments to give him time to conduct a far-reaching defence review, but they had the effect of making the Chiefs of Staff turn inwards to repair the potential damage to their own spending programmes, rather than working together to avoid further impairment of the nation's overall defence capability.

It would be a mistake to give the impression that these or similar problems kept Bramall glued to his desk or prowling the corridors of the Ministry of Defence. He took care to get out to visit commands and units at home and abroad just as much as, if not more than, his predecessors. Preparation of papers on subjects for discussion on tour was the task of the Military Assistant to the CGS, initially the experienced and competent Lieutenant-Colonel (later Lieutenant-General Sir) Robert Hayman-Joyce, whom he had inherited from Sir Roland Gibbs. When the time came for Hayman-Joyce to leave, his appointed successor proved to be something of a surprise. Lieutenant-Colonel Michael Wilkes was a former commander of 1st Regiment Royal Horse Artillery and of a Special Forces group in the Radfan and South Arabia campaigns of 1964–7, but had never previously served in the Ministry of Defence. Rather mystified by his selection for the post and also feeling a bit of a fish out of water, he suggested to Bramall after two weeks in the job that perhaps a mistake had been made and he would be content to be replaced. 'Nonsense,' snorted Bramall. 'You are doing a splendid job, get on with it.' Wilkes did as he was asked and eventually retired as Adjutant-General.

Bramall's travels as Chief of the General Staff took him to every station overseas where British troops were serving, in particular to Northern Ireland, where he made his most frequent visits. In addition to Berlin, where he took the salute on the Queen's birthday parade on the Maifeld, outside the stadium in which the 1936 Olympic Games had been staged and Hitler had held Nazi rallies, he visited Ascension Island, on long lease to the United States as an air base, Belize, Kenya, Nepal and Rhodesia–Zimbabwe, where he was addressed at one point as 'Comrade-General'. Wherever he went, he talked to assemblies of troops to bring them up to date on events, policies in the making and give them an optimistic sense of purpose for their future.

More carefully choreographed visits were made to the armed forces and their commanders or chiefs of staff of China, Egypt, France, India, Italy, Spain, Thailand and the United States. Each demanded, along with the inevitable inspection of guards of honour, visits to military establishments, speeches and, most importantly, conversations with the heads of his host's army and very often with Ministers. When he addressed the students of the Egyptian Defence College, he took care to visit the battlefield east of the Suez Canal where the Egyptian Army had scored a victory – albeit a short-lived one – over the Israeli forces at the outset of the Yom Kippur War.

During a huge diplomatic reception given in his honour in Beijing he gave a toast in most carefully rehearsed Mandarin. After a pause for discreet consultation, his host – the Deputy Chief of the Defence Staff – rose and called the toast 'Bottoms up', causing Bramall to reflect on whether his Madarin intonation had, after all, conveyed precisely what he had intended. During a visit to France, which included sites in the mountains where the French nuclear missiles were housed, he was accompanied by a general known as 'Le Sphinx', as he invariably wore what the more imaginative might think was a just a suspicion of a smile. 'Your country and mine are condemned to cooperate,' he once ventured, but then, noticing Bramall's momentary puzzlement, went on, 'Don't worry, General, that was a only joke.'

Italy took particular care of him and Lady Bramall, installing them in a superb hotel in Venice for part of their visit. Inspection of an Alpine regiment in the Dolomites required a helicopter flight from sea level to 10,000 feet. The CGS sprang out of the aircraft into the surrounding snow intent on demonstrating to the guard of honour, waiting on slightly higher ground, how young and fit he was. But a restraining hand touched his arm as he began to stride forward. 'Generali,' muttered his host. 'In the mountains we walk veree slowly.' On a visit to Spain, after cautious preliminary enquiries, he asked to see the Alcazar – where the Nationalist defenders were besieged by the Communist government forces until relieved in September 1936 by the Nationalist General Mola, in the opening stages of the Spanish Civil War of 1936–9. This reflected his interest in military heroism rather than implying any sympathy with the Franco regime. In all his visits to foreign armies, Bramall sought to consolidate relations as well as to form new personal friendships, something he accomplished with relative ease, chiefly because of his thorough preparation and understanding of the interests of his hosts and their personal points of view.

In consequence of Bramall's direction, 1980 saw the restoration of brigade headquarters in the British Army of the Rhine. This was a consequence of a largely failed experiment to dispense with the brigade level of command, and associated communication systems, in favour of small divisions made up of armoured, infantry and artillery units sub-grouped into task forces for specific operations. When subjected to rigorous trial during exercises, the frequently changing grouping of units hindered rather than speeded up manoeuvre and neither the divisional commanders nor their staffs were able to maintain proper control over units not engaged in the immediate battle. It had been argued that the continental armies were able to make a similar system work but, in every such case, the basic unit was the 'regiment' of all arms, commanded by a colonel, which, although not unlike a British brigade, was much more tightly knit and had a common title or number. The earlier change had been introduced to economise on manpower and expensive equipment, to meet cost-cutting demands of the 1976 Defence Review and was out of step with communication systems that existed at the time. It took some years for the costs of reversion to the brigade system to be satisfactorily absorbed.

The change from the traditional British Army staff structure to the NATO system based on those used by the French and American armies was more successful, if not popular in the early stages. It had to be accepted, however, that such arcane titles as 'Deputy-Assistant Adjutant and Quartermaster-General', indicating the major responsible for personnel and logistics at brigade level, sounded absurd in the latter part of the twentieth century. Although not allowing the brigade level of command to be restored in the United Kingdom at this stage, Bramall gave instructions that the NATO staff system was to be taken into use there, with minimum delay and severe cuts made in Headquarters UKLF in the same time-scale. This was quickly accomplished – some officers considered it ruthlessly so – but the savings in manpower at the higher level allowed for the brigade level of command to be restored. (Later, economy in the number of 'District' headquarters allowed for an increase in brigade staffs, so that all field force units had the advantage of a brigadier responsible for directing their training for war.)

Back at the Ministry of Defence, Secretary of State John Nott was getting ready for the showdown over his proposed savage reductions in the Royal Navy's fleet of surface vessels. During the consultation phase, he had found a strong ally in the Chief Scientific Adviser to the MoD, Sir Ronald Mason. Mason's scientific staffs, having made an operational and costing analysis, had concluded that the Navy was spending too much money on 'hulls' – or 'weapon platforms' in scientific terminology – and not enough on weapons themselves. Mid-life modernisation of naval vessels was also challenged as an excessively extravagant method of maintaining the fleet, not only in straightforward terms of the financial cost but also for the waste involved in having vessels out of use for periods of two to three years.

Having examined the roles of the three Services in any general war with the forces of the Warsaw Pact, Nott had concluded that the way ahead lay with concentration on the NATO commitments, but with emphasis on the defence – on land and in the air – of the NATO Central Region at the expense of the defence of the Eastern Atlantic and the UK's ability to operate on the flanks of NATO. In downgrading, in his own mind, the Navy's part in a general war, he had again been influenced by the scientific staff, who cast grave doubts on the survivability of surface ships in such a conflict and, in consequence, reduced the Navy's role to submarine and counter-submarine operations in the Norwegian Sea and, to a lesser extent, the western approaches in the defence of reinforcement convoys from the United States. In crude language, the forecast appeared to be the RAF slightly better off, the Army about the same and the Navy considerably worse off. This came out into the open in Nott's Defence White Paper *The Way Forward*, published in June 1981.

Until shortly before then, the general public had been unaware of the impending crisis, but the publicity leading up to the dismissal of the Under-Secretary of State for the Navy, Mr Keith Speed MP, in May, caught the public interest in a compelling manner. There is also something about the Royal Navy that enlists the support of the man and woman in the street, in much the same way as the miners did before Arthur Scargill introduced the flying picket and tactic of fighting with policemen. Speed, a former regular officer of the Royal Navy, became so angry, frustrated and disillusioned by what the Secretary of State was proposing to do to the Senior Service that he gave a speech in his Ashford constituency that alerted the news media of the dangers to national security of what Nott proposed in face of the still-growing Soviet naval threat on the high seas. Nott requested Speed's resignation, which Speed declined to give and was dismissed. When he quit his office in the Ministry on 19 May, he was given a rousing farewell at the Palladian entrance to the building by a large crowd of naval officers, led by Admiral Sir Henry Leach, the First Sea Lord and Chief of Naval Staff. One fall-out from this whole incident was the abolition of the posts of Parliamentary Under-Secretaries for the Navy, Army and Air Force and redeployment of the individuals, other of course than Speed, to across the board functions.

Despite the public outcry – it could not be described as an 'uproar' – the die appeared to be cast in favour of the Nott proposals and, with them, a decisive switch of emphasis towards a continental European strategy for the United Kingdom and away from its former role as a world power. In the minds of the economic and political realists, this was a transition long overdue, but anything from a disgrace to a disaster in the minds of the men in dark blue and their supporters in the country. The overall effect of the Defence Review that John Nott had initiated was to reduce the growth, *in real terms*, of the defence budget to 7 per cent over the three financial years from 1979 to 1981 from the 12 per cent, including compound interest, the Services had hoped for under the Callaghan commitment to NATO. But the clear re-alignment of British defence policy towards Europe and away from her residual worldwide commitment sent what was read as a clear signal to the military junta in Buenos Aires and, if any underlining of that message was required, the small print of Nott's White Paper revealed the decision to withdraw the Antarctic patrol and survey ship *Endurance* from further service. (The Foreign and Commonwealth Office had objected to this measure, a rare example of the FCO and MoD officials acting in cohesion.)

When the Argentine forces arrived off the Falkland Islands on 2 April 1982, General Bramall was visiting troops in Northern Ireland, the CDS was on his way to New Zealand, leaving Chief of the Air Staff, Air Chief Marshal Sir Michael Beetham, in charge at the Ministry of Defence. But also available to advise the Cabinet – and raring to have a go, if only to prove John Nott wrong – was the highly professional and totally dedicated Chief of the Naval Staff Admiral Sir Henry Leach.

15

The Falklands War

When the forces of the Argentine dictator General Galtieri invaded the Falkland Islands on 2 April 1982, Dwin Bramall had just four months to run for the completion of his three-year tour of duty as Chief of the General Staff. He was visiting troops in Northern Ireland as the first whisper of impending military action came through on 31 March and still out of London when the Chief of Naval Staff (CNS), Admiral Sir Henry Leach, seized the initiative on his own account, issued orders to the fleet and told Prime Minister Margaret Thatcher that, if she and the Cabinet so required, a Royal Navy task force could sail in three days' time to effect recovery of the islands either through threat of force or by its use. This was very different from the pessimistic advice she received from Defence Ministers and civil servants, but was exactly what she wanted to hear.

Studied dispassionately, the lead-up to these circumstances casts doubt on the competence of the British Foreign and Commonwealth Office, the Intelligence Services and the Cabinet, the last for not reacting to possibilities about which they had been warned specifically. But in fairness to all of them, it has to be said that similar alarms had been sounded before. Moreover, despite their authoritarian nature and the increasingly desperate economic circumstances in which they found themselves, no one expected the Argentine leaders to commit international political suicide by an act of naked aggression. Yet that is exactly what took place, leaving the British government with an awkward choice between accepting Argentina's hold on the Falklands by right of possession or opening a military campaign 8,000 miles from home in the

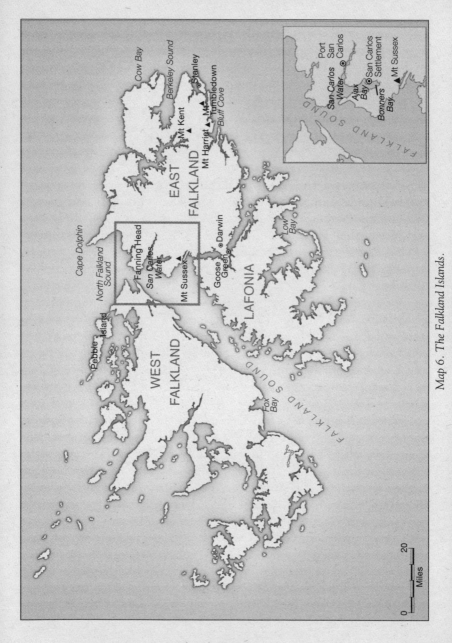

Map 6. The Falkland Islands.

hostile climatic conditions of a region where, in the absence of an airfield, gaining air superiority for the protection of the fleet and any landing sites would be extremely difficult if not impossible.

While these daunting circumstances were welcomed by the CNS, as they offered a heaven-sent opportunity to show that Britain needed the balanced fleet capability for which he had consistently argued in face of Defence Minister John Nott's determination to cut the surface fleet down to the needs of NATO, Bramall was able to view them more objectively and, in the preliminary stages at least, more sceptically.

Returning from his visit to Northern Ireland, his main task, whatever his initial reservations about the role of the Naval Task Force, was to commit the Army wholeheartedly to the huge effort to equip the men who were to sail for the South Atlantic. This particularly included the Army units with Number 3 Commando Brigade, that is the artillery regiment, engineers and signallers and the logistic support units. He knew that if the Falklands were to be recovered, it would be no use showing righteous indignation from a distance; effective power had to be projected into the South Atlantic. How the Task Force would be used once it got there was an entirely different issue, which would depend on a number of factors which would become clear later on. On this, Bramall not unnaturally reserved his position, reacting to requests for his views by stating that for the moment this was predominantly a naval matter and that it was to be hoped the Argentine junta would be sufficiently sobered by the sailing of the Task Force to put forward a plea for negotiation. He did question the Chief of Naval Staff point blank, however, on whether the Task Force as constituted could defend itself and received an affirmative answer.

Privately, he railed against the series of failures which had allowed the situation to arise. A virtually identical crisis had been averted during the winter of 1976/7 by the prompt despatch of a nuclear-powered submarine to Falkland Waters and the stationing of a couple of frigates in the South Atlantic. While these deployments had been carried out in secret, the Argentines could scarcely avoid hearing about the frigates, and their naval staff would have been quick to assume that a more serious threat to their shipping lurked beneath the surface, should an invasion fleet put to sea. In the early days of the 1982 crisis, while the Cabinet briefly hesitated over the order for the task force to sail, he supported the widely expressed view that the act of sailing might be sufficient to do the trick. But he harboured misgivings on the level of casualties if military action proved unavoidable.

In his determination to persuade the Prime Minister and Cabinet of the certain success of a naval task force, the CNS gave little emphasis to the importance of gaining air superiority over the area of operations. This is not to suggest that he failed to appreciate this threat; he had served at sea in operational theatres during the Second World War and his father's ship had been sunk by Japanese bombers off Malaya. He had also served as Director of Naval Plans and Assistant Chief of Naval Staff (Policy), so he knew the score. But it did not suit his book to advertise any doubts his subordinates put to him – and he was not a man to harbour doubts of his own.

The question of air superiority was to cause Bramall increasing concern. As the Chiefs of Staff collectively began to consider the various options available to the C-in-C Fleet and the Task Force Commander and, with Argentine obduracy persisting, the likelihood of military engagement increased. During the campaign in North-West Europe in 1944–5, he had witnessed the devastating effect of the overwhelming Allied air power on German army deployment and was aware that British Intelligence assessed the Argentine Air Force as the most modern of their three services. Equipped with high-performance American and French aircraft, their competent and high-spirited pilots were supremely confident of their navigational systems and state-of-the-art anti-ship missiles, including the French Exocet, which was also in service with the Royal Navy. Although he had not taken part in the Dunkirk evacuation, he was acutely conscious from what had occurred there of the vulnerability of a high concentration of men and vehicles on a confined beach.

By the time the task force had been joined by the destroyer group in mid-Atlantic on 24 April, it had become clear that the Argentine leadership was not going to crumble in the face of simply a *threat* of use of military force. Such negotiations as had taken place through the United States and other third parties, sponsored by the United Nations in New York, had brought forward only entirely unacceptable suggestions. Expectations of an early Argentine climb-down having evaporated, the next hope seized upon eagerly by those wishing to avoid out-and-out conflict was that the arrival of the task force off the Falklands would produce the required result. In the meantime, planners in the Ministry of Defence and at the Commander-in-Chief Fleet's headquarters at Northwood were working out in detail what to do if that result failed to materialise.

In the Army Department of the Ministry of Defence two strands of opinion competed. The first, reflecting the mood of front-line units, was that the Army must have a greater involvement, 'get into the act', if only because most soldiers had spent their working lives training for war, often with only the seldom rewarding toil of patrolling the streets of Northern Ireland for their trouble. The understandable but short-term view that 'the Marines must not be allowed to hog this one' was not reflected on the fourth floor of the Ministry, where the Military Operations and Staff Duties offices are situated side by side. Jointly responsible for recommending what should best be done with the forces available, MO and ASD recognised that, short of an outright defeat leaving the islands in Argentine hands, the Army would have to pick up the pieces by providing a long-term garrison.

There was also a more immediate difficulty. The formation designated for 'out-of-area operations', that is to say outside the NATO area, was the 5th Airborne Brigade situated at Aldershot. Formed in 1980 to take on some of the contingency plans previously the responsibility of the disbanding 16th Parachute Brigade Group, this new formation lacked the supporting and logistic units essential for independent operations. This was in part due to the belief that 'out-of-area operations' were unlikely to require more than one reinforced battalion group and, in consequence, units previously assigned to the 16th Parachute Brigade had been reallocated to 1st Brigade, part of the United Kingdom force with contingency plans for the reinforcement to

NATO's northern or southern flanks. If 5th Brigade was to be sent off on its designated 'out-of-area' role, not only would it require operational and logistic support units – at the expense of a NATO-assigned formation – an additional battalion would be needed to replace the 3rd Battalion The Parachute Regiment, which had been switched to 3 Commando Brigade as part of the Task Force, to give greater strength to any landing force.

Working out from where these additional units could be found was bread-and-butter stuff, but conditions for their actual deployment depended on whether they were to be used in battle or as an occupation force. Views on this differed widely and it has to be said that some of those supporting the army-of-occupation scenario did so largely in the certain knowledge that a prolonged fight would, among many other things, call for quantities of artillery ammunition only available from NATO stock. On the one hand, operational realists such as Brigadier Peter de la Billière – the Director of the Special Air Service (SAS) Group – held the view that 'We could get a real hiding down there unless we are properly prepared', while on the other, those hoping to conserve troop strengths to maintain other operational needs, primarily in Northern Ireland, tended to play down the risks.

As Chief of the General Staff and head of the Army who had to reconcile these views and decide between them, Dwin Bramall faced an individual dilemma which it would be wrong to ignore. The task force had been thrown together and the first element sent to sea with virtually no Army Department consultation. Admiral Sir Henry Leach, the CNS, had declared the operation a 'naval matter' and, at that stage, at least a majority of the Cabinet clung to the opinion that sending the Task Force was little more than a 'political demonstration'. Few members of the public believed a war was likely, the majority dismissing the potential enemy, who had not fought a war for 100 years, as opposition easily seen off by the UK's highly professional armed forces, ignoring the fact that the Argentine population is descended from German, Italian and Spanish immigrants with the smallest dilution of indigenous Indian blood of any of the South America states.

Against this background, Bramall had not only the opportunity but also, in a sense, a responsibility to stand back and await events. He was due to take over as Chief of the Defence Staff in just six months' time. To seek to influence decisions now, other than when his view was specifically sought, might be thought presumptuous. More importantly perhaps, in the event of a disaster – for example the Task Force being turned back at sea owing to lack of political will for a fight – or a naval reverse at Argentine hands, by standing back he would leave himself untarnished by any such event.

More than simple professional self-preservation can be attached to such a line of thought, even if subconscious. No matter how any failure to recover the islands might occur, the Royal Navy would be left in a weaker situation than when the CNS was attempting to counter John Nott's proposals to slash the surface fleet and the government would be seeking a scapegoat. By standing back and giving advice only on aspects on which he was unquestionably correct, for example on the key operational question of air superiority, his authority would remain intact, leaving him ready to pick up the pieces and assemble them into a new coherence. This was not a particularly risky line to adopt, but it was both sensible and responsible.

From the outset of the crisis, he was concerned for the medium- and longer-term outlooks, rather than simply reacting robustly in the face of the humiliation the Argentines had imposed upon Britain. That was bad enough, he argued, but it would be far worse if the UK was obliged through international pressure to recall the Task Force or, having reached the South Atlantic, suffered some incapacitating reverse. At the first meeting of the Chiefs of Staff after the Argentine invasion, on 5 April, while the CDS, Admiral of the Fleet Sir Terence Lewin was still visiting New Zealand, Bramall set out his views in a forthright way and demanded of his colleagues answers to four questions before they submitted any collective advice to Ministers.

First, he asked, 'Assuming we win any naval encounter, will Ministers take the warlike action to ensure success? Now, it looks as though they would, but a lot could change over the next fortnight.'

Second, 'Are we ready to stress to Ministers that, in order to impose a naval blockade of the islands, we shall have to sink one or more Argentine ships, possibly the aircraft carrier?' Third, 'If the Argentines are not prepared to negotiate, are we prepared to invade irrespective of casualties?' Fourth, 'Once rescued, what are we going to do with the Falkland Islands?' These were questions that, of the three Chiefs of Staff present, only he was keen to address. The Chief of Naval Staff had his eyes fixed on saving the Fleet and the Chief of Air Staff, Air Chief Marshal Sir Michael Beetham, knew the RAF would have a mainly supporting, transport aircraft role to fulfil, chiefly by skilful use of air-to-air refuelling techniques. (Later, using these techniques, the RAF confined Stanley airfield to the use of short-take-off-and-landing aircraft only by high-explosive bombs dropped by a Vulcan bomber.)

In mid-April, ten days after the naval carrier group had sailed, the Army's involvement began to ratchet up. Under the auspices of the UK C-in-C's Committee (UKCICC) the Commanders-in-Chief Fleet, United Kingdom Land Forces (UKLF) and RAF Strike Command had arranged to meet twice a week at Fleet Headquarters, Northwood, from where operations in the South Atlantic were being directed by the C-in-C Fleet, Admiral Sir John Fieldhouse, a shrewd and imperturbable Yorkshireman. A briefing of the entire situation was given and then Fieldhouse would seek such advice and material assistance as he needed from his fellow Cs-in-C.

C-in-C UKLF, General Sir John Stanier, invariably took along his Chief of Staff, the author, who knew the Land Force Commander designate, Major-General Jeremy Moore of the Royal Marines, from their service in the Far East. When Moore expressed his urgent need for 'another brigade', Stanier put this to the C-in-C Fleet and agreed to take the request to London without delay. After a telephone call to make an appointment to see the CGS, Stanier and I flew to the Thames helicopter port and were soon seated in the CGS's office. With an eye to coming in with more authority if necessary, Stanier asked me to open the discussion.

Not much progress was being made, chiefly because the CGS introduced, only to dismiss, a case for a 'breakout from the eventual bridgehead' on the grounds that such could well be obviated by 3 Commando Brigade landing in a strategically key position leading to an Argentine collapse. 'This is not going to be another Normandy invasion,' he added for good measure. At that point, the CGS's Military Assistant interrupted the conversation to ask whether a moment could be spared for the CGS to meet the newly appointed acting Chief of Public Relations, Mr Ian Macdonald, who was ushered in. He introduced himself in the sepulchral tones shortly to become his hallmark on television and at London press briefings.

As soon as he had gone, Stanier – a former Director of Public Relations (Army) and no mean communicator – switched the discussion to the need for facilities for the information media representatives with the Task Force, warning the CGS of the Royal Navy's institutional distrust and dislike of the press. The original topic of an additional brigade was shelved but, later that day, a specific request was put to Bramall by the Chief of Naval Staff.

Still conscious of the hopes of Military Operations and Staff Duties not to commit more troops if it could be avoided, he did agree that the Spearhead battalion should be released further to reinforce the Commando Brigade. By sheer chance, this was 2nd Battalion The Parachute Regiment, which was also the 'in-role' parachute battalion to be held in readiness for any emergency situation demanding a parachute drop but, hardly surprisingly, Bramall was not going to hold it back for a hypothetical crisis, when there was a major one already ongoing. The effect was to reduce the 5th Airborne (out-of-area) Brigade to one battalion only, the 7th Gurkha Rifles.

Seventy-two hours later, continued pressure from Northwood resulted in the Army Department agreeing to 5 Brigade being assigned to a follow-up role and Lieutenant-General Sir Richard Trant, commanding South-East District in which the brigade was based, was appointed military adviser to C-in-C Fleet as Major-General Moore was due to leave for the Task Force's staging post at Ascension Island. At the instigation of the CGS, Trant warned the commander of 5th Brigade, Brigadier Tony Wilson, to prepare for a tough test exercise in Wales under the direction of the Deputy

C-in-C UKLF, Lieutenant-General Sir Frank Kitson and asked HQ UKLF to replace 2nd and 3rd Battalions of The Parachute Regiment in 5th Airborne Brigade's order of battle.

Although the CGS had no direct hand in the selection of the other two battalions to go to the Falklands, in view of subsequent charges of their selection being based on grounds of 'elitism', the actual process of events is worth mentioning. The criteria excluding units specifically assigned to NATO in the short term prevented commitment of the ACE Mobile Force battalion, even though it was trained, equipped and experienced in Arctic conditions. Units very recently returned from Northern Ireland or shortly due to serve there were not to be used. The 1st Battalion Welsh Guards was free, having just completed a period as 'Spearhead' Battalion without being committed. The 1st Battalion The Queen's Lancashire Regiment was available, as was 2nd Battalion Scots Guards if relieved from London duties. HQ UKLF put these options to General Trant, who had set up a briefing for the exercise in Wales the following afternoon. Based solely on the relative ease with which the two Foot Guards commanding officers could travel to Aldershot, he chose them.

When Bramall mentioned to John Nott that the 7th Gurkha Rifles would be going to the Falklands with 5 Brigade, the Secretary of State reacted with alarm, pointing out that the Indian government would almost certainly object, perhaps even giving rise to further difficulty at the United Nations.

The CGS stood his ground, arguing that not to send Gurkhas on this operation could prejudice their deployment in the future. Nott had served as a young officer with the 2nd Goorkhas, of whom Bramall was still Colonel. Reminding Nott of this, Bramall continued, 'Look, Secretary of State, I am the Colonel of your Regiment and I am telling you that they must go and I am requiring your support to fight our corner with the Foreign Office.' Nott accepted this mission with good grace and later, when he told Mrs Thatcher that a Gurkha battalion was going to the South Atlantic, the Prime Minister exclaimed, 'What? Only one!'

General Trant's original thinking behind his choice of battalions reflected the current view that 5 Brigade would not be required, except to relieve 3 Commando Brigade of occupation duties. Indeed on 12 May, when 5 Brigade sailed for the South Atlantic in the liner QE2, having been allocated a six-gun battery, an engineer element, a mixed squadron of three Scout and six Gazelle helicopters, a field ambulance unit and logistic support elements, there was still hope in Whitehall that imposition of the total exclusion zone round the islands on 30 April by Rear-Admiral Sandy Woodward's carrier group would eventually lead the Argentine junta to call for new negotiations. That said, when Bramall went to Aldershot to speak to the 5 Brigade units before their embarkation, he told them they were going to the Falklands as the Task Force Commander's reserve, which might require not only taking over from 3 Commando Brigade, but a breakout from the bridgehead alongside them.

Before despatch of 5 Brigade, the Argentine cruiser *Belgrano* had been torpedoed by the Royal Navy submarine *Conqueror* on 2 May with the loss of 368 lives and on 4 May HMS *Sheffield* had been lost to an air-delivered Exocet missile. A plan devised by Rear-Admiral Woodward and his staff for a landing by 3 Commando Brigade on beachheads at Port San Carlos and on San Carlos Water, on the west coast of East Falkland, was submitted for approval by the Chiefs of Staff with Admiral Lewin back in the chair. It was time to look at the ground plan, and Bramall was not enamoured of it.

The Army's General Staff were of the opinion that, from the point of view of future land operations, the proposed landing area was too far from the high ground overlooking Port Stanley that it would be essential to take if the Argentines were to be defeated. The marching distance of some 75 miles would take time to cover, especially in deteriorating weather conditions and with the likelihood of enemy air attack. The outcome might consequently be a cease-fire, brought about by international pressure, before the decisive battle could be fought. But, having heard the arguments of the C-in-C Fleet in favour of San Carlos as the landing area, in the vital interests of safeguarding the ships during the landing phase, Bramall and the General Staff gave the landing plan their full support.

The outline plan for the landing and subsequent repossession of the island of East Falkland was presented to the War Cabinet for the first time on 27 April. Before this meeting, the Prime Minister had taken Bramall aside and said, 'I hear you are not entirely happy about the operation,' to which he replied, 'My concern, Prime Minister, is over the approach and landing, but this is a matter on which the Navy should advise you. Once ashore, I believe the dangers of the air threat will decrease markedly and the ground force should be able to do their job.' He also stated during the meeting that once a landing had been achieved it would be essential, in the absence of any significant opposition in the area, for the troops to move out of the bridgehead and stake claim to the vital ground dominating Port Stanley. He was aware that there were plenty of historical precedents of the initiative being lost through troops being slow to exploit a successful beach landing, a fact quickly appreciated by the war veterans William Whitelaw and Francis Pym. It was unfortunate that, although this concept of operations was well understood by the Land Force Commander, Major-General Jeremy Moore – who was still en route by sea – and it was impressed on the 3 Commando Brigade Commander at San Carlos by the C-in-C Fleet, it still took time to implement, chiefly owing to the loss of the heavy lift helicopters when the container ship bringing them in, the *Atlantic Conveyor*, was struck by an Exocet missile as she entered San Carlos Water and sunk on 25 May.

Before this dramatic setback and the Argentine junta's rejection of the final proposals of the United Nations Secretary-General, Bramall had felt it necessary to summarise his concerns and views on the conduct of the campaign for the benefit of the Secretary of State. This was in advance of the Chiefs of Staff's briefing of the Prime Minister and the War Cabinet on 18 May. It was characteristic of him to begin a speech or memo with an anecdote to catch the interest of his audience or reader. It was also typical of him that he would try to wring a wry smile out of the Secretary of State in an effort to cheer him up while he was still bruised by the reception of his disastrous winding-up speech in the emergency debate in the Commons on the first Saturday of the crisis. It was the story of the stationmaster who, when asked why his four clocks all showed a different time, retorted 'What would be the use of having four clocks if they all showed the same time?' The point was intended as a lead-in to advice from the Chief of the General Staff which was not entirely in step with that of the CDS or CNS.

He went on to say that differing shades of opinion put things in some sort of perspective and balance, then made the three points he believed were paramount at that point in the crisis. First, he confirmed his view that there was now no option but to invade and, as long as the enemy's air strength had been sufficiently reduced, the sooner the better. Second, after accepting that he had 'always looked at final repossession of the islands with less relish than perhaps some others', he returned to his contention 'that we should not have got ourselves into this position in the first place, so I naturally grudge the casualties that may now have to be suffered to recover from our mistakes'. He concluded with a hope that any settlement would not require a permanent stationing of land and naval forces in what he held to be 'entirely the wrong part of the world'.

On 18 May, the Argentine junta rejected the final British proposals put through the United Nations Secretary-General and the Chiefs of Staff were summoned by the Prime Minister to give a presentation on what was to be termed 'Operation Sutton' to the War Cabinet. Bramall's distaste for the situation in which politicians and servicemen alike found themselves and his continued apprehension over the likely air situation were all too apparent in the opening words of his verbal briefing. He pulled no punches. 'I believe that there is now no option but to invade,' he began, 'and provided that *attrition by air* and by special forces (SAS and SBS) has been given full scope and allowed to take its toll, the sooner it takes place the better.'

After referring to the undoubted advantage to Britain's status in the world that a triumphant success would achieve, he pointed out that it would need a 'bit of luck' and added,

This final act of repossession does, in my judgement, produce larger risks particularly in respect of the air threat and in the initial stages – that is the landing and build-up before troops are firmly established there, than would normally have been considered appropriate in an operation of this sort. Air superiority is, after all, one of the principles of war and we have not yet achieved it.

The landings in San Carlos Bay began on 21 May; from that moment onwards there was little that Bramall or anyone else in Whitehall could do to bring positive influence to bear on the situation in the South Atlantic. There was, however, a need to hold back attempts at political interference because of anxiety or impatience. The attack on the Argentine garrison defending the airfield at Goose Green, at the southern end of the isthmus linking East Falkland with Lafonia, is often attributed to purely political pressure from 10 Downing Street, but the truth is rather more complex.

On his first routine visit to Northwood after the San Carlos landings had begun, the C-in-C UKLF, General Stanier, was asked by C-in-C Fleet, Admiral Fieldhouse for his advice on what the commander of 3 Commando Brigade, Brigadier Julian Thompson, should do next: 'I've put five thousand troops ashore and absolutely nothing has happened! The weather is deteriorating and I'm taking stick. What are *you* going to do?'

With no express executive authority in this matter, as the command responsibility rested with Fieldhouse, Stanier withdrew into a side room with the senior Army representative at Northwood, Lieutenant-General Sir Richard Trant, and together the two made an appreciation of the situation based on the intelligence available to them. Aware that the campaign could be won only by the capture of the Islands' capital, Stanley, they were also conscious of the threat posed to the approach route and lines of communication by the garrison and still-active airfield at Goose Green.

Deciding that, at least, any aircraft at Goose Green should be prevented from interfering with the approach to Stanley, Stanier drew up a proposal that a battalion group with artillery support should eliminate the threat from Goose Green and, accordingly, passed this recommendation to Admiral Fieldhouse. The following day, while in London, Stanier explained to the CGS what had occurred. Bramall's only comment was, 'I hope you were right to recommend only one battalion.'

Unfortunately, the selection of Goose Green as the first land objective had to be communicated to the 10 Downing Street press office, which led to the Argentines being warned by a premature announcement on BBC's World Service broadcast. This naturally infuriated Brigadier Thompson and the commanding officer of the 2nd Battalion The Parachute Regiment, Lieutenant-Colonel 'H' Jones, who was subsequently killed at Goose Green. The World Service broadcast, probably more than any other factor, gave rise to the belief that the action to take Goose Green was initiated in the interest of political 'spin'. While it is true that there was political pressure for some movement to be made out of the San Carlos bridgehead, no one involved in the recommendation to Admiral Fieldhouse or formulation of the message to Brigadier Thompson was influenced by anything other than operational considerations. The CGS's view on the issue was that the matter called for a command decision to be taken by those on the spot.

There was an incident in London during May. A 'flash' radio message giving warning of a suspected Exocet attack on one of the naval vessels came through to the Operations Room in the Ministry of Defence. At that moment, quite unaccountably, all the lights fused. They were quickly restored, but Major Colin Groves, who was on duty, noticed that one of the WRAC clerks was in tears. When asked why, she replied, 'I'm frightened, sir.' As he took her hand to give what comfort he could, the CGS walked into the room. After enquiring why Groves was holding the girl's hand, General Bramall read the flash message, then walked over and, taking the girl's other hand, said, 'Don't worry – I'm quite frightened too.'

From the moment the main body of Marines and troops set out from the beachhead on 27 May, it took just 19 days to bring about the Argentine surrender on 14 June. This was despite the loss of the container ship *Atlantic Conveyor* and her cargo of troop-carrying helicopters, which would have been used to lift the men across East Falkland to Stanley, and the disaster at Fitzroy, where fifty-one

Welsh Guardsmen lost their lives in an Argentine air force attack on the landing ship *Sir Galahad* on 8 June. The Argentine collapse was as complete and humiliating a surrender of a large force to a smaller but more courageous and professional one could be.

General Bramall flew down to Ascension Island to meet the 2nd and 3rd Battalions The Parachute Regiment and elements of other army units on their way back to England. The men were assembled on MV *Norland* to be addressed by the head of the Army. He spoke briefly and crisply and, after thanking them for their courage and determination during the campaign, he advised them,

Well, you are about to start on your last leg home, where your Colonel-in-Chief, I know, awaits to greet you and you won't want to be delayed, even for a moment, by waffle and flannel from someone who has seen the Falklands crisis through from the safety and comfort of Whitehall! But I thought the least I could do, as the professional head of the British Army and one of those who sent you to war, was to come out and thank both Battalions together for all you have done for the country, for the British Army and for your proud and splendid Regiment, in carrying out, against great odds, however difficult, every task given you and in restoring the British flag to the Falklands.

You have done an outstanding job by any standards – and even that word is inadequate – and have justified a thousand-fold the confidence *we* placed in you and you can now fully take your place alongside those of the previous generation who fought with great glory at Bruneval, in North Africa, Sicily, Normandy, across the Rhine and at Arnhem. You have earned the admiration of all of us old soldiers, who may even be prepared to admit that you are probably actually fitter and more professional and just as, if not more, courageous than your fathers were.

And both Battalions share equally in the glory. 2 PARA, as your Padre and others have reminded us and no doubt will continue to remind us, were the first ashore, the first to break out of the bridgehead with your most courageous and tough battle at Goose Green – almost a 'mission impossible' but you did it and it was the turning point – and the first to enter Stanley; and 3 PARA took part in the staggering 'bash' across East Falkland to surprise and unbalance the Argies and push them off the dominant high ground, and then fought the crucial and also very tough engagement on Mount Longdon which made such a major contribution to the turning of and the final crumbling and collapse of the Argentine position. So share the honour between you. And of course, both Battalions will have seen plenty of some of the horrible aspects of battle and have lost good and brave men and fine comrades, whose death or serious injury we greatly mourn. 2 PARA has in the course of a few months lost two outstanding COs in 'H' Jones and Colin Thompson (the immediately previous CO who had died of cancer). You will never forget them and we must see that the country and the Army also never forget them, or the families that some of them have left behind. I think I can reassure you on this point.

And in all this, do not forget those in the Task Force who supplied you and backed you up and made your hard-won success possible, the Royal Navy who put you ashore under very difficult circumstances and did their level best to keep the enemy Air Force off your back. The helicopter pilots who flew you heroically in all conditions, the Gunners, the Sappers, the Doctors and Padres who helped your wounded, and the logistic organisation who went through the remarkable exercise of keeping you supplied with essential stores and ammunition 8,000 miles from home.

And perhaps a thought might not even be amiss for your own 1st Battalion, for whom no doubt your hearts bleed, sweating it out in Fermanagh, Northern Ireland. It was not their fault they were not alongside you in these last few difficult and dangerous days, where I have no doubt they would have preferred to have been.

So now you go home to a great and well-deserved welcome from your loved ones and friends and the country as a whole, who rightly rate the Falklands campaign – for which incidentally there will be a special medal – as one of the most brilliant and bravest in British military history.

Accept the praise and applause with modesty and dignity and try very hard not to do a single thing back home which will compromise that dignity or lose the respect that everyone in the land feels for you. You have, after all, nothing left to prove to yourselves or to anyone else. In the armies of the world, they come no braver or tougher than those in Great Britain's Parachute Regiment, full stop. So if anyone tries to pick a fight or lure you into unwise behaviour, treat them with the contempt they deserve and tell them to get some service in! Besides, it may even make a nice change to make love, not war, for a bit!

So I bring gratitude from everyone for your collective stamina, professionalism, courage and spirit and I wish you a safe and marvellous return to your families and a well-earned leave. In the years ahead when you are old men, you will be able to say, as they said after Waterloo, after Alamein and Arnhem, 'I marched and fought, and won in the Falklands, and showed to the world the incomparable quality of professionalism of the British Army and the spirit and strength of the regimental system' – no doubt you will bore successive generations of children and grandchildren into the bargain, but such is life.

So, once again, thank you very much indeed, and well done all of you.

From Bramall's personal standpoint, the campaign in the South Atlantic had cleared away any uncertainties of how the Chiefs of Staffs system was intended to work in the determination of defence policy in a crisis situation and present it in a concerted and coherent fashion to the Overseas and Defence Cabinet Sub-Committee. During the Falklands War a sub-group – ODSA (Overseas and Defence South Atlantic) – had been formed and the CDS, Admiral of the Fleet Sir Terence Lewin, had reported direct to that group and attended all its deliberations. Although decisions taken by the War Cabinet were passed to C-in-C Fleet by the CDS, the Chiefs of Staff were consulted collectively and during their frequent invitations to Chequers, enabling them to maintain an informed debate on the conduct of the war. On both 27 April and

18 May, when the War Cabinet was briefed, the Chiefs of Staff had been given individual opportunities to express their own views direct to the Prime Minister before the final decision to launch the land campaign was taken. In sum, the system had worked well, much supported by the mutual confidence between the Chiefs and the fact that they had all had combat experience in the Second World War.

Bramall's relations with John Nott, the Secretary of State for Defence, had been good throughout. Whereas Bramall's reservations on the merits of launching the Task Force had never been as strong as Nott had held at the outset of the crisis, their minds worked in similar ways, each perceiving quickly the line of the other's thoughts and so avoiding time-wasting sparring. They had similar senses of humour and, mercifully, neither was remotely inclined towards pomposity or offended dignity.

Despite his personal disagreement with Nott's proposals to slash the surface fleet and the Services' amphibious assault capability, Bramall had sympathy for Nott's position as a markedly unpopular Minister of Defence. This arose not simply because of the swingeing economies in defence spending that he proposed but because, through no fault of his own, he did not fit the image the armed forces looked for in their Minister. Skinny, bald and with large black spectacles, he looked what he was – a merchant banker. Nott was also not good at talking to servicemen, senior or junior, being clever and confrontational when a less inquisitorial approach would have elicited the information he required rather more easily.

When the crisis was over, Bramall wrote to Nott a letter typical of him:

My dear Secretary of State,
If I may say so (and it doesn't sound patronising) I think you have done splendidly in every possible way. You have always ensured that political decisions were ready to match the military needs; you have performed brilliantly on television (*Panorama* last night was another triumph) and never shirked being in the front line when bad news was around; and you have skilfully and admirably

prepared Parliamentary and public opinion for all the steps and shocks which were needed to complete the difficult and dangerous operation; and you stood up to the PM when necessary which is never easy.

Yours ever, Dwin.

Not everyone around at the time would concur with 'performed brilliantly on television', on which he could appear both arrogant and contemptuous of the interviewer and alternative opinion, but the rest of the CGS's letter has the clear ring of truth. Nott was the first to recognise his failings and mistakes, most of which were acknowledged in his frank and amusing memoir *Here Today Gone Tomorrow*, echoing the phrase used of him by the BBC veteran interviewer Sir Robin Day, published in 2002.

As the tumult began to subside and the 1982 summer holiday season began, Bramall could look forward to handing over the post of Chief of the General Staff at a point when the Army was held in high esteem by the public at large and the Falklands War had demonstrated that future defence policy required some radical re-thinking, although not within the purely NATO-aligned confines advocated by John Nott. He had survived Britain's most serious military challenge since the disastrous Suez Campaign of 1956 with results for the country, its political leadership and armed forces as different as they could be. New challenges lay ahead of him as Chief of the Defence Staff, following his taking up of that post from Admiral Lewin that October, but there was a distinct sense of decks having been cleared and much muddled thinking washed over the side. Here was not an exhausted man about to shoulder the greatest responsibilities a British service chief can be given with any sense of them being a burden, but one full of energy, ideas and good humour.

16

Chief of the Defence Staff

Having received his Field Marshal's baton from the Queen two months earlier, Sir Edwin Bramall took over as Chief of the Defence Staff on 1 October 1982. This was a post for which he had been destined, almost as a certainty, since his selection as Commander British Forces Hong Kong nine years earlier. The task ahead did not daunt him, although the recent war in the South Atlantic had shown up serious deficiencies in Britain's defence policy. It had also brought him into close working contact with the senior officers of the other two Services, allowing him to build on the confidence exchanged during his time as a member of the United Kingdom Commanders-in-Chief Committee and, later, as Vice-Chief of the Defence Staff (Personnel and Logistics), when he had been striving to staunch the haemorrhage of skilled manpower from all three Services by introducing radical improvements in pay and conditions.

Other members of the Chiefs of Staff Committee had also changed, or were about to do so. The highly articulate General Sir John Stanier, who had been Vice-Chief in his early days as Chief of the General Staff, had succeeded him, the amiable but very professional Air Chief Marshal Sir Keith Williamson had become Chief of the Air Staff and the calm and stalwart Admiral Sir John Fieldhouse, fresh from his triumph as C-in-C for the Falklands Campaign, was due to take over as Chief of Naval Staff in December. Scarcely in the history of the Service Chiefs meeting to determine the defence issues of the day had there been such potential for harmonious and profitable debate and cooperation.

267

For some reason of her own, Margaret Thatcher had decided to keep John Nott on as Defence Minister until the end of the year, possibly because he made public his intended resignation early in the Falklands crisis without going through the formalities with her. In his political memoir *Here Today Gone Tomorrow*, Nott frankly acknowledged that it was his mistake not to insist on giving up his post the moment the Falklands War was over. Despite the respect he had gained in Bramall's eyes during that conflict, the Royal Navy hated his guts for his plans to decimate the surface fleet, and he had become a figure almost of ridicule in the House of Commons and in the eyes of the press. But, whether by accident or design, by remaining at his post he allowed the Chiefs of Staff an opportunity to get their feet under the table before the next Minister arrived on 1 January 1983.

At least on first sight and by reputation, Michael Heseltine was an altogether different Secretary of State from John Nott. Whereas barely anyone outside the Treasury or House of Commons had heard of Nott before he became Minister of Defence, Heseltine was one of the country's best-known political figures. Nicknamed 'Tarzan' for his flowing blond hair and bravura style in the Commons, middle-ranking officers and men and women in service units welcomed him as someone they thought would fight their corner and, when necessary, stand up to the Prime Minister. In the Ministry of Defence, senior officers and many civil servants took a less sanguine view. They recognised the new Minister's driving ambition, and as with similar figures before him – for example, Duncan Sandys in the late 1950s – it was expected that his short-term high-profile interests would come first, broader issues of government policy on which he could speak in order to attract favourable attention second and longer-term but currently more pressing defence issues a poor third. Many had not enjoyed where they had found themselves standing with John Nott, but at least they had been able to identify the location.

To his credit, John Nott had started to chart the way forward before leaving his post. His Defence White Paper, *The Falklands Campaign* of December 1982, had stated: 'We shall now be devoting substantially more resources to defence than had previously been planned. In allocating these, we shall be taking measures which will strengthen our general defence capability by increasing the flexibility, mobility and readiness of all three Services for operations in support of NATO and elsewhere.' NATO still came first and the wished-for 3 per cent rise in the growth of defence expenditure *in real terms* was guaranteed but, most significantly in Bramall's view, 'elsewhere' was now firmly in the frame.

He had inherited the armed forces and their supporting programmes for expenditure in much better shape than had been the case a few years earlier. The forces were immensely respected by the majority of the population, both for their fighting qualities and for the incredible feat of organisation that had enabled them to win the war in the South Atlantic so far from home. The government's financial commitment was such as to permit expectations of restoring a more sensible operational balance between the NATO continental commitment and a broader maritime strategy. There was a very real possibility that the financial momentum generated by Margaret Thatcher after the Falklands success would allow correction of the more glaring equipment weaknesses by the end of the decade, making the armed forces better placed to face an increasingly uncertain threats to the national interests.

While this looked encouraging from the Thames side of Whitehall, it was welcomed neither by the Treasury nor the other government spending departments. In their opinion the Services had had their war and won it; now matters had to be returned to the niggling normal.

Civil servants on both sides of the street regarded the new Secretary of State and CDS with different degrees of reserve. While Heseltine was perceived as a powerful but unpredictable Minister, Bramall was seen as a man of integrity and intellectual breadth akin to that of the formidable and uncompromising Field Marshal Lord Carver (CDS 1973–6) and Bramall had a winning charm such as Carver never sought to acquire. While Vice-Chief of the Defence Staff (Personnel and Logistics), Bramall had shown that he had no difficulty in raising his sights above single Service rivalries and also his understanding of Ministry of Defence mechanics, not least because he had had a close hand in assembling them twenty years earlier under Mountbatten. He was also recognised as a skilful advocate and one not easy to predict because of his technique of the oblique approach, moving off on one tack only to home in on the key issue from another.

These factors were noted by the civil side of the Ministry with a touch of concern in case any might limit the control or at least the restraint civil sevants obliged to try to exercise over the military staffs. Working as they do at the interface with the Treasury, which usually has the ultimate whip hand, civil servants – while loyal to the common objective – invariably see themselves as essential messengers of a financial position not always in accordance with military aspirations. Aware of this situation from previous experience, Brammall sought to show that he understood it by his friendly and considerate attitude to civil servants of all grades.

The options for anyone in senior office are well known: one may either sit back to conserve one's strength and influence, ready to react decisively when 'events' suddenly determine the agenda, or move forward with new ideas and try not to allow the inevitable 'events' to blow one too far off course. Bramall belonged to the latter school and sent a memorandum entitled 'Note by the CDS on the Way Ahead' to the single Service Chiefs at the end of his first month in the job. This was intended not so much as a hint towards a stronger 'out-of-area' strategy, although after the Falklands War this was bound to occur; it was more a reference on how he envisaged them all working together.

He began by emphasising the value of the power base at their disposal in the form of the Chiefs of Staff Committee and encouraged the Chiefs to act through the Committee from the earliest stage of any project involving more than one Service. He asked them individually to indicate areas with which they could find themselves in general agreement and also those on which they had major or minor reservations. This may seem an obvious point, but open-minded consultation at an early stage would help to avoid differences later on, when single Service attitudes had been formed separately, arguments had hardened and points against any policy generated from the centre rehearsed from every angle.

Personally, the principal proposal he wished to air was the urgent need for greater readiness to meet the unexpected from outside the NATO geographical area, as demonstrated by the Falklands crisis. But he knew, if he was not to put his own credibility at risk, Ministers and his fellow Chiefs had to be reassured of the inviolability of the country's NATO commitments. So his 'Note' rehearsed this hallowed ground before going on to break fresh earth. It listed the key issues he wished to pursue:

- To support and protect the Country's interests and, without eroding our freedom, avert a European war which would almost certainly overwhelm the continent if not the world. [Before collapse of the Soviet Union, this translated into any confrontation with Moscow.]
- To avoid maritime/continental arguments. [This was not intended as a hint towards an out-of-NATO-area strategy, but reference to the argument between a predominantly seaborne or continental land strategy which had soured Navy and Army relations for centuries – and which he regarded as now entirely outmoded.]
- To nudge our middle and long term defence procurement towards greater strategic mobility and flexibility to meet the unexpected.
- To refine force mix studies in the maritime areas for unexpected out-of-area operations.
- To develop our ability to support and make more dynamic our country's foreign policy, particularly out-of-area, by *helping our friends to help themselves.*

The final point was his first sally as Chief of the Defence Staff on his philosophy of the 'Fifth Pillar' explained in Chapter 1. There was a long way to go and he was to be interrupted by the unexpected.

The same 'Note' also included a steer to the VCDS (Personnel &

Logistics) to persist with the policy, which Bramall had started while in that post, of ensuring that servicemen's and women's pay, allowances and conditions of service kept pace with their equivalents in civilian life. He was to be disappointed in this, chiefly because of difficulties the new VCDS encountered in dealing with his civil servants, probably themselves inhibited by the prospect of direct interference by the Secretary of State for political presentational purposes.

Although contact with senior civil servants had been a daily event since his return to the Ministry in 1978, Bramall was to receive a blunt reminder of their attitude shortly after taking over as CDS. During a meeting with Mr John Stanley, a junior Defence Minister, he heard an Assistant Under-Secretary exclaim to the Minister, 'You do not take military advice from the military, you take it from us.' Bramall's response is unprintable.

In setting out his philosophy to the single Service Chiefs, he took great care to emphasise his commitment to them and their professional views as a counter to the development during the Falklands crisis of the CDS tendering advice to the War Cabinet on his own. Although this only occurred during the campaign, the Prime Minister still maintained her links with the Chiefs of Staff, individually and as a whole.

His 'Note' of 29 October 1982 contained this important reassurance:

I intend to keep the Chiefs of Staff Committee very much a living entity, by seeing that it meets regularly, has directed to it those matters on which HMG should, through the Secretary of State, be getting military advice, e.g. on strategy and commitments, and that it produces a consensus when it can and certainly not, as some might fear, *by merely asking the Committee's advice when this is convenient.*

Having given clear marching instructions to the single Service Chiefs, he turned to the central Defence Staffs, now operating on his direction in line with the Nott/Lewin system developed even before the Falklands crisis. He commissioned studies to review strategy in the light of perceived threats to national security, rather than by the Treasury to save money.

By keeping this work within the confines of the Defence Staffs he did not seek to deny the single Service Departments a view. He wished them to be kept in touch with the lines along which he was thinking to allow them to stimulate the work either by indicating broad agreement or by raising major reservations. This method of systematic consultation did much to ensure that relationships with his fellow Chiefs of Staff remained harmonious throughout his tenure as CDS.

Before addressing problems arising from the 1982 Defence White Paper on the Falklands experience, he decided it would be prudent to get the political and financial matter of the Trident programme out of the way. The Government decision to acquire Trident II D5 to be fitted into replacements for the British Polaris submarine hulls was noted by the Chiefs of Staff without adverse comment. By that stage, the nuclear versus conventional forces argument had largely, but not conclusively, given way to that of Europe and NATO versus unexpected, and therefore unevaluated, commitments elsewhere. While the Falklands crisis gave some credibility to the latter eventuality, it was vulnerable to dismissal as a one-off event with no similar circumstance either on the horizon or beyond it.

Every CDS since Mountbatten had faced a financially driven Defence Review or serious curtailment of expenditure. With procurement plans in fairly good shape when he took over, Bramall sensed that the time was ripe to launch his review of strategy outside the NATO area because war in Europe had become most unlikely, as the confronting alliances knew the rules of the game too well. In contrast, the rest of the world, the Middle East in particular, concealed uncertain dangers, making the likelihood for military intervention much more probable there.

In doing this, he was testing out the system agreed between Sir John Nott and Admiral of the Fleet Lord Lewin, when the former was Secretary of State and the latter CDS, whereby the Defence

Staff operated on the instructions of the CDS, with the single Service Chiefs brought in at a later stage to comment and amend where necessary.

Bramall had no quarrel with the four-pillars concept as such, but had concluded that, provided the UK continued to match its commitments to NATO and did nothing that would lower its guard or break the implied link between forward conventional defence in Central Europe and the last-ditch nuclear deterrent, war in Europe would be most unlikely. He consequently told the Central Staffs to adopt a two-handed approach by setting in train a fresh analysis of commitments and eventualities, likely and less likely, within the NATO area and on possible and hitherto undefined contingencies outside it. The former presented staff planners with the difficulties of matching Britain's resources with a wide range of NATO commitments, while the latter called for imagination to identify possible scenarios as unlikely as the Falklands War, yet remaining within the bounds of credibility.

His desk-level experience in MO 4, and on the staff of the 3rd Division in Egypt, had given Bramall insight into the complexity of Middle East affairs not shared by many of those about him when CDS. To his mind, the Arab–Israeli confrontation provided the greatest threat to stability in the region and for heightened East–West tension, or even war by proxy. But the outrages in Israel/Palestine obscured other prejudices, rivalries and uncertainties that bedevilled development of any coherent foreign policy towards either the region or its constituent countries. Britain's attitude of trying to be nice to everyone, while keeping undertakings to the absolute minimum, had become little more than a week-by-week expedient of muddling along as inexpensively as possible.

Public opinion and outrage over atrocities also had to be taken into account. While it was acceptable for Her Majesty's Government to stand smilingly clear of the Iran–Iraq War in its earlier stages, demand for something to be done quickly arose when British tankers and oil supplies were threatened by indiscriminate attack in the Arabian Gulf. Royal Navy ships deployed accordingly. A token ground force was despatched to the Lebanon in an effort to help stabilise a situation of chaotic violence, which would have been better addressed by the United States 'ordering' its irresponsibly aggressive dependant – Israel – to get out of the country and stay out.

Aside from the risks to regional and international security arising from these and other tensions in the Middle East, sordid competition in the arms trade fomented bad blood between NATO allies. Hostage taking, in the Lebanon in particular, inhibited government attitudes in public for fear of reprisal against the victims, leading to policy paralysis. All these distant but acutely distressing and prohibitive problems gave a clear guide to the relentlessly increasing importance of the Middle East as a focus for defence contingency planning, and the Chiefs of Staff gave Bramall their full support for the studies he directed towards the region.

Essentially, the Chiefs of Staff reached collective agreement to abandon the 'Critical Level' of forces implicit in the Mason–Carver 1975–6 Defence Review and make adjustments to reflect the need for a greater out-of-NATO-area intervention capability. This involved maintaining the Navy's strategic delivery and assault capabilities and assigning the ships, 3rd Commando Brigade and the 5th Airborne Brigade to out-of-area operations, as well as to NATO contingencies. The retention of the Navy's assault ships and those held by the Army for the transportation of tanks proved a shrewd investment when it became necessary to reverse Saddam Hussein's invasion of Kuwait in 1991.

The 'out-of-NATO-area' studies he initiated concentrated on steps to improve the strategic flexibility of the British forces assigned to NATO to allow them to be double-earmarked and, given an increased ability to deploy quickly elsewhere in the world, a proper capability to react more quickly to unforeseen crises like the Argentine occupation of the Falklands. In terms of geographic priorities, the Middle East was by far the most prominent region from the standpoint of maintaining world peace and looking after Britain's economic interests, in particular its oil supply. The Chiefs of Staff agreed that a stable Middle East situation was in the national interest but, because of the costs and political difficulties of stationing more forces there than the token element on Cyprus, the way forward lay in using such links as the country still had in the area to help friends to help themselves.

The value of *indirect military influence* had been Bramall's philosophy since writing his thesis 'The Application of Force' in 1970. Now, faced with a kaleidoscopically changing world situation, he saw the urgent need to pull together the strands of military assistance and contacts abroad under an out-of-area coordinating group. Only by introducing this control in support of a Fifth Pillar of British strategy would it be possible to maintain coherent political, military and economic direction.

But before those strategic studies could be brought to fruition by changes in emphasis in defence policy and consequent defence spending, he, the single Service Chiefs and their staffs were distracted by studies based on a wholly different area of examination initiated by the Secretary of State. Not unexpectedly, Michael Heseltine began by devoting his considerable energies to organisational reform of the Ministry of Defence, rather than to strategic innovation. He had arrived with a reputation for business acumen and, to put it cynically, it was easier for him to apply techniques that had served him well in the past than to apply his mind to complexities of strategy or demands for scarce military resources to match competing priorities. To his credit, his structural reforms were designed to make such matters easier to resolve and execute – and they did so.

The coincidence that Bramall was CDS when Heseltine decided on a re-organisation of the Ministry beyond the point where Mountbatten had left off, twenty years earlier, is in itself remarkable. Had he drawn on the experience of his principal military adviser at an earlier stage than he did, his proposals would have had fewer raw edges and consequently found easier acceptance by the CDS and single Service Chiefs. As it was, the Secretary of State made a conscious decision not to take the CDS into his confidence, but to present him with a *fait accompli*.

In his autobiography *Life In The Jungle*, Heseltine described this course as 'the least *undesirable* way forward': 'To have done other would either have required him [Bramall] to keep the information confidential, opening him up to charges of betrayal by his fellow military officers, or have made him feel compelled to consult them and in that case the process would have unravelled at bewildering speed.' In the same passage, he asserts that Bramall was 'deeply hurt that I didn't consult him about my plans'. In fact, Bramall was usually able to see the amusing side of an event, which might give rise to offence being taken. From a professional standpoint, however, he considered that his earlier participation would probably have brought a better overall result than was achieved by Heseltine and his Private Secretary, Richard (later Sir Richard) Mottram, working together in their closeted review of the MoD policy-making and management structure.

The aim of designing a structure capable of determining defence policy and managing its execution more efficiently and quickly than the current one while, simultaneously, reducing the number of people working in Whitehall, could scarcely be faulted. Concern arose when it became known that reducing civil service rather than uniformed staff numbers was his priority, but otherwise there was a co-operative response to Heseltine's Management Information Service (MINIS) enquiries. These were addressed to different departments to establish current methods of conducting business and introducing means of improving them. Behind these enquiries, however, the Secretary of State was planning a more radical review, that of strengthening the 'centre' of the Ministry by introducing a 'functional' structure as an alternative to the one where policy was decided at the centre and execution left to the single Service Departments to perform.

Many aspects of administration lend themselves to functionalisation – food and raw materials procurement and delivery, buildings repair and furnishing are obvious examples – but care for the interests of the end user, which can easily vary, is essential if operational efficiency is not to be compromised. Scrutiny of this, in both the development and working stages, is rapidly diminished in value if the specialists of each Service – Navy, Army and Air Force – are removed from the supervisory role. The pre-

Heseltine structure comprised a small central policy-making core with three adjacent single Service executive staffs.

Once this structure was changed to one of segments responsible for a function on behalf of all three Services, little or no place would remain for the single Service Chiefs or their staffs to apply their specialist expertise or professional knowledge. Hence the argument resolved into the *extent* to which it would be applied and where the limitations on the single Service Chiefs and their staffs would begin and end.

Whatever his other characteristics, Michael Heseltine's secretive manner of constructing his proposals and presenting a *fait accompli* to the CDS afforded Bramall the opportunity to take the proposals to the Chiefs of Staff Committee with a clear conscience. They could scarcely take issue with the Secretary of State's wish to strengthen his hand in his own Ministry, nor with pooling their similar requirements into one functional department. Nevertheless, it was necessary for them to recognise that, whatever compromise would eventually be achieved, some erosion of their authority was inevitable. As the aim of the reforms was to improve the machinery for decision-making, they could hardly take issue with that either, so they were left with responsibility only for recommending *how* the Heseltine reforms could be implemented to best effect for their own Service and its operational functions.

After careful consideration of the central proposals, the Chiefs of Staff Committee put forward their views, both supportive and critical, to the Secretary of State immediately before he was due to put the broad outline of his plan to his Cabinet colleagues. This took the form of a Note signed on 13 June 1984. Subsequently the Chiefs met the Secretary of State on several occasions to discuss points of detail. Not assured that this would be sufficient to reserve their positions, the Chiefs addressed a new Note to Heseltine on 29 June 1984 and, as he was anxious to maintain a constructive debate, Bramall took it to the Secretary of State personally and waited while he read it. Here is what it said.

DEFENCE REORGANISATION

1. You will shortly be telling your Cabinet colleagues what you propose on Defence Reorganisation, and we feel it appropriate to remind you of our views – supportive as well as critical. These were forwarded to you under our four signatures on 13 June. Since then you have met us on certain points of detail, but our overall reservations and serious misgivings remain valid.

2. The Chiefs of Staff feel responsible for ensuring that any new organisation will stand up in a crisis irrespective of who occupies the highest positions at the time and this is where our greatest concern lies.

3. We believe that we can make your proposals work satisfactorily in peacetime, and that central control and allocation of resources may well be improved and certainly made easier for you to handle by the arrangements we have now agreed upon. We also accept that the Ministry of Defence is too large and fully support your determination to streamline the system wherever possible.

4. However, we cannot accept that the new proposals will provide the Government with sound professional advice in a crisis involving warlike operations. Your proposals undoubtedly aim at reducing the influence of individual Chiefs of Staff on defence policy and distancing them from the development of that policy. They will also inevitably dilute the expertise that the Chiefs of Staff can call upon, blur the lines of their responsibility for the effectiveness of their service and ultimately diminish the quality of advice available to the Government in a crisis. Thus, since we may live to regret these decisions in the event of war, we believe Cabinet Ministers should fully understand these implications and appreciate our grave concern.

5. We request that this note should be laid before the Cabinet when they consider your White Paper.

The Note was initialled by the CDS and the three single Service Chiefs of Staff. After reading it through, Michael Heseltine looked up and remarked, 'I think this is the biggest piece of political chicanery I have ever come across.' 'Well, Secretary of State', Bramall replied with his usual wry smile, 'I would expect you to recognise that when you see it.'

At noon on 4 July, the CDS had an audience with Margaret Thatcher to explain the principal areas of concern that he and the single Service Chiefs held regarding Michael Heseltine's proposals. After assuring the Prime Minister that he and his fellow Chiefs were in no sense seeking to provoke a confrontation with the Defence Minister, Bramall explained his qualifications for adopting a strong position on defence organisation, namely his service with Lord Mountbatten in the 1960s, his careful observation of the disastrous experiment with unification of the Canadian Armed Forces and his recent participation in the changes brought about so successfully by Sir John Nott and Lord Lewin. Then, having accepted that the new proposed changes would be manageable in a *minor crisis* and for the routine allocation of resources, he made clear that a functionalisation beyond the point where Mountbatten had halted would impair the sound management and effectiveness of the individual and separate Services and the balance between policy and management.

Turning to the Note sent to the Secretary of State on 29 June, which the Prime Minister had seen, he explained its purpose 'to emphasise our deep concern and to bring it home that we were going down a quite discernible and different path as regards the position of the Chiefs of Staff, the implications and consequences of which should be taken fully into account'. In essence, the heart of the matter was that if the single Service Chiefs were to be distanced from the development of policy and yet keep three separate Services, expertise would be diluted, lines of responsibility would be blurred and ultimately the quality and credibility of specialist advice to Her Majesty's Government in a real crisis would be diminished.

An elegant way out of this *impasse* had to be found. Even though Michael Heseltine was not, even then, the apple of Margaret Thatcher's eye, her instinct was to support her Secretary of State. She decided therefore to adopt the view that, under the Heseltine proposals, the Chiefs of Staff felt they would lose control of their respective Services and so their ability to influence events effectively in a crisis. In the mind of a politician, 'control' and 'influence' can be taken to mean either quite different things or virtually the same thing, depending on whether one is seeking a difference or a similarity. Margaret Thatcher decided on this occasion that they meant virtually the same thing and so turned the issue into one of the Chiefs' access to her and the Cabinet, rather than of actual day-to-day control of the individual Services.

In the record of the meeting between the Prime Minister and the Chief of the Defence Staff, her Private Secretary – (later Lord) Robin Butler – after giving an account of the views expressed, concluded with two key statements:

> The Prime Minister recognised that there was a reluctance about proceeding from the known to the unknown but she believed that if the Chiefs of Staff gave the new organisation a chance they would find it to be an improvement. [In simple terms, 'Nice try but now get on and do as you are told'.] The Prime Minister said that it would be right to review the new organisation when it had been given a reasonable time to settle down and to work. She also repeated that the Chiefs of Staff would continue to have right of access to the Prime Minister and she would see advantage in annual meetings with them.

Although controversial at the time, Heseltine's reforms of the Ministry of Defence do not appear to have inflicted serious damage on the efficient functioning of the Navy, Army or Air Force. That this can be explained away through the seemingly endless adaptability of the Services, and the fact that some of the functions drawn to the centre were later 'clawed back' to the single Service Departments, but this does not excuse the extent to which the Chiefs of Staff were distracted from their primary planning functions by the *manner* in which the reforms were introduced.

One immediate outcome was the introduction by Bramall of Heads of Department meetings, or 'HODs', involving the Deputy

Under-Secretary (Policy) and all Deputy Chiefs of Staff and senior members of the Defence Staff. While this would not necessarily prevent another *coup de maître* by the Secretary of State, it would make the exclusion of the military members of the Defence Staff more difficult to achieve, as it emphasised the position of the Defence Policy Staff under the CDS.

From the single Services' standpoint, however, the reforms inflicted a serious blow by removing the powerful Vice-Chiefs of Staff. Invariably very experienced men with plenty of fire in their bellies, the Vice-Chiefs had customarily formed a powerful partnership capable of frustrating almost any initiative from the centre that did not suit their collective book, which the civil side found difficult if not impossible to brush aside.

If the single Service Chiefs needed reassurance of their continued influence, Bramall provided it by re-emphasising the importance of the Chiefs of Staff Committee and its position firmly over the top of and in control of the Central Staff. This situation and the Chiefs' influence with those of their own Service within the Central Staff allowed watch to be kept on the Office of Management and Budget, which had been set up to look ahead for storms arising in the seldom tranquil waters of the ten-year-ahead rolling defence budget. The clear link between this Office and the Treasury was a constant reminder of how tempting it would be for the civil servants to discern defence economies that might be used to help the Treasury out of a hole caused by an unexpected financial crisis or mismanagement somewhere or other.

The final year (1985) of Dwin Bramall's tenure as CDS was dominated by explaining the impact of the Heseltine reforms (which came into effect on 1 January 1985) to the three Services and reassuring them that no damage to their operational capabilities should result. He also had to explain two other difficult financial issues. The first of these was the government's decision, in the light of the country's deepening recession, to 'come off', in effect renege on, the commitment to maintain the 3 per cent growth in NATO-related defence expenditure for seven years from 1979 agreed by the Callaghan administration. Michael Heseltine helped him in this with his formidable salesmanship in encouraging closer cooperation with the UK's European allies in defence equipment design and development. Even so, when the UK was often in a position to set a good example to NATO partners, Bramall did not relish the prospect of explaining, either directly or indirectly through the military and civil service representatives at NATO headquarters in Brussels, what amounted to a failure of the UK to keep an important promise.

The second financial issue was the decision to stage the implementation of the 1984 pay awards to servicemen and women recommended by the Armed Forces Pay Review Body. This was a Treasury-driven decision occasioned by the UK's economic circumstances, but it was a difficult matter to put across to servicemen and their families who were to suffer the result. Worse, Bramall faced the possibility of the next pay award being similarly staged – thereby losing its positive impact in avoiding recurrence of the haemorrhage of skilled Service manpower that characterised the late 1970s and early 1980s. There was also the danger that the Secretary of State, Michael Heseltine, skilful politician that he was, would contrive some politically appealing sleight of hand which would look good, but leave nothing extra in the serviceman's pocket.

Events had not allowed Bramall to leave his post as Chief of the Defence Staff on such a peak of achievement as characterised the departure of his predecessor, Lord Lewin, after the Falklands War. He had handled the Heseltine MoD restructuring with skill and tact, however, and, more significantly from the operational standpoint, he had got the Chiefs of Staff off the hook of allocating resources to NATO commitments when they were more urgently required to meet the less obvious but rumbling threats outside the NATO area. He had resolutely drawn the attention of Ministers to the dangers evident in the Middle East and arising in south-west Asia, seemingly to little avail, but subsequent developments were to prove him uncannily perspicacious.

He had shown himself to be a shrewd manipulator of the long-term costings of the defence procurement programme, while leaving the year-to-year management of the actual acquisition and bringing the weapon systems and equipment into service to the senior officers responsible. This field had been one of comparative plenty in the early years of his period as CDS, but the situation had reverted to one of cheese-paring, because of economic factors beyond governmental control. Throughout, he had demonstrated a strict impartiality over the funding demands from rival programmes sponsored by the three Services, making plain not just a sense of fairness but, rather more importantly, a comprehensive grasp of the strategic issues, which led to priority being accorded to those most urgently needed in the broad national interest.

In terms of handling those around him, he had maintained a sense of harmony and trust in the Chiefs of Staff Committee, perhaps most particularly over the initial discussions and then the implementation of the reforms to the MoD structure. His relationship with Ministers and top civil servants had been subjected to severe strain, most significantly at the time of being quite excluded, by design, from the deliberations of the Secretary of State and his Private Secretary over the blue-print for the greater centralisation of control in the MoD. Even then, he had skilfully avoided being isolated by his good humour – if just a touch rueful at times – and innate good manners. This had helped to strengthen his own hand in the crafting of policy without diminishing the authority of the single Service Chiefs of Staff, indeed – where he judged it appropriate – he had encouraged the clawing back of some power lost by them to the centre in consequence of the Heseltine restructuring.

When he left the Ministry of Defence Main Building for the last time as CDS, he left behind staffs who felt they knew him well and respected his dedication and personal care for their views and well-being – and there was no doubt about the genuineness of his taking even relatively junior staff into his confidence and his wish to hear their views. Primarily, however, the insistent need for him to react to events, rather than be proactive, had left him with the personal unease of unfinished business. This was especially the case of his 'crusade' to bring foreign and defence policy into much closer cohesion in the future and in the country's essential interests. So he resolved not to let this matter rest.

17

Covering the Waterfront

Completion of Dwin Bramall's term as Chief of the Defence Staff in October 1985 deprived him of his personal staff and office, while leaving him with a rapidly extending range of demanding public, charitable, military and other responsibilities. One or two of these might have been discharged from his recently acquired home in a village in north-east Hampshire, but he would have needed a full-time secretary and a base in London. The question of a base was largely resolved in January 1986 when, on the advice of the Prime Minister – Margaret Thatcher – he was appointed Her Majesty's Lord Lieutenant of Greater London and was able to move into the Lieutenancy Office, at first in the old County Hall and then in the Westminster County Offices in Victoria Street. The appointment also provided him with the services of the Clerk to the Lieutenancy, the wise and humorous Mr George Gordon-Smith, who was responsible for guiding the Lord Lieutenant through the intricacies of the London scene and organising his participation as Her Majesty's representative. Gordon-Smith became a firm friend to the Field Marshal, giving him his loyal and enthusiastic backing over the wider field during the next phase of his public life.

The office of Lord Lieutenant dates from the reign of Henry VIII and is of military origin, the incumbent originally being responsible for law and order in the capital and, from 1715, for the readiness and training of the local militia. This task was removed by the Regulation of Forces Act of 1871, but it was not until 1921 that he was deprived of his power to call on all able-bodied men of the country to fight, should the need arise, leaving the post largely ceremonial in nature but nevertheless a significant call on the Lord Lieutenant's time, as he is kept in touch with the reserve forces and cadets by being the *ex-officio* President of their respective associations. The Lord Lieutenant is the Queen's representative in the thirty-two boroughs of Greater London, which excludes the City, where the Lord Mayor acts as the Lord Lieutenant during his year of office. As all the royal households are based within Greater London, the Lord Lieutenant's direct involvement with the detailed planning of royal visits within the capital is less than it might otherwise be. The very frequency of such visits would make even his attendance at all of them quite impossible.

The Lord Lieutenant is invariably required to attend upon the Queen on Her Majesty's departure on official visits overseas and to receive foreign heads of state on their arrival in London on state visits. After the monarch, the Lord Lieutenant heads the receiving line – even before the Prime Minister and members of the Cabinet. On the first occasion Bramall appeared in this way, the Prime Minister, Margaret Thatcher, said to him with a distinctly pained expression, 'I think you are supposed to go in front of me,' as if to imply that such an arrangement was quite bizarre.

The Lord Lieutenant also presents certain medals on behalf of the Queen, for example, the Queen's Police and Fire Service medals and Commendations for Brave Conduct. He also holds *ex-officio* appointments with a range of Greater London charitable bodies and receives more requests to attend official and semi-official functions than he could possibly fulfil. An essential part of Bramall's character was to treat every event in an individual way, to research the background to the occasion and the principal individuals attending, so that he could deliver a speech appropriate to the moment.

A little-known responsibility of the Lord Lieutenant of Greater London, and of those of other counties or county boroughs, is the handling of recommendations for honours and awards to deserving individuals living within his region of responsibility. This pre-dates the introduction of the 'citizen's awards' system introduced by John Major when he was Prime Minister, which does not appear to have reduced the burden on the Lord Lieutenant, particularly when the nominations are submitted through him or where any going direct to the Nominations Unit in the Cabinet Office require a local enquiry because of insufficient supporting evidence or other information.

There are many anecdotes about Bramall's time as Lord Lieutenant, usually highly complimentary about his relaxed style and ability to talk easily with people from all walks of life. Frock coat and decorations were almost invariably the costume for day occasions. His role as a trustee of the Imperial War Museum, undertaken before leaving the Army, came in useful on the occasion when he discovered he had left his Field Marshal's baton at home halfway to an occasion in London by car. A telephone call from the museum's Director-General to the National Army Museum led to the baton of the late Field Marshal Sir Evelyn Wood VC being borrowed from its display case and delivered to the place of parade in the nick of time. A more serious concern arose after a ceremonial tree-planting; during his return to the office, he realised that his Garter Star was missing, but a telephone call and a bit of surreptitious excavation revealed that he had planted it with the tree.

A strong republican undercurrent was evident in the capital in the mid-1980s, making the tasks of many of the thirty or so Representative Deputy Lieutenants in the London boroughs distinctly uncomfortable. Bramall did what he could to encourage them and made a personal effort to talk up the Monarchy whenever possible. His interview by the BBC's early morning Today programme following the death of Diana, Princess of Wales, was especially effective. The fact that his elder brother, Sir Ashley Bramall, was a London Labour councillor and a former Chairman of the Greater London Council and the Inner London Education Authority proved a great help, as his brother was widely known and had great standing – and not just in the socialist sphere. Even so, the Lord Lieutenant's furrow was not always easy to plough in those days and demanded much of his patience and tact.

Following the mandatory six months' pause after relinquishing his post as Chief of the Defence Staff, Bramall joined Vickers Defence Systems as a Director. At first, some board members suspected that his air of acute concentration during board meetings might be due to him surreptitiously drafting speeches for other occasions – until he began to ask questions! His nerve, and that of others, was tested at the opening of a publicity launch, when a Mark III Vickers tank from the company's museum was driven down the centre isle as he prepared to make his preliminary remarks, then halted with the gun barrel just inches from his ear – a fine demonstration of precision driving. His commitment to the company's interests was perhaps no more forcefully demonstrated than when, during a reception at Lancaster House, he took a senior British civil servant, who was recommending purchase of the United States M1 Abrams tank for the Army, by the lapels of his jacket and – in the words of the Chairman, Sir David Plastow – 'Shook him until the chandeliers jangled'. He was not to regret this display of enthusiasm, but rather to delight in Vickers winning the contract to supply the Army with the far superior Challenger II tank.

He had become a member of MCC's Committee in 1986, so was as familiar with the problems at Lord's as with the challenges facing the trustees of the Imperial War Museum. In 1988 he became President of MCC and in the following year chairman of trustees of the Imperial War Museum. Both institutions faced difficult and demanding problems. The renovation of the Imperial War Museum's main building in Lambeth Road was completed under Bramall's chairmanship and the Museum now covers conflicts from 1914. The new permanent display on special forces was supported by the late Sir Paul Getty, whose love of cricket brought him and Bramall together at Lord's and at Getty's home at Wormsley in Oxfordshire, providing an intriguing link between Lord's and Lambeth.

As President, Bramall was a member of MCC's newly formed Executive Committee at the end of the 1980s when MCC's relationship with the Test and County Cricket Board (TCCB) had all but broken down, following the erosion of MCC's powers by the TCCB, which had assumed responsibility for English cricket. Understandably it was felt to be impossible to hand over government funding to a private club, however distinguished. From 1968, therefore, the TCCB had become the official ruling power in

English cricket, despite Lord's remaining the Mecca of the game and the venue at which every national team wished to play.

This dichotomy was to cause difficulties and misunderstandings for years to come. Communication between the Club and the Board might have broken down altogether but for the trump card MCC held. The money generated by a test match at Lord's was far greater than the receipts of any other test match ground. MCC needed its test match and the Board needed the money this generated. Such issues as advertising and television rights led to regular wrangling, but gradually the relationship began to settle down, not least because of the diplomatic skills of Lord Bramall and others, who were often cast in the role of mediator both during his term of presidency and when it had finished.

The greatest test of his diplomacy arose during his chairmanship of the International Cricket Conference (ICC) in 1988–9. The outstanding point of contention was the increasing number of individual players taking part in matches in South Africa at a time when the majority of ICC member countries felt that a ban on such participation would add significant weight to the international campaign against apartheid in South Africa, where there is such enthusiasm for sport of all kinds. The other side of this argument is that England's cricketers, in particular, have only six-month summer contracts, unless they are selected for a winter tour abroad, and a winter tour in South Africa provides an opportunity for round-the-year employment. This point was taken up by the Cricketers' Association of county players, which together with the Freedom Association in the United Kingdom, argued that any ban on their playing in South Africa would be a 'restraint of trade'.

The ICC met under Lord Bramall's chairmanship in the Committee Room at Lord's on 24 January 1989 to address this issue. Although it was predicted in some sections of the press that England would try to impose what might amount to a veto on any sanction against 'rebel' players who continued to play in South Africa, the eventual outcome was a unanimous vote in favour of a ban from playing test cricket on any player breaking the embargo. The sanction was severe, five years' exclusion from test cricket on any player who had 'sporting contact' in South Africa, but the ban was not to be retrospective, leaving so-called 'offenders' with clean sheets. After two days' deliberation, the press were invited into the Long Room to hear Lord Bramall announce,

> I want to make it absolutely clear that I am speaking to you as the impartial chairman of ICC, provided traditionally by the President of MCC. Throughout, the aim of everyone has been the health, the unity and the continuity of international cricket. I am confident that the unanimously agreed steps will clear up the current uncertainty and disarray of international cricket.

The 'amnesty' that prevented players who had gone to South Africa being penalised went a long way in taking the sting out of the ICC ruling. It was also revealed that the then Commonwealth Secretary, Sir 'Sonny' Ramphal, had seen the resolution in draft and said he was available for consultaion should the ICC so desire.

Lord Bramall had done all in his power to establish a more congenial atmosphere, not just over the South Africa tours issue but also over the relationship between MCC and the TCCB. But his brief chairmanship of ICC terminated with his presidency of MCC at the end of September 1989, as the two roles went together. He supported successfully the proposal that future MCC presidents should serve for two years, to give better opportunity for them to tackle and solve such problems as arose during their tenure. The idea was adopted for almost a decade, but the presidency then reverted to the single-year system on grounds that two-year tenures excluded too many candidates of quality from holding the office.

Subsequent to his presidency of MCC, Bramall worked closely with the new chairman of the ICC, Colin Cowdrey, later Lord Cowdrey, whose appointment he had sponsored in the light of the wishes of other cricketing countries not to have the chairmanship of the international body permanently linked to the MCC and therefore to the United Kingdom. He also worked harmoniously with Raman Subba Row, Chairman of the TCCB, to enable the South African Cricket Board to come back into the fold of international cricket, as soon as politics allowed and on terms acceptable to all the test-playing nations. The success of his presidency owed much to his cricket background and his understanding of the game at all levels. He had been a fine club player as a young man and was determined to do all in his power to safeguard the standards of fair play and good behaviour upon which the game ultimately depends. He remained on MCC's Main Committee until 1997 and then became an Honorary Life Vice-President of the Club. One of the happiest memories current at Lord's of his presidency was the part played by Lady Bramall. As hostess of the President's Box in the test matches she made every guest feel special, never forgetting a name or neglecting an introduction.

His own energy and breadth of interest were never more evident than in his dealings with young people. This was apparent in his years on the Council of Radley College. His regular attendance at meetings of the Council was astonishing when the enormous workload he shouldered is taken into account. He enjoyed talking with the boys, discovering what motivated them and appreciated drawing them out, advising them and putting them in touch with people who could help them in their career plans.

During this same period, he and his friend General Sir William Jackson had been working together writing an anecdotal history of the Chiefs of the Naval, General and Air Staffs and – from inception of the post – the Chief of the Defence Staff. Bill Jackson, former Quartermaster-General and the Governor of Gibraltar during the Falklands campaign, was a historian of repute and had previously published several books. Their combined work, titled *The Chiefs*, reflects the writing styles of both men but results in a cohesive account of the thoughts and actions of the Service Chiefs when confronting the wide span of crises facing Britain and its vital interests from 1904 to 1991. It was well reviewed on both sides of the Atlantic.

At the time Bramall joined the Imperial War Museum trustees, the Chairman was the late Marshal of the Royal Air Force Sir John Grandy, a Battle of Britain pilot, former Chief of the Air Staff and a man of great drive and self-confidence. The first phase of the restoration of the main building of the one-time Bedlam Hospital, and the modernisation of the displays it contained, was completed under Grandy's chairmanship. Bramall was left to carry through the second phase, but more immediately to secure the agreement and funding for the American Air Museum to be built at Duxford, which had been an American air base during the war, a project that Grandy had begun but had been unable to launch before becoming seriously ill shortly after handing over to him.

The project was controversial, in that not everyone, certainly not all the trustees, considered it appropriate for a museum displaying the aircraft and weapons of the US Air Force to be established in Britain. Like Grandy before him, Bramall was strongly of the view that the exploits of the 8th US Air Force, which had been based in Britain since mid-1942 and had played a critical part in the strategic bombing offensive against Germany and in securing air superiority over northern France in time for the D-Day invasion, was most worthy of recognition by present and future generations. The project was dependent on the cooperation of the appropriate authorities in the United States as well as in Britain, and, before handing over, Sir John Grandy had established an excellent working relationship with Charlton Heston, the American actor and Chairman of the United States Museum Appeal. Sir John had also arranged for high-level royal family and political support for the fund-raising enterprises across the Atlantic.

Bramall and Dr Alan Borg, Director-General of the Imperial War Museum for the first six years of the nine of his chairmanship, made fund-raising tours to the United States. Dinners in the American fund-raising style were arranged with the Duke of York on several occasions and with Margaret Thatcher on one occasion in Houston, Texas, attending as a special supporter. Bramall made speeches in Dallas, Houston, Los Angeles, New York, Washington and many other American cities. One of the Field Marshal's several minor vanities was his undoubted skill as a map-reader and consequent ability to find his way in territory unknown to him. En route to the dinner venue in Los Angeles the taxi driver confessed to being lost. Bramall, who had the city map open on his knee, leant forward with, 'I think if you take the next right and then second left, you will find what we are looking for.' They did.

Bramall's and Borg's joint powers of persuasion led to a grant from the British Heritage Lottery Fund of £6.5 million, which established the initial viability of the project, and a total of $22.8 million from private and public subscriptions from the United States between 1989 and 2003. The Museum was opened by the Queen on 1 August 1997. An average of 450,000 visitors per year have since viewed the display of the twenty-two types of US aircraft flown in combat in the twentieth century.

During the twelve months up to May 1995, as Lord Lieutenant of Greater London, Lord Bramall had been a knowledgeable and greatly valued member of the Second World War Commemoration Team, under the chairmanship of Viscount Cranborne, charged with the arrangements for the events in London to mark the fiftieth anniversary of the end of the war in May 1945. This was much more than keeping an eye on the military niceties and correctness in what was being planned. No one on the team had his knowledge and understanding of how the celebrations had to be staged, the proper sequence of events or what should be included and what, if pressure so required, might safely be left out.

His role as Lord Lieutenant was to receive the Queen and the Duke of Edinburgh at the Ceremony of Peace and Reconciliation in Hyde Park on Sunday, 7 May and, on the previous evening, to receive Queen Elizabeth the Queen Mother and Princess Margaret at the dramatic opening ceremony in Hyde Park. Throughout the long parade of veterans and those representing organisations taking part, the Lord Lieutenant could be seen at the Queen's side assiduously and enthusiastically explaining each group, however small, to Her Majesty and pointing out individuals of special account: a Gurkha VC, a survivor of a long-forgotten campaign or wartime incident and especially civilians who had endured great hardship during the war.

More challenging than the American Air Museum was the proposal to establish an exhibition depicting the 'Holocaust' – the mass murder of Jews in Nazi-occupied Europe between 1941 and 1945 – at the Imperial War Museum site in Southwark. The project had developed from Bramall's conviction that the concluding element of the Museum's redevelopment scheme should confront the theme of ethnic violence, and the many terrible instances throughout the twentieth century of 'Man's inhumanity to Man'. It soon became apparent that there was a strong demand – from the educational sector in particular – for a narrative exhibition on the history of the Holocaust. And so it was decided to devote the greater part of the new spaces released in the Museum building to this depressing but historically important theme. (A 'sister' exhibition on the top floor dealing with the broader notion of genocide would open in 2002.)

The Holocaust project was not without its critics. Within the Museum staff and among some of the trustees, there was concern over whether the Holocaust was not too radical a departure from the Museum's central theme of war. Would the public really come to such a display, or would it just be extremely depressing and therefore repelling? Outside the Museum, there was a nervousness – among Jewish academics in particular – at what the Imperial War Museum might 'do' with the Holocaust, and whether a national museum would be free to comment on the less palatable aspects of Britain's involvement, such as why the Allies had failed to bomb Auschwitz or the railways on which the Jews were being transported to death camps.

While understanding these reactions, Bramall was able to counter them on both intellectual and practical grounds. To him, the Holocaust was a horrific event in the history of conflict in the twentieth century, which the Museum had already started to portray (an exhibition on the relief of Belsen had been initiated by the Museum's Director-General, Alan Borg, in the early 1990s). He argued that an exhibition set up under Jewish auspices, no matter how prominently sited or publicised, would primarily attract Jewish visitors, while a permanent exhibition in the Lambeth Road site in Southwark would provide a memorial that many other faiths could see and remember. On matters of historical balance, Bramall reassured the doubters that the Museum had a long tradition of delivering historical subject matter to the public and promised a fair and honest interpretation.

He set about the task with determination and sensitivity to the various cultural and historical issues raised. Fact-finding visits to Holocaust museums provided both inspiration and support. The United States Holocaust Museum in Washington – opened in 1993 and created in part by filmmakers who had worked on the famous *World at War* television series which the Museum had partnered back in the 1970s – provided a reassuring model of how the story of the Holocaust could be told in exhibition form. This acclaimed Museum – which had received over a million visitors in its first year of opening – would later give the IWM team much valued advice on acquiring artefacts for the showcases.

A visit to Israel with Robert Crawford (who had succeeded Alan Borg as Director-General of the Museum in 1995) and Suzanne Bardgett (the Holocaust Exhibition's director) afforded other examples of exhibition-making on this theme, with tours of Yad Vashem, the memorial museum in Jerusalem, and Lohamei Hagetaot, the ghetto fighters' museum in the north of Israel. Bramall found especially moving and illuminating a number of encounters with Holocaust survivors, including the historian Professor Yisrael Guttman, the survivor of the Warsaw ghetto who went on to become an eminent historian of Polish Jewry. A visit to the Museum of the Diaspora in Tel Aviv brought the opportunity to meet its inspired creator, Jeshajahu 'Shaike' Weinberg – the remarkable Polish-born computer developer turned theatre director turned museum creator, whose concept of narrative-led exhibitions did much to inspire the IWM team.

A press conference was held in April 1996 – presided over by Bramall – at which the exhibition proposal was given unequivocal support. Lord Runcie, the former Archbishop of Canterbury, described his terrible shock when, as a young officer, he entered the concentration camp at Bergen–Belsen. Sir Martin Gilbert, the well-known historian and biographer of Churchill, spoke movingly of Britain's relationship with the Holocaust story. Rabbi Hugo Gryn – at that time Britain's best-known Holocaust survivor and a regular contributor to Radio 4's *The Moral Maze* – emphasised the huge educational importance of the enterprise.

In November that year, Bramall was invited to Israel to give the prestigious Balfour Memorial Lecture – an occasion that allowed him to look back over Britain's relationship with Israel and to explain to those present the Holocaust Exhibition plans. He began by paying tribute to Doctor Chaim Weizmann for his work as Director of the British Admiralty laboratories 1916–19 and his part in the preparation of the Balfour Declaration of November 1917. He touched on the problems Britain had encountered in discharging the League of Nations mandate for Palestine impartially between the Arab and Jewish populations and interests, and the complexities of the search for political settlement in the Middle East, but his main theme was the Holocaust Museum.

Changing his tone of voice, he explained:

I wish to take this opportunity to say why we think it is so important that Britain should have its own record, at national level, of those terrible events which Winston Churchill described as the most horrible crime in the whole history of the world, and to be able to disseminate the vital lessons of those ghastly days to as wide a public as possible and, particularly as we approach the next Millennium, to the young who already have it in our National Education Curriculum. The Imperial War Museum has already over a million visitors a year and rising, so we will be spreading the net wide and not just preaching to the converted.

The first reason why we think it is not only vital for future generations to learn about the Holocaust but it is entirely and properly within the remit of our Museum, and here I speak as part of the Second World War generation which took part in the Normandy invasion and final conquest of Nazi Germany, is that nothing convinced us young soldiers more that we had been fighting a just war, and whatever steps we had to take to achieve victory were justified, than discovery by British forces of the concentration camp at Bergen-Belsen, those at Dachau and Buchenwald discovered by the Americans and Majdanek and Auschwitz by the Russians.

As usual, however daunting the topic, he sought to introduce a touch of humour at the beginning, in the middle and – if it were not likely to cloud his message – at the end of a speech. He knew a good Jewish story but was experiencing some doubts as to how well it would be received by the Tel Aviv audience but, egged on by George Gordon-Smith, Clerk to the Lord Lieutenancy and the British Ambassador in Tel Aviv, David Manning, on whom he tried it out, he told it towards the end of his address. It concerned the occasion, perhaps apocryphal, when the Chief Rabbi was having lunch with King George VI at Buckingham Palace just after Dunkirk and before the Battle of Britain, when the King was very worried and asked the Chief Rabbi how he thought events would turn out. 'Don't worry, your Majesty,' came the reply, 'I'm sure it will be all right in the end, but have you thought of putting a few of your colonies in your wife's name?'

The relatively brief and most impressive reply was given by Mr Ehud Barak, previously Chief of Staff of the Israel Defence Force and future Israeli Prime Minister. He expressed his sincere regard for the British Armed Forces, which he had seen under training in Britain, sent a clear message on the importance he attached to the Middle East peace process and ended with the fervent hope that the twenty-first century would later be termed 'The Century of Peace'. Both men were heard in silence, a rare compliment in Israel, and the response to the sentiments they expressed was enthusiastic. On the following day, Lord Bramall received a personal letter from Mrs Amina Harris, wife of the Chairman of the Anglo-Jewish Society, in which she wrote,

The clarity with which you presented the British position on Palestine, moving from events in Egypt in 1915 and culminating in your personal response to the Second World War and the Holocaust, was inspiring. I now understand your deeply personal commitment to establishing the Holocaust wing at the Imperial War Museum. Thank you.

In the United Kingdom, a number of key individuals in the Jewish community gave their support to the IWM scheme. Lord

Wolfson of Marylebone – formerly one of the Museum's trustees – hosted a meeting of what became the 'Founding Patrons' to take the plan forward. It included a number of leading members of the Jewish community in Britain, together with the historian Sir Martin Gilbert, a leading survivor Ben Helfgott and the Israeli ambassador. Bramall took Lord Wolfson up to the roof of the Museum and showed him the site of the proposed exhibition, at that stage an unsightly jumble of Victorian-era outbuildings. The scale of the project was immediately apparent, and Lord Wolfson shortly afterwards pledged one million pounds. A similar sum was promised by Stephen Rubin, the sportswear manufacturer who devotes much effort and funds to supporting Holocaust education.

Armed with these generous pledges, Bramall sought support for the project, and letters from the leaders of the three main political parties were obtained and added to the very substantial prospectus, which Bramall then laid before the Heritage Lottery Fund. 'The trustees', he told them, 'are unanimous in believing that the time had now come to record permanently that horrific chapter in twentieth century.' He then went on to remind his listeners of the unequivocal all-Party support that had already been given, adding that it would have been scarcely sensible to proceed with the project at all if the ground had not been cleared politically. In doing this and, at the same time, establishing the argument for the exhibition being set up permanently in the museum, he referred to the launch of the public appeal that the former Archbishop of Canterbury, Lord Runcie, and he had made in April 1996.

Quoting, he said:

Having said the Trustees were unanimous in believing that the time had now come to record permanently that horrific chapter in 20th century European history, the calculated and systematic extermination of over six million Jews in Europe, which had become known as the Holocaust, I explained that the wartime generation, like Lord Runcie and myself, which had taken part in the Normandy invasion and the conquest of Nazi Germany, believed themselves justified in what they were doing because

Hitler and his evil regime had to be beaten, and this was confirmed by discovery of the concentration camps at Auschwitz, Bergen–Belsen, Buchenwald and Dachau.

Eventually news came that the Lottery bid had been successful, and – boosted by the promise of a grant of £12.6 million for the building and its exhibition – the Exhibition's creative and curatorial team started work. Lord Bramall would regularly drop in on this young and highly motivated team – which included Polish, German, Czech and Russian speakers – whose research work took them all over Europe. Phone calls from Bathurst House would bring recommendations of television programmes the team were urged to watch, and suggestions of especially strong quotes that might convey particular points to the public. On 27 February 1997, the Museum was visited by Mr Izer Weizmann, President of Israel and nephew of Dr Chaim Weizmann the first President, and his wife. Lord Bramall welcomed them and explained the plans for the Holocaust Exhibition, concluding with the words, 'On all counts we believe that this is the place (in Britain) to tell the story as it happened and, as we approach the Millennium, as a lesson and a warning to future generations that such evil must never be allowed to happen again, as it so easily could if we are not on our guard.'

It was with some apprehension that the completed exhibition was unveiled to the press in June 2000, but verdicts on it were extremely positive. The sombre black-and-white photographs and voices of survivors (whose testimony can be heard on a series of videos) bring an absolute hush on visitors. But the cattle truck, in which so many thousands of the Holocaust victims were transported to the death camps, is perhaps the most poignant exhibit. The scale and ruthless method of mass murder are apparent in the model of the 'ramp' at Auschwitz Birkenau, where Jews deported from Hungary are shown being selected either for slave labour or for immediate murder in the gas chambers.

By 2005, the Holocaust Exhibition has had nearly one and a half million visitors. It has brought new audiences to the Imperial War Museum, and has more than vindicated Bramall's determination that knowledge of so terrible a crime should reach as wide an audience as possible. In February 2001, the President of the International Council of Christians and Jews – Sir Sigmund Sternberg – presented Lord Bramall with the Inter-Faith Gold Medallion at a special reception staged at the Imperial War Museum. In his speech of acceptance and thanks, he paid generous tribute to those who had inspired him with the idea of the Holocaust Exhibition and had done so much to see it through to completion. Making particlar mention of Dr Alan Borg and Mr Robert Crawford, Directors-General of the Museum over the period, and to Miss Suzanne Bardgett, the Project Director and Miss Penny Ritchie Calder, the Museum's Director of Exhibitions, he said: 'These are the ones who deserve the praise and I am so glad they are here this evening with me as I receive this medallion because I feel I am accepting it on behalf of their whole team.'

Bramall ceased to be Lord Lieutenant of Greater London in 1998 and gave up the chairmanship of the Imperial War Museum Trustees that year. He therefore felt able to accept an invitation to become Chairman of the Travellers Club, of which he had been a dedicated member save for a brief interval shortly after the war. As a young officer of unusually broad interests, including a passion for travel, he had originally chosen the Travellers rather than one of London's several military clubs.

The Club had been founded in 1819 by the then Foreign Secretary, Lord Castlereagh, together with other distinguished British travellers, to provide a congenial forum in which to meet and entertain foreign visitors. Its building in Pall Mall, designed by the young Sir Charles Barry, is modelled on a classical Florentine palazzo, and contains some of the finest public rooms in London. In his lapidary *Companion Guide to London*, written in 1980, David Piper described the Club as 'modest in its small elegance but immensely smart, both easy in manner and very sophisticated'.

Bramall thrived within this stimulating and eclectic mix of serving and retired diplomats, lawyers, journalists and such travel luminaries as Sir Patrick Leigh Fermor and Sir Wilfred Thesiger. Despite Piper's eulogy, the Club had actually gone through a relatively difficult period in the 1980s. Fortunately, an era of reform and renewal was initiated towards the end of the decade when George Webb became Chairman. He was succeeded by two other equally able and committed former diplomats in Frank Brenchley and Sir Peregrine Rhodes. Bramall was therefore able to build on a solid financial and aesthetic foundation. Characteristically, he took energetic advantage of this heritage and plunged into a comprehensive programme of further reform, strongly supported by the Club's General Committee and its Secretary, the devoted and hard-working Malcolm Alcock. The Field Marshal and his temporary 'Military Assistant' constituted a formidable team for whom stones existed only in order to be overturned.

The agenda was considerable: the completion of the redecoration of the Club's public rooms, in particular the repainting of the Smoking Room; the construction of a new garden bar (now the 'Bramall Room') leading out to the communal gardens at the rear of the club house shared with the Athenaeum and Reform Clubs; and the further upgrading of the Club's accommodation. In addition to these material improvements, Bramall presided over the creation of a new members' subscription scheme, devised by the then Honorary Treasurer, Michael Garvin and the publication of *Travellers' Tales*, a slender volume of stories edited by Frank Hermann and Michael Allen written by members, himself included, who were able to draw on a wide range of personal experience. But his greatest achievement on behalf of the Club and the one which, as a talented amateur painter since his youth, gave him the most pleasure, was the acquisition on loan of a fine collection of early eighteenth-century paintings by artists such as Reynolds and Romney owned by a distinguished Anglo/South African family. These joined the magnificent Angelica Kaufmans already in the Smoking Room and other paintings lent by the Dulwich Picture Gallery, which now hang alongside a striking crimson portrait of a Venetian fencing master in the Inner Morning Room, the work by an unknown Venetian master.

This massive programme of change was carried through in Bramall's customary style, combining a full mastery of complex briefs with an engaging but formidable ability to persuade. The

Club, members and staff alike, responded with a parallel measure of enthusiasm. By the end of his term as Chairman in the summer of 2003, he could fairly say, although he would never do so, that he had more than done his duty by his three able predecessors and had left the Travellers at its highest point, financially and aesthetically, for many years. Throughout his five years as Chairman of the Club, much as he had done as Chairman of trustees of the Imperial War Museum, he had taken a close interest in all members of the staff, knowing all but the newest recruit by name – and fixing him or her in his mind from first acquaintance – never failing to greet them and ask how they were. It was an example of 'real leadership', learned early in his military service and never forgotten.

18

Cross-bencher

Elevation to the Upper House in January 1987 brought Dwin Bramall and his family quiet satisfaction. Moreover, as an assiduous observer of international affairs and, until relinquishing his post as Chief of the Defence Staff in October 1985, the United Kingdom's principal professional adviser on defence, he welcomed the opportunity to express his opinion free from the constraints of military office. Some might have expected that the socialist influence of his mother, which continued until her death in 1984, could have persuaded him to take the Labour whip, but, having all his professional life prided himself on being non-political and wishing to have freedom to speak his mind on any issue on which he was well informed or felt strongly, he took his seat on the cross-benches as an Independent.

Today, debate in the Lords is generally thought to be of better quality than in the Commons. This is chiefly due to the age, experience and in some cases expert knowledge of the speakers, most of whose ambitions have largely expired. Conciseness and brevity are also exercised to a greater extent than 'in another place'. Bramall of Bushfield lost no time in mastering the courtesies of the House, attended the majority of defence or defence-related debates and quickly made new friends.

He confined his maiden speech on 25 March 1987 to setting out his own credentials and convictions. In 1945 he had seen the devastating results of massive conventional air attack on Hamburg and later that of the atomic bomb on Hiroshima. These experiences had led him to reject the view that if it were possible to remove nuclear weapons from both West and East, conventional war would somehow become tolerable. But he argued that a *credible* conventional opposition to the Soviet threat in Central Europe was more likely to deter aggression than a mere 'trip-wire' force hinting at an early nuclear release. Looking to the broader scene, he concluded with the appraisal that, except where a threat of nuclear war acted as a restraint, the members of the human race still seemed all too willing to fight among themselves.

His easy style of speaking, military standing and readiness to listen to others in the corridors and tea-room soon drew admirers, yet, despite his confidence that what he had to say was heeded in the House, his reliance on their having the least impact on government policy steadily ebbed away.

His comments in the early years were chiefly confined to defending the reputation of the armed services, arguing for their proper remuneration and conditions of service and, perhaps most determinedly, against structural changes or government-inspired forays overseas likely to put service resources under more pressure than could be sustained. He took pains to avoid being perceived as the holder of extreme views, as Field Marshal Lord Carver had become on the usefulness of the nuclear deterrent, *vis-à-vis* its drain on the defence budget, or the need for the Royal Air Force. Unlike the Commons, where military experience and knowledge are today in conspicuously short supply, the Lords held both in some measure and he was careful to acknowledge this in his statements, despite the fact that his understanding of the mechanics and machinations of defence finances and related issues was probably greater than that of any other member of the House, other than Lord Carver, and more currently relevant.

When, in the summer of 1989, Mikhail Gorbachev made clear to his East European allies that the Soviet Army would no longer be available to bolster regimes resistant to political change, the Warsaw Pact collapsed as a military force and with it the most high-profile threat to the West. Only an uneasy atmosphere of uncertainty prevailed, until the festering dangers of the Arab–Israeli conflict filled the vacuum and came into proper focus. This came as no surprise to Bramall, but no event in the Middle East at that point was of sufficient international impact to allow him to turn the minds of his fellow peers away from euphoria to danger until Saddam Hussein annexed Kuwait, thereby raising the political temperature in the Muslim world, increasing the menace to Israel and threatening the supply of oil.

During the Lords' debate on 6 September 1990 to take note of developments in the Persian Gulf and the British government's response to them, Bramall lost no time in pointing out,

> I reminded your Lordships' House in the debate on the defence estimates on 17 July that the Middle East might explode at any moment; and if that happened, it would not be a question of meddling in the affairs that did not concern us, because we would perceive that our interests were much affected and because the result of our not becoming involved was likely to be more serious still.

He had a valid and important point, with relevance beyond the immediate crisis in Kuwait, but he went on – in a closely argued speech of some length – to offer advice on key issues to be addressed if the use of force proved unavoidable. These again were consummately valid: winning the air battle, acquisition of up-to-date and accurate intelligence, use of sufficient force to put fear into the hearts of the enemy, induce confusion in its leadership, have a proper chain of command and a good, experienced commander-in-chief.

No sensible person would dispute any of these suggestions, and it is likely that their Lordships left the debate with these points uppermost in their minds. It might be argued, however, that the relative ease with which they could be grasped led to more difficult questions he raised being obscured. For example, he expressed the hope that the government would discount any argument that because troops have been deployed they automatically have to do battle, citing the instance of the vast German mobilisation of 1914. He emphasised this point by quoting the Chinese General Sun Tzu of 500 BC: 'The best general may be the one who achieves his political and strategic objectives without having to fight.' Despite these cautionary remarks, he made it clear that he considered the stance of the American-led Coalition to be justified and carefully avoided giving any impression to the contrary. In the event, Saddam Hussein declined to withdraw before a show of force and had to be driven out of Kuwait by military action.

When the First Gulf War came to a less than decisive end in February 1991, to the extent that Saddam Hussein was left in control in Baghdad, Bramall took an interest in the Defence Review entitled *Options for Change*. The Conservative government had begun this inquiry before the war and blithely renewed it immediately afterwards. Scant note was taken of the shortcomings in defence preparedness the war had revealed and the same set of threat assumptions was slavishly maintained, despite many being invalidated by the military deployment to the Middle East.

The review had its origins in the country's – or more particularly the Treasury's – persistent demand for a 'peace dividend' for the end of the Cold War and was not due to be presented to Parliament until 1992. Before that could happen, another vicious conflict erupted in the Balkans. With no political framework available to deal with such circumstances, European governments were paralysed. Initially they expostulated hotly against such events on their collective doorstep but did very little until UN Security Council Resolution 743 of 1992 established UNPROFOR, the United Nations Protection Force mandated to protect aid convoys to refugees, but not to protect the refugees themselves.

Bramall had no first-hand experience of UN peace-keeping or enforcing operations, although he had overseen the participation of the small British contingent with the Multinational Force in Lebanon in 1983. No one had foreseen the rapid fragmentation of Yugoslavia, but it was clear to everyone with an eye to defence issues that the Army and the RAF would be drawn inexorably into the Balkans situation, either as part of the UN effort to restore order, or within some European initiative.

John Major's Conservative administration reacted to this new situation by taking a timorous look at the Army's manpower situation in February 1993. Opening the Lords debate on the subject, Viscount Cranborne, the Under-Secretary for Defence, read a statement to the Commons by the Secretary of State for Defence, Malcolm Rifkind, which asserted:

> The judgements made in the *Options for Change* remain valid. The threat to our national security is much less than it was. Since 1991, however, there have been a number of developments which have added *significantly* to the commitments the Army is required to meet at the same time that it is in the process of reorganising.

This was followed by the announcement that the planned reduction of the infantry to thirty-eight battalions was to be moderated by reducing only to forty, with a consequent increase of Army manpower by 3,000 posts – but to be met within the existing budget. In other words, only two rather than four battalions were to be cut, but no extra funds were allocated to maintain the two retained.

Although Bramall knew enough about army manpower calculations to have tied the Under-Secretary in knots, he limited himself on this occasion to pointing out that it would be wiser to restore 5,000 posts, rather than only 3,000, to allow the two extra battalions and others to be fully manned and so reduce the strain on the individual soldier. A week later, in the debate on military commitments and resources, he revealed the sham of the government's manpower announcements with what some would describe as uncharacteristic ruthlessness. Drawing attention to the trick of allowing extra manpower without extra funding, he challenged, 'By not finding extra resources to meet new and unplanned commitments, they [the Government] are merely shifting £80 million from one part of the highly-stretched budget to another. It is all being done by mirrors!' But he kept his key point until last: 'If the Cabinet cannot produce more resources or at least stop taking them away, then they must shed commitments and have the courage to do so. The assumptions and judgements on which *Options for Change* were drawn up three years ago are today no longer valid.'

Options for Change was followed by another review encouragingly but deceptively entitled *Front Line First*. This title was deceptive, because it was in fact a scouring search of the three Services' logistics support structure to find financial savings from there, with no intended benefit to the front line, and Bramall was among the first to recognise this. He had been in the Lords for seven years, and his patience with what he saw as ministerial chicanery had worn thin. In consequence, his speeches began to show some irritation and even occasional irascibility, but never petulance, as he laid the facts bare.

The debate on this and the Defence Estimates for 1994–5 took place in the Lords on a hot and sticky July afternoon in 1994. First to speak, after the statement made in the Commons by the Secretary of State had been read by the Under-Secretary of State, was the Opposition spokesman on defence, Lord Williams of Elvel, who, as Lieutenant Charles Williams, had accompanied Bramall on the desert drive to Kufra oasis in 1957. Although witty in his delivery, he challenged the government's presentation of the costs to be saved, the acute shortage of essential equipment spares revealed by the First Gulf War and the threat of a collapse of servicemen's confidence in the arrangements for their support on active operations.

Bramall was the third to speak and, after thanking Viscount Cranborne for his 'frank if rather curate's egg-like statement on the *Front Line First* exercise', made clear that the government proposals required 'very careful study, a stripping away of the gift-wrapping and a full debate'. This last observation had particular pertinence, as the debate was taking place on the final day before the summer recess. It was decidedly hot and the sceptics in the House might be forgiven for thinking that the government hoped to get the debate over and done with rather quickly and without undue fuss.

Time was short and Bramall confined himself to two observations. First:

> Whatever the merits and demerits of the proposals, they must be viewed against the background of the draconian cuts in front line manpower, support services and budget holders imposed since the beginning of the decade [which] by 1997 will have reduced defence expenditure by 25 per cent in real terms to bring it down to below 3 per cent of gross national product.

His second point dwelt on the need for the Lords to analyse most carefully whether the manpower cuts and civilianisation proposals really did represent enhancement in areas in need of them or were largely cosmetic. He concluded with the real-life barb, 'I am sure that we will be looking for reassurance from the noble Viscount on that *and he may like to quote an add-back figure to reassure us.*'

Nine years after Bramall had relinquished the post of Chief of the Defence Staff, there were officials in Whitehall, some in uniform and some not, who felt it was time that he 'let go' on major defence issues in the Lords and in his speeches, because they judged that he was out of touch. While it is true that he could only guess at the pressure the Treasury was applying to the Ministry of Defence, in comparison with what he had sustained, no one in either House had his command of the harsh realities of the damage inflicted on defence capabilities by swingeing or even niggling cost-cutting. Equally, few – if any – were able to see through the seductive presentation of such cuts as 'modernisation' or 'reform'. Lord Carver understood the issues as well as he did, but neither he nor Marshal of the Royal Air Force Lord Craig, Chief of the Defence Staff 1988–91, appeared eager to use his experience and knowledge quite so fearlessly.

In this debate, the Minister – Viscount Cranborne – dealt with Bramall's question about an 'add-back' with a courtesy fully in keeping with the ways of the House but, probably inadvertently, let the cat out of the bag. He replied:

When it became apparent that there was additional money over and above the reduction in the defence budget that we had been asked to find, Ministers immediately consulted the Chiefs of Staff on how it should be spent. I am content to rest on their judgement.

In this seemingly positive reply, he conceded – probably artlessly – that *Front Line First* was not about strengthening the front line by stripping out the logistic support services, but simply about reducing defence costs to meet Treasury demands.

Bramall returned to this theme in the defence debate that took place on 26 July 1994, during which the intentions and results of *Front Line First* were again debated. He began by seeking to establish that the review was in fact a drive for greater effectiveness of the armed services or, as the Under-Secretary had earlier let slip, simply a means to satisfy Treasury demand for still further financial economy. He sought clarification on a series of questions concerned with service manpower strengths, the application of financial savings achieved and the degree to which the current 'over-stretch' of the armed forces had been taken into account. He concluded his speech with a warning of the 'great unease and discontent and considerable lack of confidence in the higher management of defence' and a disconcerting question (for the Minister) about a term being used in Whitehall about 'de-enriching' the Services. As he put it: 'If one de-enriches the services one will, as surely as night follows day, de-enrich the nation.'

He then turned to the implications for foreign policy.

Is this [he asked] a new deal for the forces, constructed with vision and due regard for the future in the very uncertain and dangerous world that we live in? If the latter, will it be allowed to work as it should before further cuts, no doubt in the name of still greater efficiency, make us infinitely weaker all round and virtually impotent to support an honourable and *positive foreign policy* and protect our national and international interests?

Then he reminded the House: 'Sadly, all this occurred in the 'twenties and 'thirties when the Chiefs of Staff had repeatedly to warn Ministers that they must carry out a policy of appeasement because we lacked the military strength to support any other policy or even to protect our own country.'

Lord Carver, speaking later in the same debate, urged the government 'to have a radical rethink of the organisation for European security, within the framework of NATO, incorporating a European security and defence identity'. This was a subject on which he had previously spoken in the House and written a number of articles, all to no apparent avail.

Closer to home, speaking in the Defence Estimates debate in July 1995, by which time the damage to the Army's medical services by the *Front Line First* cuts in defence spending had become apparent, because of the extent to which these vital support services had been stretched by deployments in the former Yugoslavia, Lord Bramall said: 'The Army's medical services are in a particularly parlous state, with no reason to believe that the National Health Service would be able to provide all the consultants, surgeons and anaesthetists needed in any conflict, because the Royal Army Medical Corps can no longer provide them.' This was a theme to which he was to return time and again, no doubt mindful of the excellent medical attention he had received when wounded in the Normandy campaign of 1944.

He also took every opportunity to try to achieve a distinction in the minds of his fellow peers and – as far as reports of his words allowed – in those of the general public, between European defence cooperation and what the information media chose to term a 'European Army'. Commenting during the debate on the Queen's Speech, in November 1995, he said:

I was pleased to see a reference to the development of more effective European defence arrangements under the Western European Union [the European Treaty which preceded NATO and is without United States participation] because whatever may have been implied, or perhaps misunderstood, we must, if we are ever to match our resources and commitments, have greater coordination and harmonisation of our defence policies with our European partners. Of course we do not want, and I am glad to say are unlikely ever to have, a 'Maastricht Rifles' or totally impractical and unnecessary mixed manning; but our research and development programmes need to be developed on a European basis.

After registering his approval for the government's intention to encourage a cooperative relationship between NATO and Russia and new legislation dealing with the British Reserve Forces, he returned to the subject to which he was by then concentrating increasing attention in the Lords, that of foreign policy.

I am perhaps more concerned with what was *not* in the speech. History must have taught us that the price of the peace we all seek is not only eternal vigilance but also a clear commitment and a balance of power which is seen to be acceptable. That inevitably requires sufficiently strong military forces to give credibility to our *foreign policy* and good intentions. There are a number of matters which should still be of concern to your Lordships' House if our Armed Forces are to continue to make a contribution to that commitment.

He then went on to explain to their Lordships the intricacies of 'trained Army manpower', now reduced to 100,000 men from the 168,000 of just a few years previously, and the impact this curtailment inevitably had on the nation's ability to keep up to 15,000 men monitoring the 'peace' in Bosnia-Herzegovina for an indefinite period. This was something he understood perfectly and had explained on several previous occasions; but there was a risk in returning to a previous theme, as he was inclined to do over the value of Gurkha troops, of automatically switching off the hearing aids of those around him. The counsel on speeches intended to persuade – 'Make three points in the hope that 10 per cent of the audience will remember one of them' – remains sound advice.

In placing the concluding words of this speech in context, it is important to remember that it was delivered two years before the end of John Major's Conservative administration. It was also close to the end of the decade when day-to-day financial management, with specific budget levels, had first been imposed on unit commanders. 'Morale, motivation and dynamic leadership as opposed to cautious financial management, are the key to success,' Bramall explained.

If this problem is not solved, as we approach the millennium, we shall either not be able to meet all the commitments which the country's role as a leading international power and as a member of the Security Council places on our Armed Forces; or, we shall once again experience the traumas of military defeats and disasters such as we have been able to avoid for the past half century.

The Lords debate on medical provision took place in March 1997, by which time the damage done to the medical services by cuts under the *Front Line First* Defence Review had become too serious to ignore. This had never pretended to be an efficiency-driven reform, but one to provide the same level of secondary medical support with drastically reduced staff and facilities. It had gone far beyond what had been agreed under *Options for Change* when, having taken its peace dividend from the end of the Cold War, the Treasury had come back for more. The cut-backs and economies resulted in the Army's medical services retaining only one tri-service hospital in the United Kingdom, at Haslar in Gosport, with other minor wards or wings inside existing National Health Service hospitals.

The principal casualties of these economies, aside from the patients who had to travel greater distances for treatment and receive it in competition with the general public courtesy of the NHS, was the 'skill fade' of medical staff motivated and trained to treat servicemen and women, who found themselves working in environments devoid of the camaraderie and ethos of Service life. Not surprisingly, they were leaving in droves, abandoning an apology of a structure manned to wholly inadequate levels and dependent on reservists and volunteers to step in when front-line units deployed on active service overseas.

As with others who spoke in the debate, except for those speaking *for* the government, Bramall's comments were severely critical of what had happened. 'From what all noble Lords have said, it is very obvious that nothing that has been instigated and executed during the whole series of defence reviews, studies, squeezes and cut-backs over the past five to six years has turned out quite so disastrously as these new medical arrangements,' he began. Although he did not say so, his wrath was by no means reserved for the Ministers and civil servants who had instigated the restructuring of the medical services but also, as he put it in the debate, for the 'oddly supine attitude being taken by some of the most senior medical officers'. And they were not the limit of his criticism.

The Chief of the Defence Staff during the course and implementation of the Armed Forces Medical Provision review was Field Marshal Sir Peter (later Lord) Inge, who had unexpectedly been appointed to that office by Prime Minister John Major when the CDS, Air Chief Marshal Sir Peter Harding, had been obliged to resign over a social indiscretion in 1994. Inge was well known as a safe pair of hands and, since the rank of major, as a man who didn't make mistakes.

Bramall considered Inge's error over the medical services restructuring was that he failed to give the matter his detailed attention, a technique in which he was skilled, and left the work very largely to the senior medical officers of the three Services. Their discussion consequently focused, with a few honourable exceptions, on which Service should have which key facilities, rather than on the essentials of how best to continue to provide servicemen and their families with the high-quality medical care they deserved. That said, it should be recognised that the senior medical officers were working to a very tight remit imposed by the Secretary of State, Mr (later Sir) Malcolm Rifkind, who had allowed himself to be persuaded by others of the merits of combining service and National Health facilities on a large scale.

Following the destruction of the twin towers of the World Trade Center in New York on 11 September 2001, Lord Bramall made clear that he was in full support of action against al-Qaeda wherever the terror organisation was to be found, but he questioned whether high-level bombing was the most appropriate weapon. He had been strongly opposed to the high-level bombing of Serbian cities, bridges and communication centres prior to the launch of ground operations to protect the Kosovo-Albanians in 1999. In the case of Serbia, he had taken up the issue with the then Chief of the Defence Staff, General Sir Charles (later Lord) Guthrie.

As his predecessors, including Bramall himself, had done,

Guthrie gave occasional informal briefings to the House of Lords' Conservative Peers Defence Group, to which non-Conservative peers were usually invited. The briefings were largely a one-way traffic as, except for former Defence Ministers or Chiefs of Defence Staff present, the members' knowledge of defence issues was limited. On the occasion in question, Guthrie – an essentially relaxed and urbane individual – responded courteously to questions but became impatient when Bramall pressed him on the precise aims of the operation, as well as on the issue of the high-level bombing of Serbian cities and key facilities. The briefing took place in an annexe to the House of Lords in The Abbey Gardens and, uncharacteristically perhaps, Bramall returned to the issue with some vehemence as Guthrie was leaving.

Black Rod, General Sir Edward Jones, a fellow former Royal Green Jacket who had also attended, witnessed the brisk exchange between Lord Bramall and General Guthrie that followed. The incident did no harm to his reputation with his fellow peers, but it gave point to the argument of Guthrie and other senior officers that it was time for him to 'let go' on current defence matters, but Bramall did not see it that way. Passing Black Rod in the House of Lords a short time later, he remarked, 'Well, I'm clearly not in the CDS's good books,' or similar words, to which Black Rod replied, 'Well, I'm scarcely surprised.' The two men were eventually reconciled after Bramall had written to Guthrie explaining his concern at the bombing.

Subsequently, Bramall was to concede that the bombing of Serbia had brought about the removal of Slobodan Milosevic by his own people, but he continued to regret the damage done to a country with a distinguished cultural heritage and the alienation of the population that had had a record of alliance with Britain in the two world wars.

Speaking in the Lords debate on the situation in Afghanistan in November 2001, four weeks after the start of American military operations against the Taliban forces apparently sheltering the presumed perpetrator of the attack on the twin towers in New York – Osama bin Laden – Bramall welcomed the intervention and particularly the 'relatively low tempo of operations rather than rushing in where wise men fear to tread', but then returned to the issue of high-level bombing:

> But an indefinite continuation of that type of bombing, sadly and inevitably causing further casualties among non-combatants, not only risks losing some of the moral high ground in the propaganda war, it also puts the Coalition, already affected by the situation in Palestine, under increased pressure.

Ending this speech, he referred to the Chiefs' of Staff role in providing expert advice to Ministers, something he considered had been lacking, or possibly ignored, during the Kosovo operations. In doing so, he permitted himself some implied advice to the new Chief of the Defence Staff, a distinguished naval officer, with the warning, 'When active operations are imminent there can be no substitute for the depth of expert knowledge as regards operational detail which the professional heads of the Services *particularly involved at the time* are in the best position to impart.'

This was sixteen years precisely after he had relinquished the appointment as CDS, and in the absence of a more authoritative voice on defence, he still felt the strong pull of national responsibility. By this time, only one of his successors, Lord Craig, was active in the Lords, and none was nearly so broadly active as he, being either preoccupied with national or international projects of his own or retired from public life. Bramall might be vulnerable to criticism for not 'letting go' so long after holding military office, but no one younger or better informed was pushing forward to take his place.

The political manoeuvrings in London, New York and Washington over the summer and autumn of 2002 over whether a pre-emptive attack on Iraq, allegedly to deprive Saddam Hussein of weapons of mass destruction, could be justified, provoked Bramall to write a comprehensive appreciation of the situation in a letter to *The Times*. Published on 29 July, six months before the US air attack was launched, it bears reproduction in full.

Sir, The question we should be asking ourselves is not whether the Americans can invade Iraq, or indeed whether they will invade, but whether they should do so and, of course, whether we should follow in their wake.

Apart from the difficult moral questions of lesser or greater evils, there seem to be two distinct but tenable schools of thought on what the outcome of such action would be.

The first is that if Iraq is successfully attacked, by whatever means, and as a result Saddam Hussein is removed, preferably with the help of a popular uprising, the terrorist-ridden, war-torn Middle East would unravel beneficially. It would then become a more benign, tolerant area in which moderate Muslim governments would take heart, a Palestine solution would become possible and the ability of terrorists to strike another dramatic blow at the US (or indeed Europe) with or without weapons of mass destruction could be effectively neutralised. The flames of resentment and protest which exist in the area today would have then, at least, been doused, and the 'war against terrorism' achieved a major victory.

The second viewpoint is that conflict with Iraq would produce, in that area, the very display of massive, dynamic United States activity which provides one of the mainsprings of motivation for terrorist action in the region, and indeed over a wider area. Far from calming things down, enhancing any peace process and advancing the 'war against terrorism', *which could and should be conducted internationally by other means*, it would make things infinitely worse. Petrol rather than water would have been poured on the flames and al-Qaeda would have gained more recruits. It would be interesting to know to which of these two points of view the British Government is more inclined.

America, with all the power at its disposal, and with no other superpower to gainsay it, can presumably and eventually achieve any military objective it wishes. I cannot help, however, but be reminded of that remark by a notably 'hawkish' General (later Field Marshal) Gerald Templer who when, during the Suez crisis (1956), Britain was planning a massive invasion of Egypt through

Alexandria, said something to the effect, 'Of course we can get to Cairo but what I want to know is what the bloody hell do we do when we get there?'

Seldom can such a public expression of the options and their probable consequences have been more concisely put or, subsequently, so cursorily disregarded. It is a curious phenomenon of British public life that, while retired diplomats, judges and scientists can be hauled away from their rose bushes to advise the government of the day on a question related to their expertise or experience, retired Armed Service Chiefs – with the exception of Wellington – are steadfastly ignored. The argument is usually, 'Ah, but this is *different*,' while it generally turns out to be almost exactly the same, the politicians having been taken by surprise only by the slightly different guise or motivation of the crisis.

As it was, the invasion of Iraq became inevitable – as Bramall recognised – because of events elsewhere. From an early stage, President George W. Bush and his advisers had perceived that a change of regime in Iraq was their only politically dynamic response to the 11 September attack on the World Trade Center, and, after deployment of massive US forces to the area of the Arabian Gulf, to apply pressure on Saddam Hussein to comply fully and openly with the UN inspectors seeking weapons of mass destruction, the path to war had become irreversible.

Initially, the swift execution of the American-led invasion of Iraq brought widespread jubilation in Britain and the United States, together with scornful derision of the still-cautious attitudes in Berlin, Paris and Moscow. The lack of preparedness of the US Army, in particular, for the fierce reaction to their presence in the 'Sunni triangle' west of Baghdad and for the collapse of the civil infrastructure everywhere except in the Kurdish-controlled north was then obscured by the shrill political outcry in London, and to a lesser extent in Washington, over failure of the invasion forces and the specialist inspectors who followed on their heels to discover any weapons of mass destruction, or evidence of their recent presence. In Britain, there was satisfaction over the relative quiet of the predominantly Shia region around Basra, tactfully controlled by the 7th Armoured Brigade under the experienced and pragmatic Brigadier Graham Binns, but the implications of no weapons of mass destruction being found led to near-hysterical exchanges in the House of Commons, the Parliamentary Defence and Intelligence Sub-Committee and through debate in the news media.

On 2 July a letter from Bramall, intended to help still this tumult and lead to concentration on the new, rapidly deteriorating situation, appeared in *The Times* alongside the first leader bearing the querulously optimistic heading: 'Baghdad and Saigon – More troops are needed but *Iraq is no quagmire*'. No evidence in the body of the leader bore out the 'no quagmire' assertion, which appeared to have rested on hope rather than on fact. Bramall's letter put the issue of intelligence into context:

Sir, When the unedifying smoke-screens, recriminations and counter-recriminations as to who did what to intelligence dossiers have dispersed, two things should emerge with clarity. The first is that the significance of intelligence lies not only in the information, be it empiric or uncorroborated conjecture, which is thought fit to put into this or that document, but more importantly in what interpretation is placed upon it.

The second, leading on from this, is that on the basis of the way in which whatever was said or written was presented, the British people obtained the distinct impression that the threat from Iraq was more massive and imminent than has since proved to be the case, or indeed may ever have been.

There were other tenable reasons, which could have been used to justify military force, but none which could have satisfied Parliament and the country as regards the necessity and legality of such action.

This confronted the principal political issue of the day of whether the country had been taken to war on what became euphemistically known as a 'false prospectus'. Even on the basis of the 'evidence' of Saddam Hussein's inferred hostile intentions, as presented by the

American and British political leaders, Bramall had opposed going to war on the grounds that it would inflame the war on terrorism, rather than help to subdue it. Now, he was unequivocally arguing that the 'evidence' as presented had misled the British people as to the real dangers, so far as they had actually existed.

There are some who argue that individuals who write to *The Times*, or any other newspaper, do so only to see their opinions in print or to advertise some expertise. Neither accusation fitted the case here, but one might reasonably ask why Bramall did not take the issue further, bearing in mind his strong feelings about what had occurred in government circles and the rapidly worsening situation in Iraq. The answer lies in a government with an overwhelming majority in the Commons and a consequently blithe disregard for public protest such as was made in the streets of London, before the invasion was launched, by many thousands of people from across the entire political and social spectrum – despite the then largely believed 'evidence' of Saddam's WMD capability. No doubt he would have received a courteous reception had he sought interviews with the Prime Minister or Defence Minister, but what would have been achieved?

In terms of public protest in recent times, only the 'poll tax' riot in Trafalgar Square on 31 March 1990 has had any significant impact on the policy of the government of the day, in that instance bringing down the Prime Minister and resulting in the scrapping of the tax in the form initially conceived. The Iraq situation in which the Blair government had become involved was not susceptible to extrication without huge loss of British prestige and, one might assume, the resignation of the Prime Minister. So, in company with the majority of responsible citizens, Bramall focused his interest on making the best of a thoroughly messy military and political situation.

His letter to *The Times* published on 18 November 2003 sought to draw a line under what had passed, without in any way excusing what had been done, and to point out the risks of the military strategy seemingly adopted by the US forces in Iraq.

Sir, Now that weapons of mass destruction have turned out to be something of a damp squib, the justification for what is happening in Iraq is concentrating [i.e. in statements by Ministers or their spokesmen] more and more on the war against terrorism. However, wherever else al-Qaeda and other terrorist groups were before the war, they were not in Iraq – Saddam Hussein saw to that; but they are certainly there now, attracted like bees around a honey pot.

The United States seem therefore, wittingly or unwittingly, to have adopted what I might describe as a 1954 Dien Bien Phu [Indo-China] strategy. In this, instead of having to deal with a more dispersed threat in more inaccessible places, you contrive a more concentrated focus and threat, which you are then in a position to destroy with greatly superior force, backed, hopefully in Iraq's case, with massive aid and self-government for the indigenous inhabitants.

This strategy may work; I hope it does, but as the name implies it carries serious risks, and it is difficult to see how it can be successful if there is any premature withdrawal of American forces.

The 'Dien Bien Phu strategy' was that adopted by the French High Command in Saigon in November 1953. A force of divisional strength with artillery and engineer support was air-lifted to the remote village of Dien Bien Phu, on the North Vietnam/Laotian border, deep inside territory controlled by the guerrilla forces under the Viet Minh General Vo Nguyen Giap. The aim was to force Giap to concentrate his forces to attack the French stronghold and then destroy them with superior strength. The plan failed owing to the unexpected weight of artillery Giap was able to bring to bear and inability of the French Air Force to supply the besieged garrison in face of Viet Minh anti-aircraft fire and bad weather. The French lost the battle and with it Indo-China.

The strategy was not new in 1953 and had succeeded on other occasions. It is therefore conceivable that, in order to associate an invasion of Iraq with the international 'war against terrorism', officials and other advisers in Washington presented to themselves – and also to the President – the fatal proposition that an invasion of Iraq would draw in al-Qaeda, which it has done, so that the organisation could be closely identified and destroyed. But, despite all the efforts of intelligence and application of technology, the United States has manifestly failed to do this. In their part-defence, it has to be recognised that their pre-war intelligence was at fault, not only about the existence of weapons of mass destruction but also on the reaction of the Iraqi people to a freedom none had ever experienced at home.

Bramall wrote again to *The Times* on 18 March 2004 to draw a distinction between the action taken by America, Britain and others against the Taliban regime in Afghanistan, which was certainly sheltering if not actively supporting al-Qaeda, and the continuing operations to try to contain the increasing level of violence in Iraq. He also made a point in his own defence with the words

> We should reject the largely political argument that those who have been less than enthusiastic, particularly over the reasons behind going to war in the first place, are somehow being pusillanimous about the so-called war against terrorism, which is a separate issue, but which must remain the highest priority at the moment.

This letter was reprinted by *The Week* magazine in its collection 'Pick of the Week's letters'.

He spoke in the Lords on a number of occasions as the euphoria over the swift end to conventional operations in Iraq degenerated into confusion and then into near-total chaos. As one who had opposed the war from the moment it seemed likely, he took care to avoid the 'I told you so' theme, but concentrated on the positive. Speaking in the Foreign and Commonwealth Affairs debate in the Lords on 26 May 2004 he made two key points. First, in the sense of current realism, he said,

> Of course, having brought Iraq to a state of manifest disorder, whatever our motives, it is not unreasonable to feel that the Coalition ought to see the occupation through to a more benign

conclusion. Certainly, handing over political power early would restore some legitimacy in the eyes of the rest of the world.

Secondly, he tellingly conceded,

The judgement of history as to whether the advantages of invading Iraq would ever outweigh the short term disadvantages, would have to wait. It certainly would not depend on the Government continually telling the country it had done the right thing; nor whether the country was taken to war under false pretences, which it probably was, but on how Iraq and the rest of the Middle East looks in two or three years' time.

Finally, he turned to the future.

We really should know by now that, unlike naked aggression, terrorism cannot be defeated by massive military means, but by concentrating on competent protection and positive diplomacy. By protection, I mean building up our home and overseas intelligence, which would greatly reduce the risk to us and to others and then, based on that intelligence, rooting out those planning and perpetrating criminal acts.

This was a wide-ranging debate, for which four hours of their Lordships' time had been allocated, and Iraq was only one of the many topics addressed. It has not been possible to identify any positive outcome arising from it, bringing to mind a statement Lord Bramall made in the Defence Debate on 12 May 2000.

The fact that defence has been relegated to a Friday indicates yet again the low priority in political terms which government accord it. Once upon a time it was considered the prime responsibility of any government. Today, the apparent imperviousness of the Ministry of Defence to any criticism, however constructive, means that these debates do not appear to get us anywhere.

Epilogue

At the time of writing in the late summer of 2006, there are five on-going situations that warrant analysis against the background of Lord Bramall's question mark over the application of force in dealing with international disputes and the merits of his Fifth Pillar strategy of a pro-active foreign policy, closely supported by military expertise and facilities.

In Afghanistan, the anarchic situation outside Kabul is moderated only by warlord rule or on the spot presence of Coalition troops. The Taliban are resurgent, especially in the historically lawless and independent south of the country and British troops deployed there, ostensibly in a reconstruction role, have had to be reinforced. As Lord Bramall expressed it in a House of Lords debate as long ago as December 2001, troops are there 'to do heaven knows what for heaven knows how long.'

This situation is a result of mission creep in the absence of a clear overall strategy. The initial bombing campaign against terrorist training camps and al-Qaeda hideouts, supported by special forces on the ground, seriously restricted al-Qaeda's ability to operate and contributed to the ousting of the Taliban from central Government. But when parallel diplomatic moves failed to bring about the capture of Osama bin Laden, the United States and Britain – and later some Nato partners – allowed themselves to be drawn into deploying large bodies of ground forces just as the collateral damage and civilian casualties from the bombing had begun to alienate the Afghan people.

These troop deployments were presented to the world as a means of introducing democracy into Afghanistan – a concept alien to the local culture – and installing an elected government, for which it transpired 25,000 troops were required. Later, as it became apparent the elected government was not self-sustainable, the mission changed again. Troops were deployed further afield in an attempt to break the Taliban's hold on areas outside Kabul where reconstruction work was scheduled and help the central government in its struggle to bring the resurgent poppy trade under control.

The history of foreign interventions in Afghanistan tells us that none of the subsequent missions is achievable. Consequently, short of some dramatic turn for the better, the Coalition troop-providing nations are faced with either an open-ended presence or humiliating withdrawal.

Use of large-scale force in this instance brings to mind the response of the head of the United States Navy when asked by Secretary of State John Foster Dulles whether the Sixth Fleet could do anything to prevent the Anglo-French invasion of Egypt in 1956, 'We can defeat them – the British and the French and the Egyptians and the Israelis – the whole goddam works of them we can knock off, if you want. But that's the only way to do it.' But we now know that *massive* force was not the only way. It was not, for instance, the route to apprehension of Osama bin Laden. Save for a lucky strike, his demise will be achieved by consistent high-level diplomacy backed by patient and subtle intelligence gathering, using local proxies. In the Afghan border regions every man has his potential betrayer.

The US-led invasion of Iraq began principally because President Bush's rhetoric against Saddam Hussein and complementary troop deployment had gone beyond the point of retraction or recall. In consequence, selected negative intelligence, i.e. *no evidence* of the destruction of certain chemical weapons and their production capability known to be in Iraq in 1992, had to be presented in a manner to appear to justify invasion. Boasts that the world is better off without Saddam Hussein have to be set against the upset to the balance of power in the Middle East and the stark reality that the Iraqi people now live at greater risk than under his misrule. Even worse, international terrorism has been further provoked, not reduced.

The diplomatic route would still have been available. Inspection of the suspected chemical weapon manufacturing and storage sites by the UNSCOM teams could have been resumed, allowing time for the building of a broader coalition for action, if action was ultimately perceived to be both justified and the only course. The cat and mouse game with Baghdad would have dragged on but without the horrendous loss of life that has occurred or the upsurge of resentment in the Muslim world generated by the invasion and subsequent tactics of Coalition forces. The rush to war has resulted in what Lord Bramall referred to in a Lords' debate of February 2003 as 'a cauldron of anti-Western feeling', alienating Muslim states which might well, if sensitively approached, have eventually been of help.

With Iran, there is still time for carefully orchestrated diplomacy to succeed in defusing the apparent crisis over the regime's nuclear enrichment programme – but it will have to be conducted in a more subtle manner than hitherto. The Iranians are an ancient and proud people. Although economically and socially diverse, the 91% Shia Muslim population is susceptible to centralised religious-based leadership. Neither the people nor President Mahmoud Ahmadinejad are likely to be swayed by the, 'Do this or else,' type of diplomacy nor by economic or industrial development bribes, even should they be taken.

Continued dialogue offers a better way forward, together with carefully acquired, objectively assessed intelligence on Iran's nuclear and missile development programmes. Containment in this situation should also be applied to Western impatience, rather than by any threatening naval deployments or aggressive over-flights. Events in nearby Iraq have rendered the use of force in this instance a non-viable option.

Although defiantly pursuing a ballistic missile and nuclear weapon programme, North Korea calls for consideration quite different from Iran. Although rich in minerals, North Korea's economy is stagnant through inept or communist doctrinaire management. Death of almost three million people during the famine of 1995-98 has left the hard-line communist regime discredited although not yet challenged domestically, as there is no coherent opposition. Fostering an internal uprising would, as the Duke of Wellington famously described revolutionising a country for a political objective, be 'a fearful responsibility'.

Sabre rattling by the financially and intellectually bankrupt administration of Kim Jong-il is the old political card of distracting the electorate from ills at home by drumming up trouble abroad. Threats of force would be counter-productive. The Koreans are a tough and ruthless people who would respond to any external threat virtually as one – and they have large, well-equipped armed forces. Calm and patience are required until China decides to intervene in her own interest. Beijing does not want a failed communist economy on its doorstep any more than an open local confrontation with the West. This is a matter best left to China to resolve in the role of friendly ally. Japan also has a lever, in that the Korean economy leans heavily on remissions home from Koreans working there.

Finally we must consider the Arab-Israeli dispute, the solving or at least the *moderation* of which is key to removing the currently most acute threat to world stability and the internal security of countries in the region and others more remote. Force in ruthless and brutal form is being used by both sides to no discernible useful effect. Support from outside simply strengthens the will of each party, leading to demands for more of the same. A halt to military aid or subsidies to both sides in Palestine, and to the Israelis from the United States in particular would help but the United States, from its position of economic strength, must insist on the Israelis getting round the table with all the locally interested parties with the unequivocal intention of giving up the illegal settlements and forging a lasting peace. Only such a process could produce borders for Israel susceptible to international approval and a viable state for the Palestinian Arabs.

Even this might not work and there may be no peace, because it will undoubtedly be difficult to reconcile what appears to many people to be the irreconcilable. Yet a peace process is the only route to future stability in the region. In all of this Britain bears an historic responsibility stemming from the Balfour Declaration of November 1917, made without a plan, or even a proposal, of how the Zionist aspirations on the one hand might be achieved without 'prejudice to the civil and religious rights of existing non-Jewish communities in Palestine' on the other; and her unilateral abandonment of the United Nations mandate to administer Palestine in May 1948. The recent anguish and suffering experienced by both sides in the Gaza Strip and Lebanon, behoves Britain to 'bend every sinew to bring about a settlement' as Prime Minister Blair belatedly expressed it, in what may be the last opportunity before the conflagration spreads.

Throughout his long career in the army and public life, Lord Bramall has stressed the importance of understanding the point of view of one's opponents. It is difficult for many westerners to imagine that those of another culture do not necessarily want what we want or what we decide they should have. This is not a monolithic truth, in the case of the Muslim world there are many people who desire Western pleasures but seldom advertise such interests. The more conservatively minded perceive many outward features of Western life as a challenge to the role of elders and the family in the ordering or influencing of conduct in their own society. While cynics may argue that each cultural group has to settle for the best that is achievable for them in their lifetime, the awkward generalisation is that Westerners crave power and possessions while the majority of Muslims seem content with their faith and associated moral code.

The use of overwhelming force in Iraq, after the weapon inspectors failed to find something that evidently did nor exist, has proved counter-productive, critically damaging the credentials of the West in the global context. The situation in Afghanistan appears to be deteriorating towards something disturbingly similar. Lord Bramall pointed out the limitations on the use of force in 1970 and suggested an alternative way forward when in a national position of authority a decade later. It is not yet too late to heed his warning and advice to use *some other way*.

So it is time to demand of ourselves whether – tarnished by association with the USA in a reckless rush to war in Iraq – Britain is in any position to take or even suggest a theme for a positive way forward. There are two arguments for doing so. We still have a permanent seat on the UN Security Council and, despite expressed doubts at home, an edge of authority over our hesitant or heads-in-the-sand fellow Europeans.

Certainly a radically new approach is urgently required before the worst happens and, in this potentially explosive situation of seething Muslim resentment and enmity, we lurch inexorably into a more general conflict involving the whole of the Middle East. This will need a carefully thought out strategy, subtly and not just cravenly different from that of the United States, and dynamic diplomacy to help bring it about, as Dwin Bramall has so consistently advocated.

Index

INDEX

INDEX